# CAMBRIDGE

# GRAMMAR

# FOR first certificate

## WITH *ANSWERS*

Self-study
grammar reference
and practice

**LOUISE HASHEMI** and
**BARBARA THOMAS**

PUBLISHED BY THE PRESS SYNDICATE OF THE UNIVERSITY OF CAMBRIDGE
The Pitt Building, Trumpington Street, Cambridge CB2 1RP, United Kingdom

CAMBRIDGE UNIVERSITY PRESS
The Edinburgh Building, Cambridge CB2 2RU, UK
40 West 20th Street, New York, NY 10011–4211, USA
477 Williamstown Road, Port Melbourne, VIC 3207, Australia
Ruiz de Alarcón 13, 28014 Madrid, Spain
Dock House, The Waterfront, Cape Town 8001, South Africa

http://www.cambridge.org

First published 2003
Third printing 2004

Printed in Dubai by Oriental Press

Text typeface GammEF  11.5/13pt System QuarkXpress® [KAMAE]

A catalogue record for this book is available from the British Library

Library of Congress Cataloguing in Publication data

ISBN 0 521 53336 8

Produced by Kamae Design, Oxford.

# Acknowledgements

The authors would like to thank their editors, Alison Sharpe and Anna Teevan, and also the following people for their comments and advice: Shahla Hashemi, Neca Huntic and Christina Wylie.

The authors and publishers would also like to thank the following teachers from around the world who commented on the material in its draft form: Roger Scott, Bournemouth, UK; Mairi Beaton, Lyon, France; Elisabeth de Lange, Beckum, Germany, Helen Gialias, Bournemouth, England; Mechthild Hesse, Bad Homburg, Germany; Diana Hopkins, Bath, England; Scott Lusher, Izmir, Turkey; Mark Nettle, Bath, England; Graham Palmer, Royston, England; Martin Parrott, London, England; Dmitris Primolis, Archanes, Greece; Susan Rastetter-Gies, Aschaffenburg, Germany; Nick Shaw, A Coruna, Spain; Anna Sikorzynska, Warsaw, Poland; Sylvia Sommer, Lyon, France; Roy Sprenger, Troyes, France.

The authors and publishers are grateful to the following for permission to reproduce copyright material. It has not always been possible to identify the sources of all the material used and in such cases the publishers would welcome information from the copyright owners:

p.23: adapted extract from 'The rise and rise of news girl Katie' by Lisa Millard, *Cambridge Evening News*, 26 April 1999, reproduced with permission of Cambridge Newspapers Ltd.; p.32: adapted extract from 'Hurled through the door' by Max Wooldridge, *Observer*, 6 February 2000 © Max Wooldridge, reproduced with permission of Max Wooldridge; p.198: adapted extract from *The Language of Clothes* by Alison Lurie, published by Henry Holt and Company (Owl Books) © Alison Lurie, reproduced with permission of A. P. Wyatt on behalf of Alison Lurie; p.213: adapted extract from 'World Standard English', *The Cambridge Encyclopaedia of the English Language*, 1997, by David Crystal, reproduced with permission of Cambridge University Press.

Photographs: p.6: Powerstock Zefa; p.11: Picture Desk/Kobal; p.12: Powerstock Zefa; p.21: Stockbyte; p.23: Rex Features; p.31: Art Directors and Trip; p.32: Robert Harding Picture Library; p.56.1: Network Photographers; p.56.2: Robert Harding Picture Library; p.56.3: Art Directors and Trip; p.56.4: Art Directors and Trip; p.64: Alamy.com; p.70: Robert Harding Picture Library; p.77: Corbis UK Ltd; p.87: Anthony Blake Picture Library; p.91a: Greg Evans Picture Library; p.91b: Greg Evans Picture Library; p.91c: Robert Harding Picture Library; p.91d: Rex Features; p.100: Art Directors and Trip; p.104: Powerstock Zefa; p.125: Art Directors and Trip; p.135.1: Corbis UK Ltd; p.135.2: Photofusion; p.153: Popperfoto; p.182a: Popperfoto; p.182b: Rex Features; p.182c Powerstock Zefa; p.182d Robert Harding Picture Library; p.187 Robert Harding Picture Library; p.196: Art Directors and Trip; p.197: Rex Features; p.216: Powerstock Zefa; p.222: Rex Interstock.

# Contents

## To the student

### Who is this book for?
This book is for anyone preparing for the Cambridge First Certificate in English exam and covers the grammar needed for the exam. You can use it with a general English language course for extra grammar practice or with practice tests as part of a revision programme. You can use it in class or for self-study.

### How do I use this book?
There are two ways to use this book. You can either start at Unit 1 and work through to the end of the book, or you can do the Entry test on p.vii to find out which units you need most practice in and begin with those.

### What is in this book?
This book contains 25 units. Each unit is in four parts:

**A: Context listening** This introduces the grammar of the unit in context. This will help you to understand the grammar more easily when you study section B. It also gives you useful listening practice. Play the recording and answer the questions. Then check your answers in the Key before you read the Grammar section.

**B: Grammar** Read through this section before you do the exercises. For each grammar point there are explanations with examples. You can also refer back to this section when you are doing the exercises.

**C: Grammar exercises** Write your answers to each exercise and then check them in the Key.

**D: Exam practice** Each unit has a writing task and one other exam task. These have been designed to give you practice in the

grammar for that unit as well as helping you to get to know the different parts of the exam. The Use of English tasks test the grammar presented in that unit, but they also test other areas of grammar (which are presented in the rest of the book). In the actual First Certificate exam, each question would test a different grammatical point.

### The Key
The Key contains:
- answers for all the exercises. Check your answers at the end of each exercise. The Key tells you which part of the Grammar section you need to look at again if you have any problems.
- sample answers for exercises where you use your own ideas to help you check your work.
- sample answers for all the writing tasks in the Exam practice section. Read these after you have written your own answer. Study the language used and the way the ideas are organised.

### The Recording Scripts
There are recording scripts for the Context listening in each unit, and for the Exam practice listening tasks. Do not look at the script until after you have answered the questions. It is a good idea to play the recording again while you read the script.

### Note on contractions
This book generally uses contractions, for example *I'm* for *I am*, *wasn't* for *was not*, because these are always used in speech and are common in written English. The full forms are used in formal written English.

# To the teacher

This book offers concise yet comprehensive coverage of the grammar students need for the Cambridge First Certificate in English exam. It can be used for self-study or with a class. It will be particularly valuable for revision, for students retaking the exam and for candidates in classes where some students are not entered for the exam. Sections A, B and C are designed to be useful for all students, whether entered for the First Certificate exam or not.

### The Entry test

The entry test can be used diagnostically as a means of prioritising the language areas to be covered, either for a class, or for individual students.

**A: Context listening** This section is suitable for classroom use. Many of the tasks can be done in pairs or small groups if appropriate.

**B: Grammar** This section is designed for private study, but you may wish to discuss those parts which are particularly relevant to your students' needs.

**C: Grammar exercises** This section can be done in class or set as homework. Students can be encouraged to check their own work and discuss any difficulties they encounter.

**D: Exam practice** This section can be used to familiarise students with the exam task types while offering further practice in the grammar for each unit. Each task is followed by a Grammar focus task, designed to raise students' awareness of a particular language point covered in that unit. The book contains at least one task from each part of the Reading, Writing, Use of English and Listening papers. There are more tasks from the Use of English paper than the others because it is a grammar-based paper. The writing tasks cover the full range of tasks which students may come across in the exam, including articles, compositions, short stories and letters. The Writing hints offer extra support in the form of useful words and expressions.

In classes where only some of the students are entered for the First Certificate exam, you might prefer to set exam tasks as extra work for exam candidates only. Alternatively, you could set the tasks for all students, as a further opportunity to practise the grammar of each unit.

You can do this test before using the book to help you choose what to study. Choose the correct answer, **A**, **B** or **C**, for each question. When you have finished, check your answers on p.226. The key tells you which units are most important for you.

1   Teresa ...................... Russian at evening classes this term.
   A   is studying
   B   studies
   C   study

2   I don't know what this sentence ...................... .
   A   is meaning
   B   means
   C   mean

3   Clive was driving into town when he ...................... out of petrol.
   A   was running
   B   run
   C   ran

4   I don't enjoy computer games now, but I ...................... like them when I was younger.
   A   was used to
   B   used to
   C   would

5   We expected George at 7.30 but he ...................... yet.
   A   hasn't arrived
   B   has arrived
   C   didn't arrive

6   The film started ...................... so you've missed quite a lot.
   A   for half an hour
   B   half an hour ago
   C   since half an hour

7   When ...................... the picnic, they went for a swim in the lake.
   A   they'd been eating
   B   they'd eaten
   C   they've eaten

8   ...................... my sister three times today but her number's always engaged.
   A   I'd phoned
   B   I've been phoning
   C   I've phoned

9   Anna:   Shall I ring you at one o'clock?
   Ben:    No, my lunch hour is earlier tomorrow so ...................... my lunch in the canteen then. Ring me at about one-thirty.
   A   I'm eating
   B   I'll be eating
   C   I eat

10   ...................... to the dentist after college so I can't play squash with you.
   A   I'm going
   B   I'll go
   C   I go

11   I'll write to you as soon as ...................... my exam results.
   A   I know
   B   I'll know
   C   I'm going to know

12 The builders ..................... the house by the end of this month.
- A  have finished
- B  will have finished
- C  will have been finishing

13 This dictionary is ..................... useful than that one.
- A  less
- B  as
- C  so

14 I keep my grammar notes in a ..................... folder.
- A  plastic big red
- B  red big plastic
- C  big red plastic

15 Until last week, he ..................... a motorbike before.
- A  had never ridden
- B  never had ridden
- C  had ridden never

16 The day before the holiday, the men worked ..................... than usual.
- A  hardly
- B  hardest
- C  harder

17 Doesn't your brother ..................... discos?
- A  enjoy
- B  enjoys
- C  enjoying

18 Let's take a break soon, ..................... ?
- A  is it
- B  will you
- C  shall we

19 Most of the houses in this country have ..................... .
- A  a garden
- B  the garden
- C  garden

20 My father normally reads the paper while eating ..................... .
- A  a breakfast
- B  the breakfast
- C  breakfast

21 The first thing they did when they met after twenty years was to hug ..................... .
- A  each other
- B  someone else
- C  themselves

22 ..................... the children look like their mother.
- A  Either
- B  Both
- C  Neither

23 My manager says we ..................... take more than ten minutes for our break and, if we do, he'll make us work extra hours.
- A  don't have to
- B  don't need to
- C  mustn't

24 I ran all the way to the station but when I got there I realised that ..................... because all the trains were delayed.
- A  I didn't need to hurry
- B  I needn't have hurried
- C  I didn't have to hurry

25 ................... to take a spare T-shirt as you'll probably get really hot playing tennis.
   A  You'd better
   B  You should
   C  You ought

26 You look really busy. ................... I put the shopping away for you?
   A  Would
   B  Shall
   C  Will

27 When I got home I looked at the bill and realised the restaurant ................... added it up wrong so I'd paid too much.
   A  must have
   B  should have
   C  could have

28 That bicycle ................... belong to Judy – it's much too big for her.
   A  mustn't
   B  mightn't
   C  can't

29 While my car ................... I wandered round the city centre.
   A  be repaired
   B  was repairing
   C  was being repaired

30 Katie ................... her hair cut short when she left school.
   A  had
   B  did
   C  made

31 Gareth ................... he was never going to lend Robert anything again.
   A  informed
   B  said
   C  told

32 I asked Ruth where ................... her coat.
   A  did she buy
   B  had she bought
   C  she had bought

33 I always avoid ................... on the bus because it makes me feel ill.
   A  to read
   B  reading
   C  read

34 My grandfather remembers ................... into this house when he was a very small boy.
   A  moving
   B  move
   C  to move

35 If you don't know a word, you can look ................... in your dictionary.
   A  it up
   B  up it
   C  it

36 I've never really got ................... my neighbour, probably because we're so different.
   A  up to
   B  through
   C  on with

37 I'll book seats for the concert, if there
....................... any good ones available.

A   will be

B   were

C   are

38 Liam would have saved a lot of money, if
he ....................... to my advice.

A   would listen

B   had listened

C   was listening

39 We'll go for a walk ....................... it's foggy –
I hate walking in the fog.

A   if

B   in case

C   unless

40 I wish I ....................... a good memory – it
would make learning English much easier.

A   had had

B   had

C   would have

41 Alfred wears an old coat ....................... his suit
when he walks to work.

A   on

B   above

C   over

42 We're having a party ....................... the last
day of term.

A   in

B   on

C   at

43 As we can't agree ....................... this subject,
we won't discuss it again.

A   about

B   in

C   with

44 All the nurses were very kind .......................
me when I was ill.

A   with

B   to

C   of

45 I enjoyed ....................... last week.

A   the book you lent me

B   the book which you lent it to me

C   the book, that you lent me

46 This is the room in ....................... the famous
poet died.

A   which

B   where

C   that

47 I left the cinema ....................... I had a
headache and the film was very noisy.

A   as

B   so that

C   therefore

48 I'm ....................... tired to work tonight. I'll
finish my homework in the morning.

A   very

B   too

C   so

49 ....................... Martin could easily afford to go
on holiday, he never does.

A   Although

B   Despite

C   In spite of

50 Since ....................... school, Sheila has had
several interesting jobs.

A   left

B   leaving

C   to leave

## A Context listening

**1** You are going to hear Millie talking on her mobile phone to her friend Lisa. It's Saturday morning. Before you listen, look at the picture. Why do you think Millie is phoning Lisa? .................................

.................................................................

.................................................................

Lisa

Millie

NEW ROC

**2** 🎧 **1a** Listen and check if you were right.

**3** 🎧 **1a** Listen again and answer these questions. Write complete sentences.

  1 What's Millie doing this morning? *She's looking round the shops.* ...........................

  2 What does she do nearly every Saturday? ...................................................

  3 What's she looking for? ...............................................................................

  4 What's Lisa wearing? ...................................................................................

  5 What's she doing this morning? ................................................................

  6 What does she do whenever she goes to town? ...................................

  7 What's Millie looking at right now? .........................................................

  8 What does Lisa want Millie to do now? ..................................................

**4** Look at your answers to Exercise 3 and answer these questions.

  1 Look at answers 2 and 6. What tense are they? ...................................

  2 Look at answers 1, 3, 4, 5 and 7. What tense are they? .....................

  3 Which sentences are about regular actions? .........................................

  4 Which sentences are about actions at or around the time of speaking? ............

  5 Look at answer 8. Does it fit the pattern? ...........................................

## B Grammar

### 1 Present simple

| + | verb / verb + -s | *She **works** in London.* |
|---|---|---|
| – | do / does not + verb | *He **doesn't work** in London.* |
| ? | do / does ... + verb? | *Where **do** you **work**?* |

We use the **present simple**:

◆ to say when things happen if they take place regularly:
*They **eat lunch at two o'clock**.*

◆ to talk about permanent situations:
*I **work** in London.*

◆ to state general truths:
*Popular CDs **sell** really fast.*
*The moon **goes** round the earth.*

◆ to talk about habits and how often they happen:
*You **buy** new clothes **every Saturday**.*

◆ to describe the plots of books and films:
*The story **begins** and **ends** in Spain. The year **is** 1937.*

### 2 Present continuous

| + | am / is / are + verb + -ing | *He**'s working** in London this week.* |
|---|---|---|
| – | am / is / are not + verb + -ing | *I**'m not working** in London this week.* |
| ? | am / is / are ... + verb + -ing? | ***Are** you **working** in London this week?* |

We use the **present continuous**:

◆ to talk about the present moment:
*I**'m wearing** a pair of old jeans.*
*I**'m looking** at that CD right now.*

◆ to suggest that an action is temporary, often with words like *now*, *at the moment*, *at present* or *just*:
*They**'re eating** lunch **at the moment**.*
*I**'m working** in London **this week**. (= I don't usually work in London)*

◆ for an action around the time of speaking, which has begun but is not finished:
*I**'m doing** my homework.*
*I**'m looking** round the shops. (Millie isn't looking round at this moment – she has stopped to talk to Lisa – but she plans to continue looking round later)*

◆ for changing or developing situations:
*That group**'s becoming** more well known.*
*The earth's temperature **is rising**.*

◆ with a word like *always* or *continually*, if we want to criticise or complain:
*You**'re always buying** new clothes! (= you buy too many)*
*I**'m always forgetting** people's names. (= it's very irritating)*

◆ with always when something unexpected happens several times:
*I**'m always meeting** my neighbour John near the station. I guess he works somewhere near there.*

## 3 State verbs

These verbs are nearly always used in a simple rather than a continuous tense. They are mostly about thoughts, feelings, belonging and the senses:

*... that special CD **you want** to get.* (**not** ~~you are wanting to~~)
*You **don't deserve** to hear it.* (**not** ~~you aren't deserving to~~)

The following are some important **state verbs**:

◆ thoughts: *believe, know, mean, realise, recognise, remember, suppose, understand, feel* (= believe), *think* (= believe):
*I **think** you're wrong.*
*We **feel** this letter should be changed.*
⚠ *Feel* and *think* are not state verbs when they mean the action:
*I'm **thinking** about my holiday.*
*We're **feeling** cold.*

◆ feelings: *adore, dislike, despise, hate, like, love, want, wish, prefer:*
*They **despise** me because of the way I'm living.*

◆ belonging: *belong, have / have got* (= possess), *own, possess:*
*It **belongs** to my father.*
*The manager **has** the biggest company car.*
⚠ *Have* can be continuous when it does not mean 'possess':
*Steve's **having** a difficult time at college this term.*
*Can I phone you back later? We're **having** lunch right now.*

◆ senses: *smell, taste, hear, see:*
*This sauce **tastes** disgusting.*
*I **hear** what you're saying to me, but I don't agree.*
***Do** you **see** anything you want to buy here?*

We use *can* with these verbs to show we are talking about this moment:
*I **can see** the postman at the gate.*
*I **can hear** someone in the next room.*
⚠ *Taste* and *smell* can be continuous when they mean the action:
*I'm **tasting** the sauce.*

*See* can be continuous when it means 'meet':
***Are** you **seeing** Tom today?*

⚠ *Listen to, watch* and *look at* are not state verbs and can be continuous:
*I'm **listening to** music and Diane **is watching** a video upstairs.*

◆ other state verbs: *contain, deserve, fit, seem, look* (= seem), *look like, matter, weigh:*
*This medicine **contains** aspirin.*
*Mark **weighs** 70 kilos.*
⚠ *Weigh* can be continuous when it means the action:
*The shop assistant's **weighing** the cheese.*

## C Grammar exercises

**1** In five of these sentences there is a verb in the wrong tense. Underline each mistake and write the correction.

1  My brother <u>lives</u> with us until he can find a flat of his own. ..............is living..............
2  These days we're always having tests in school. ....................................................
3  I'm not having enough money for a long holiday this year. ....................................................
4  Everyone needs a break from work sometimes. ....................................................
5  I'm liking a good cup of coffee after lunch. ....................................................
6  I must lose weight – I'm weighing over 80 kilos. ....................................................
7  Maria is going to the shops every Saturday morning. ....................................................
8  What period of history are you studying this term? ....................................................

**2** Fill in the gaps with the correct form of the verb in brackets.

1  My father ..............knows.............. (know) all about mending cars, but nothing about bicycles.
2  A: Why ............................... (you wear) my coat?
   B: Oh, I'm sorry. It ............................... (look) like mine in this light.
3  This pie ............................... (smell) a bit odd. What's in it?
4  I ............................... (like) the jacket of this suit, but unfortunately the trousers
   ............................... (not fit) me any more.
5  You're very quiet this evening. What ............................... (you think) about?
6  A: I ............................... (have) no idea what this sentence ............................... (mean).
   Can you translate it?
   B: No, sorry. I ............................... (not understand) it either.
7  A: ............................... (you see) those men near the door? They ...............................
   (look) at us very strangely.
   B: Yes. You're right. ............................... (you recognise) them from anywhere?
   A: No, but they certainly ............................... (seem) to know us. They
   ............................... (come) across to speak to us.
8  A: What ............................... (you do) in the kitchen?
   B: I ............................... (just make) some coffee.
   A: Well, go away. I ............................... (not want) your help. Our guests
   ............................... (wait) for their dessert, and you ............................... (get)
   in my way!
9  I played football at school, but now I ............................... (prefer) swimming
   or tennis.

**3** Fill in the gaps with the correct form of the verbs in the box.

| behave | come | cost | eat | enjoy | feel | ~~go~~ | have | have | have |
|---|---|---|---|---|---|---|---|---|---|
| like | love | realise | say | serve | show | smile | stay | take | visit |

Dear Stephanie,

How are you? We're fine. Our trip round the States ............is..going............ (1) well and we
.............................. (2) ourselves very much. One good surprise is that things .............................. (3)
less here than back home. For example, this weekend we .............................. (4) in a motel beside a
lake. We .............................. (5) a room with a beautiful view for only $35 per night.

The only thing we .............................. (not) (6) much is the food. Restaurants
.............................. (7) dinner rather early. We .............................. (never) (8) at six o'clock
at home so we .............................. (not) (9) hungry then and Americans .............................. (10)
very big meals. Apart from that, we .............................. (11) a wonderful time. We
.............................. (12) lots of interesting little towns and we .............................. (13) the scenery.

People here .............................. (14) in a very friendly manner towards strangers, all the shop
assistants .............................. (15) at us, and everyone .............................. (16) 'Have a nice day!'
At home, the TV .............................. (always) (17) us bad news stories about the States, but in
fact, when you .............................. (18) here, you .............................. (19) it's a really great
place.

We .............................. (20) lots of photos to show you.

                                        Much love,

                                        Mick and Mary

**4** Write six true sentences about yourself, using the words in the box and a suitable verb in the correct form.

| at the moment | before breakfast | every day |
|---|---|---|
| most weekends | once a year | ~~right now~~ | this term |

1  I'm doing my homework right now, and I'm listening to a CD.
2  ..............................................................................................................................
3  ..............................................................................................................................
4  ..............................................................................................................................
5  ..............................................................................................................................
6  ..............................................................................................................................
7  ..............................................................................................................................

## D  Exam practice

### Listening

🎧 **1b** You will hear an interview with a university student. For questions **1–7**, choose the best answer, **A, B** or **C**.

1  Today's edition of Study Talk is about an unusual
   A  university.
   B  course.
   C  hobby.

   [ ] **1**

2  What is the subject that Ellis Graham is studying for his degree?
   A  surfing
   B  mathematics
   C  computing

   [ ] **2**

3  What does Jed suggest about most people who enjoy surfing?
   A  They waste time when they should be studying.
   B  They know a lot of unimportant information.
   C  They are not very intelligent.

   [ ] **3**

4  Ellis says the course he is doing at university
   A  is extremely popular.
   B  accepts people who failed on other courses.
   C  attracts applications from other universities.

   [ ] **4**

5  What does Ellis make Jed understand?
   A  Jed needs to practise seriously to be a good surfer.
   B  Jed had the wrong idea about Ellis's studies.
   C  Jed does not have to work as hard as the students.

   [ ] **5**

6  What plans does Ellis say he has for the future?
   A  to travel to other countries
   B  to join a research project
   C  to start a business

   [ ] **6**

7  Ellis has problems with Jed's last question because
   A  it involves discussing something secret.
   B  he is unsure of the facts.
   C  it's hard to find uncrowded beaches.

   [ ] **7**

These are some extracts from the first part of the interview. Underline the tenses that the speakers used.

1 And today, someone *sits* / *is sitting* beside me to give us some info ...
2 ... there are some people who *think* / *are thinking* it's not really a subject for serious study ...
3 ... he actually *does* / *he's actually doing* a degree ...
4 ... in something I *enjoy* / *am enjoying* from time to time ...
5 ... you're a mathematician who *goes* / *is going* surfing in his free time ...
6 So what *do you do* / *are you doing*? You have classes on the beach?
7 We learn about ... how waves *form* / *are forming* ...

## Writing

You are on holiday in a place where the way of life is rather different from the area where you live. You want to tell a friend about the customs of the place, the way visitors are treated, and describe how you feel and what you are doing. Write a **letter** in **120–180** words in an appropriate style. Do not write any addresses.

This task gives you a chance to practise:
using the present simple for the customs.
using the present continuous for what you're doing on your holiday.

**Useful words and expressions**
*to enjoy, to miss, to stay with, to make friends, to have problems with traditional, typical, strange, difference*

> See also the letter in Grammar exercises, Exercise 3.

# 2

## Past tenses

past simple; past continuous; *used to* (and *to be used to*); would

<table>
<tr><td>A</td><td>Context listening</td></tr>
</table>

**1** You are going to hear Jack talking to his grandmother. Before you listen, look at questions 1–8 and guess who did what. Write *J* (for Jack) or *G* (for Gran) or *M* (for Jack's mother). Did Jack, his Gran or his Mum:

1 go to London? ...J...
2 go to the cinema? ........
3 see a famous footballer? ........
4 collect autographs? ........
5 go up to town alone? ........
6 scream at pop concerts? ........
7 worry about homework? ........
8 go to a club? ........

**2** 🎧 2 Listen and check if you were right.

**3** Look at your answers to Exercise 1 and answer these questions.

1 Which things did Jack do last Saturday? ...........................................................................................
...................................................................................................................................................................
2 What tense does he use? .....................................................................................................................
3 Which things did Gran do when she was young? ...........................................................................
...................................................................................................................................................................
4 Did she do them regularly? ...............................................................................................................

**4** 🎧 2 Listen again and complete these sentences.

1 We did some revision for our exams while we ...................................................................................... .
2 When we ..................................................... for the cinema, we saw a really famous footballer.
3 He ..................................... a burger and all the crowds ............................................... past but nobody noticed him except me.

**5** Which tense is in the gaps in Exercise 4? ........................................................................................

## B Grammar

## 1 Past simple

| + | verb + -ed* | *I **wanted** it.* |
|---|---|---|
| − | *did not* + verb | *I **didn't want** it.* |
| ? | *did ... + verb?* | *What **did** you **want**?* |

*Regular verbs add -ed or -d to the verb: want → wanted; hope → hoped
Many common verbs are irregular: think → thought; make → made ⟩ See Appendix 2
To be is irregular: am, is (not) → was (not); are (not) → were (not)*

We use the **past simple**:

◆ for completed actions and events in the past:
   *We **had** an exam on Thursday.*
   *We **caught** the coach.*

◆ for a sequence of actions or events:
   *I **went** round the shops, then I **went** to the cinema.*

◆ for permanent or long-term situations in the past:
   *I really **enjoyed** myself when I was a teenager.*

◆ for repeated events:
   *Jack's grandmother **went** to lots of concerts.*
   *She always **asked** for an autograph when she **met** someone famous.*

⟩ See also Unit 3 for further uses of the past simple.

## 2 Past continuous

| + | *was/were* + verb + -ing | *They **were waiting**.* |
|---|---|---|
| − | *was/were not* + verb + -ing | *She **wasn't waiting**.* |
| ? | *was/were ... + verb + -ing?* | ***Were** you **waiting**?* |

We use the **past continuous**:

◆ for an activity beginning before a past action and continuing until or after it. The action is usually in the past simple:
   *We **did** some revision while we **were travelling**.*
   *When we **were queuing** for the cinema, we **saw** a really famous footballer.*

   we **did** some revision
   ▼
   ▲▲▲▲▲
   we **were travelling**

◆ for two things happening at the same time:
   *He **was buying** a burger and all the crowds **were walking** past.*

   he **was buying** a burger
   ▼▼▼▼▼
   ▲▲▲▲▲
   the crowds **were walking** past

◆ for repeated events, with a word like *always* or *continually*, especially if the speaker is criticising the activity:
*Your mother **was always doing** her homework.* (= She did her homework regularly and often. Jack's grandmother thinks she worked too hard!)

◆ for unfulfilled plans, with verbs like *hope*, *plan* etc.:
*I **was hoping** to find a new jacket.* (= but I didn't find one)

⚠ State verbs are used in the past simple, not the past continuous (≻ see p.4):
*I **didn't know** him.* (**not** ~~I wasn't knowing him.~~)

## 3 *Used to (do)* and *would (do)*

| + | used to + verb | He **used to read** a lot. |
|---|---|---|
| – | did not use to + verb | We **didn't use to read** a lot. |
| ? | did ... use to + verb? | **Did** you **use to read** a lot? |

| + | would + verb | He **would read** a lot. |
|---|---|---|
| – | would not + verb | We **wouldn't read** a lot. |
| ? | would ... + verb? | **Would** you **read** a lot? |

We use *used to* and *would* to talk about past habits when we are emphasising that they are no longer true:
*I **used to collect** all the autographs of film stars when I was a teenager.* (= she doesn't do this now)
*I **would go** up to town on my own.* (= she doesn't do this now)

*Used to* can describe actions and states, but *would* can only describe actions:
*All the teenagers **used to** / **would scream** at pop concerts.*
*They **used to be** crazy about the Beatles.*
(**not** ~~They would be crazy about the Beatles.~~)

⚠ *Used to* is much more common than *would*.

⚠ Do not confuse *used to (do)*, which is a past tense, with *be / get used to (doing)*, which can be present, past or future.
*Be / Get used to (doing)* means 'be / become accustomed to doing'. Compare:
*I **used to work** at weekends.* (= in the past I worked at weekends, but I don't now)
*I'**m used to working** at weekends.* (= I often work at weekends, it doesn't worry me)

The question form is:
*Are you **used to working** at weekends?*

*Be / Get used to* can be followed by a noun:
*He **wasn't used to criticism** and found it hard to accept.* (= people hadn't criticised him before so he didn't like it)

## C Grammar exercises

**1** Fill in the gaps with the past simple of the verbs in the box.

| be | ~~begin~~ | come | drink | eat | explain | feed |
| find | find | get | give | go | have | know | learn |
| meet | read | seem | speak | spread | tie | write |

# The mystery of **Caspar Hauser**

The mystery of Caspar Hauser ....began........ **(1)** in Nuremburg, Germany, about 200 years ago. One morning, the people of the town .......................... **(2)** a young man standing alone in the square. He was holding a piece of paper in his hand. The paper .......................... **(3)** only that he .......................... **(4)** the son of a soldier. Caspar .......................... **(5)** how to say a few words and when given a paper and pencil he .......................... **(6)** his name, but he .......................... **(7)** completely ignorant about everyday life. At first he .......................... **(8)** only bread and .......................... **(9)** only water, but he gradually .......................... **(10)** used to ordinary meals. He also .......................... **(11)** to talk properly.

No one ever .......................... **(12)** out the real truth about his birth, but it is probable that his father kept him in one small room for the whole of his early life. He .......................... **(13)** him on bread and .......................... **(14)** him water to drink. He .......................... **(15)** Caspar up and Caspar never .......................... **(16)** out, he never ..........................**(17)** to anyone or .......................... **(18)** other children. In spite of this extraordinary childhood, Caspar was not stupid. He .......................... **(19)** books and .......................... **(20)** discussions with teachers and philosophers. News about Caspar .......................... **(21)** through Europe and visitors .......................... **(22)** from abroad to meet him. Unfortunately, he lived only a few years, but his strange life story still fascinates many people.

**2** Fill in the gaps with the past simple or past continuous of the verbs in brackets.

1  My parents ...........got........... (*get*) to know each other when they
   .....were studying..... (*study*) at university.

2  Doctor Fisher ................................. (*travel*) widely as a young man and
   ................................. (*always keep*) a diary.

3  I ................................. (*see*) my brother and his girlfriend when I .................................
   (*wait*) for the bus, but they ................................. (*not see*) me.

4  Lily ................................. (*fill*) in the application form and ................................. (*give*)
   it to the receptionist.

5  While I ................................. (*work*) in Rome, I ................................. (*meet*) a girl who
   ................................. (*look*) just like your sister.

6  Simon ................................. (*finish*) with his girlfriend because she .................................
   (*always cancel*) dates at the last moment.

7  Anna's feeling depressed because she ................................. (*hope*) for a pay rise
   last week, but she ................................. (*not get*) one.

**3**  Underline the correct form of the verbs.

# MAKING CHANGES

*Ada Atkins, 93, explains why she has come to live in town*

Years ago, nobody in my village *would lock / was locking* (1) their front doors. We *used to feel / would feel* (2) safe in those days. Last month, I *met / was meeting* (3) my neighbour in the street when I *was walking / would walk* (4) home from the shops and she *told / was telling* (5) me some bad news. Thieves *were breaking / used to break* (6) into people's houses while they *were sitting / would sit* (7) in their back gardens.

I *realised / was realising* (8) that I *wasn't wanting / didn't want* (9) to live there any more. So last week I *was moving / moved* (10) to this little flat. I *am not used / didn't use* (11) to being in the town yet, but people are more friendly than I *was thinking / thought* (12) they might be, and I feel much happier and safer.

**4** Fill in the gaps with a suitable form of *be / get used to*.

1 Rita's very tired this morning. She ..........*isn't used to*.......... (*not*) going to bed late.

2 Don't worry about the children, they ............................................... going to school by bus.

3 My new boss ............................................... giving orders, not receiving them.

4 She ............................................... (*not*) drinking wine and it made her ill.

5 ............................................... (*you*) our climate or do you miss the sunshine?

6 I had never stayed in such an expensive hotel before, but I soon ............................................... it.

**5** Complete these sentences using your own ideas.

1 When our neighbours went to Italy, they *saw some wonderful paintings.*......................

2 I was hoping to finish my homework by eight o'clock last night, but ...............................................
...............................................

3 The film star shouted at the director, then she ...............................................

4 As a small child, I would sometimes ...............................................

5 We were coming out of the café when ...............................................

6 A hundred years ago people ............................................... but now they go by car.

7 While you were lying on a beach, I ...............................................

8 When my father was young, he was always ...............................................

## D  Exam practice

This task tests grammar from the rest of the book as well as the grammar in this unit.

### Use of English

For questions **1–15**, read the text below and decide which answer (**A**, **B**, **C** or **D**) best fits each space. There is an example at the beginning (**0**).

Example:

**0**    Ⓐ spent     **B** made     **C** held     **D** went

### A MUSICIAN IS DISCOVERED

When William was a small boy, the family **(0)** ..A.. their holidays on his grandfather's farm in the mountains. On their arrival, the children **(1)** ........ race around the yard and orchard, overjoyed to be free from the strictly correct **(2)** ........ expected of them in the city. As the days passed, their parents also **(3)** ........ increasingly relaxed, and the house rang with the laughter of old friends. It was during one of these visits that William's **(4)** ........ to remember a tune led to the suggestion that the boy should **(5)** ........ up a musical instrument. One evening everyone was gathered in the living-room, and a discussion **(6)** ........ about the differences between a piece of music which was popular at the time and a well-known folk song. Various adults tried to **(7)** ........ the similarity of the two tunes to those who **(8)** ........ with them, but without success. **(9)** ........ fell, and then William, who was about five, made his **(10)** ........ to the piano and played first one tune and then the other. His parents and their friends were astonished **(11)** ........ no one had even heard William **(12)** ........ to play before. 'That child must go to a music teacher,' **(13)** ........ one neighbour, and the others agreed. William's parents were persuaded to **(14)** ........ help with payment of the fees, and his musical **(15)** ........ began.

| | | | | |
|---|---|---|---|---|
| **1** | **A** would | **B** were | **C** might | **D** had |
| **2** | **A** manner | **B** behaviour | **C** style | **D** attitude |
| **3** | **A** showed | **B** acted | **C** became | **D** found |
| **4** | **A** talent | **B** gift | **C** ability | **D** skill |
| **5** | **A** take | **B** start | **C** pick | **D** bring |
| **6** | **A** happened | **B** came | **C** entered | **D** arose |
| **7** | **A** prove | **B** claim | **C** pretend | **D** test |
| **8** | **A** refused | **B** varied | **C** disagreed | **D** resisted |

9   **A** Silence        **B** Argument       **C** Doubt          **D** Conclusion
10  **A** path           **B** way            **C** route          **D** direction
11  **A** so             **B** although       **C** when           **D** as
12  **A** want           **B** decide         **C** try            **D** go
13  **A** told           **B** stated         **C** confirmed      **D** expressed
14  **A** accept         **B** attain         **C** achieve        **D** apply
15  **A** work           **B** living         **C** career         **D** study

## Grammar focus task

In the exam task, there are some irregular past simple verbs. Without looking back at the text, write the past simple form of these verbs.

1 arise ....*arose*....    2 become ...............    3 begin ...............    4 come ...............
5 fall ...............    6 find ...............    7 go ...............    8 hold ...............
9 lead ...............    10 make ...............    11 ring ...............    12 spend ...............

## Writing

A magazine is running a competition called 'Memories'. Readers are asked to send in stories of **120–180** words about a significant event in their early childhood. Write your **story**.

## Writing hints

This task gives you a chance to practise:
using the past simple and past continuous for events in the past.
using *used to* and *would* for past habits.

**Useful words and expressions**
*at the time, by chance, I clearly remember, I now realise, in those days, luckily, one day, there was / were, unfortunately, when I was X years old*

# Present perfect and past simple
present perfect simple and past simple; present perfect simple
and continuous

**1** You are going to hear two
people called Mike and
Lucy talking to each other.
Before you listen, look at
the picture. How do Mike
and Lucy know each
other? ..............................

..............................................

**What is Lucy's problem?**

..............................................

..............................................

**2** 🎧 3 Listen and check if you were right.

**3** 🎧 3 Listen again and write Mike and Lucy's exact words. Stop the recording
when you need to.

1 What does Mike say about finishing work? Mike says 'I finished at lunchtime today. '

2 What does he say about this afternoon? He says '..........................................................'

3 What does Lucy say about finishing her essay? She says '..........................................'

4 When does she say she started it? She says '..............................................................'

5 What does Mike say about studying history? He says '.....................................................'

6 How long has Lucy lived next door? She says '...............................................................'

7 How long has Mike lived there? He says '.......................................................................'

8 Why is Mike surprised? He says '....................................................................................'

**4** Look at your answers to Exercise 3 and answer these questions.

1 Look at answers 1, 4 and 5. What tense are they? ..................................................

2 Look at answers 2, 3, 6, 7 and 8. What tense are they? ..........................................

3 Which sentences are about a period of time which is still continuing? ..........................

4 Which sentences are about a period of time which is finished? ....................................

## B Grammar

### 1 Present perfect simple or past simple?

| + | has/have + past participle | *I've finished.* |
|---|---|---|
| - | has/have not + past participle | *She hasn't finished.* |
| ? | has/have ... + past participle? | *Have you finished?* |

Some verbs are irregular: break → broken; go → gone ➤ See Appendix 2.
For past simple forms, see Unit 2, Grammar, part 1.

We use the **present perfect simple**:

◆ with *since* or *for*, about a period of time which is still continuing:
*I've **lived** next door **since** June.* (= and I still live next door now)
*I've **lived** there **for** four years.* (= and I still live there)

◆ with questions asking *how long*:
***How long have** you **lived** here?* (= I know you still live here)
⚠ Sometimes we can use also use the present perfect continuous.
➤ See Grammar, part 2.

◆ for unfinished actions and events, often with *still* or *yet*:
*I **still haven't finished** it.*
*I **haven't finished** it **yet**.*
⚠ *Still* and *yet* are always used with a negative in the present perfect. (*Still* goes before the verb and *yet* goes after it.)

◆ for events repeated over a period of time until the present (they may continue):
*You've **played** the saxophone every night.* (= until now, and you will probably continue to play every night)

◆ for events which happened in the past at a time which is unknown and/or irrelevant:
*I've **started** my essay.* (= we don't know when)
*I've **lost** my new camera.* (= it's not important when or where)

We use the **past simple**:

◆ with *for*, about a period of time which is finished:
*I **lived** there **for** four years.* (= but I don't live there now)

◆ with questions asking *when*:
***When did** you **move** here?* (= the move is in the past)

◆ for completed actions and events in the past, often with *ago*:
*I **finished** it half an hour **ago**.*

◆ for events repeated over a period of time in the past (they are now finished):
*You **played** the saxophone every night.* (= but you don't any more)

We use the **present perfect simple**:

◆ for events that happened in the recent past (often with *just*):
*Flight 206 **has landed**.* (= in the last few minutes)
*She's **just gone** to the cinema.* (= and she's there now)

◆ when the time stated is not finished:
*I've **spent** this morning writing an essay.* (= it's still morning)

*The builders **have started** working on the kitchen this week.* (it's still this week)

◆ when we talk about a period of time up to the present:
*I've **been** to Los Angeles but not to New York.* (= in my life so far – I may go to New York in the future)
*The team **has won** several matches.* (= and may win more)

◆ when we talk about how many times something has happened:
***This is the first time** anyone **has complained**.*

◆ with adverbs like *already*, *before*, *ever* and *never*:
*Nobody's **ever complained before**.* (= until now)
*I've **never tried** Japanese food.* (= but I might one day)
*I've **already rung** the restaurant.*
*I've **met** her **before** somewhere.*
⚠ *Never, ever* and *already* go between the auxiliary and the main verb. *Before* goes after the verb.

◆ after a superlative (➤ see Unit 7):
*It's the best cup of coffee I've **had** here.*

We use the **past simple**:

◆ for events that happened at a particular time in the past:
*Flight 206 **landed** at one o'clock.*
or within a period of time in the past:
*She **was** at the cinema between midday and two o'clock.* (= but she's not there now)

◆ when the time stated is finished:
*I **spent** this morning writing an essay.* (= it's now afternoon so 'this morning' is in the past)
*I **started** my essay last week.* (= 'last week' is definitely in the past)
*I **lost** my new camera in London.* (= the place fixes it at a time in the past)

◆ when we talk about past events which are not connected to the present:
*I **went** to Los Angeles but not to New York.* (= on a particular trip which is in the past)
*The Chinese **invented** printing.*

## 2 Present perfect simple or continuous?

| + | has / have been + past participle | I've been working hard. |
| - | has / have not been + past participle | She hasn't been working hard. |
| ? | has / have ... + been + past participle? | Have you been working hard? |

The present perfect and the present perfect continuous are both used to describe events or activities which started in the past and have continued up to the present, or activities which stopped recently. Some verbs can be used in either the present perfect simple or continuous with little difference in meaning. These are verbs which describe activities which normally happen over a period of time, e.g. *live, study, learn, wait, work*:
*Martin **has lived** / **has been living** in Australia for five years.*

We use the **present perfect continuous**:

◆ to talk about how long something has been happening:
*I've **been driving** since five o'clock this morning.*
*The children **have been playing** happily all morning.*
*We've **been worrying** about her all week.*

*How long **have** you **been watching** TV?*

◆ to focus on the activity or event itself (whether it is complete or not is unimportant):
*He's **been reading** the newspapers while he was waiting for her. (= we're interested in how he passed the time − not if he read every page)*
*I've **been mending** the car. (= that's why I'm dirty)*

We use the **present perfect simple**:

◆ to talk about how often or how many times something has happened:
*I've **driven** there several times before.*

*The children **have played** four games of tennis this morning.*
*I've **worried** about her every day since she set off.*
*I've **watched** three programmes.*

◆ to focus on the results of an activity or event which is complete:

*I've **read** the newspapers. (= I've finished reading them)*

*I've **mended** the car. (= I've just finished so we can go out in it now)*

⚠ We never use the present tense to talk about how long we have been doing something:
*I've **been learning** the piano **for a long time**.*
(**not** ~~I'm learning the piano for a long time.~~)

State verbs are not usually used in the present perfect continuous (≻ see Unit 1):
*I've **known** her since she was four years old. (**not** ~~I've been knowing her...~~ )*

## C  Grammar exercises

**1** Match these sentence halves.

1  He's talked to her on the phone ...j...
2  This summer the pool was only open ........
3  The whole team felt exhausted ........
4  The rent of my flat has gone up ........
5  She's had nothing to eat ........
6  I got very wet ........
7  I spent a month in Brazil ........
8  She's always enjoyed painting ........
9  I haven't had such a good time ........
10  The post arrived ........

a  for years.
b  on my way home from work yesterday.
c  since nine o'clock this morning.
d  when the match finished.
e  ever since she was very young.
f  by 20 per cent this year.
g  a few minutes ago.
h  from April till September.
i  in 1992.
j  every night this week.

**2** Fill in the gaps with the present perfect or the past simple of the verbs in brackets.

1  This is only the second time I 've ever flown .......... (*ever fly*) in an aeroplane.

2  The child .......................... (*sleep*) from seven till seven without waking once.

3  Gabriella ........................ (*grow*) five centimetres since last month.

4  I .......................... (*send*) Ed three emails last week but he ........................... (*not reply*) to any of them yet.

5  .......................... (*you learn*) to play chess when you were a child?

6  I .......................... (*buy*) this bicycle five years ago and I ........................... (*use*) it every day since then.

7  How long .......................... (*you have*) that bad cough?

8  The train .......................... (*just arrive*), so hurry and you might catch it.

9  I .......................... (*never see*) such a beautiful rainbow before.

10  I .......................... (*dream*) about a beautiful desert island last night.

11  On Sunday we .......................... (*meet*) outside the cinema as usual.

12  When .......................... (*you get*) that jacket? I ........................... (*not notice*) it before.

**3** Fill in the gaps with a suitable verb in the present perfect or the past simple.

Dear Lewis,

I've been (1) here in Spain for two weeks now and I'm having a really good time. When I ........................... (2) at the airport I ........................... (3) very lonely. But I ........................... (already) (4) some friends and I'm staying with a really nice family. They ........................... (5) me to the seaside last weekend and we ........................... (6) in the sea. I really ........................... (7) it. I ........................... (8) some Spanish but I ........................... (not) (9) to any language classes yet – they start next week. It's now midnight and I need to go to bed as I ........................... (10) a very busy day. I ........................... (11) shopping this morning and I ........................... (12) tennis this afternoon.

Write back soon.

All the best,

Richard

**4** Read this conversation between two people in a sports club. Underline the most suitable form of the verbs.

Anna: Excuse me. *We've waited / We've been waiting* (1) to play tennis since 10.30. It must be our turn now. How long *have you played / have you been playing* (2)?

Tim: Since about 9.30. *We've played / We've been playing* (3) two matches so far this morning and *we haven't finished / we haven't been finishing* (4) the third yet. You'll have to wait or do something else. *Have you tried / Have you been trying* (5) the swimming pool?

Anna: We don't want to swim, we want to play tennis. *You've played / You've been playing* (6) for more than two hours and it's our turn. We're tired of waiting and we haven't got anything to do. *We've read / We've been reading* (7) the magazines we brought with us.

Tim: I said you'll have to wait. I always play on a Saturday morning. Anyway, *we've already started / we've already been starting* (8) the third match.

Anna: Oh well, it looks like we've got no choice, but *we've booked / we've been booking* (9) the court for next Saturday so you'll be unlucky then.

## D Exam practice

### Reading

You are going to read a newspaper article about a news presenter called Katie Derham. Choose from the sentences **A–H** the one which best summarises each part (**1–6**) of the article. There is one extra sentence which you do not need to use.

---

> **A** She decided she was not talented enough for one particular career.
> **B** Other people do not realise what her job is really like.
> **C** She is likely to do well despite some mistakes.
> **D** She does not accept how famous she really is.
> **E** The range of skills she has acquired are an advantage in her present job.
> **F** She recognises which skills she needs to develop.
> **G** There is no truth in some of the reports we read.
> **H** She does not consider herself to be ambitious.

# Katie's path to success

**0** | H

When Katie Derham went to Cambridge University to study economics, she fell in love with the place. 'I was so much enjoying my luck at being in such a beautiful place that while I was there I didn't think further than that and that's still the way I am. I enjoy what's on offer at the moment. People don't believe me, as a lot of media people I work with have had to push very hard to get where they are, but I've been lucky. When I left Cambridge I didn't believe life could be better.'

**1** |

But it has got better and continues to do so. Katie Derham is 28 and she is the new face of television news bulletins on ITN. The regular news presenter finished last year. Katie took over from her and has read the news five nights a week since then. She has survived reports of a couple of slips when she misread some news items and the media interest in her points to a bright future.

**2** |

But Katie does not really take the media interest seriously. Becoming so visible has taken some getting used to, but she does not feel it imposes on her life, despite being recognised on the street. It has not gone to her head and her response is typically modest: 'I think people more often think they were at school with me or they've seen me before in the supermarket serving cheese or something.'

**3** |

And stories of fights amongst the news girls are denied: 'There are so many channels, news programmes and air time that there is plenty of space for everyone. There have always been these kinds of rumours. You get to know a lot of presenters but I've found the others are a support to me – at least they understand the kind of pressures which come with the job.'

**4** |

Katie has just moved into a flat near Regent's Park in London. She is a keen musician and is looking forward to getting her piano into the flat so she can start playing again. There was even a brief moment when she considered trying to make a career out of her piano playing, but she says realism intervened: 'I think you should know what your limitations are. I was adequate but never brilliant.'

**5** |

During college Katie considered many 'serious' professions such as management consultancy and accountancy but journalism was always at the back of her mind although she knew no journalists and had very little knowledge of the profession. Eventually she got a job as a secretary at a radio station. She went on to produce and present a range of radio programmes and started to get noticed. She currently combines being ITN's arts and media correspondent with newsreading and brings a solid journalistic background to the job.

**6** |

For the moment, Katie loves her job despite not getting home until nearly midnight some days. 'I try to persuade my friends to have parties which start at midnight! However often I tell them, they don't take in the reality of what's involved in a media job. They just see me on the screen for a few minutes. But I don't mind missing out – I would be delighted if I was still doing this in a couple of years' time.'

## Grammar focus task

This is an extract from the text. Without looking back at the text, fill in the gaps with the present perfect simple or the past simple of the verbs in the box.

be    fall    finish    get    ~~go~~    have to
not believe    not think    read    take

When Katie Derham ..............went.............. (1) to Cambridge University to study economics, she ............................ (2) in love with the place. 'I was so much enjoying my luck at being in such a beautiful place that while I was there I ............................ (3) further than that and that's still the way I am. I enjoy what's on offer at the moment. People don't believe me, as a lot of media people I work with ............................ (4) push very hard to get where they are, but I ............................ (5) lucky. When I left Cambridge I ............................ (6) life could be better.' But it ............................ (7) better and continues to do so. Katie Derham is 28 and she is the new face of television news bulletins on ITN. The regular news presenter ............................ (8) last year. Katie ............................ (9) over from her and ............................ (10) the news five nights a week since then.

## Writing

You are a student and you are looking for a summer job in England. You see an advertisement in a newspaper for young people to work at an activity centre for children. You believe you have the right experience and decide to apply for the job. Read the job advertisement on which you have made some notes about yourself. Read also the notes you have made to remind you of some other points to include in the letter.

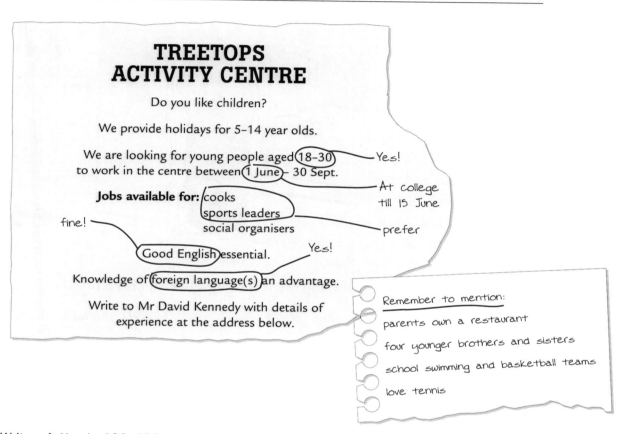

### TREETOPS ACTIVITY CENTRE

Do you like children?

We provide holidays for 5–14 year olds.

We are looking for young people aged (18–30) — Yes!
to work in the centre between (1 June)– 30 Sept.

At college
till 15 June

**Jobs available for:** (cooks
sports leaders)
social organisers — prefer

fine!

(Good English) essential. Yes!

Knowledge of (foreign language(s)) an advantage.

Write to Mr David Kennedy with details of experience at the address below.

Remember to mention:

parents own a restaurant

four younger brothers and sisters

school swimming and basketball teams

love tennis

Write a **letter** in **120–180** words in an appropriate style. Do not write any addresses.

### Writing hints

**This task gives you a chance to practise:**
using the present perfect to describe your experience.
using the past simple to say when you did something.

**Useful words and expressions**
*to be keen on, to look after, to take part in, would prefer, available, fluent, unfortunately*

# 4 Past perfect

past perfect simple and continuous

## A  Context listening

**1** You are going to hear a teenage boy called Richard talking to his mother. Before you listen, look at the picture. How has Richard spent the weekend? ..............................

..................................................................

How does his mother feel?
..................................................................

Why? ..........................................................

..................................................................

..................................................................

**2** 🎧 4 Listen and check if you were right.

**3** 🎧 4 Listen again and fill in the gaps. Stop the recording when you need to.

Richard:  I *'d done* ........................ (1) the ceiling, and I ................................ (2) one wall, when I

........................ (3) paint ...

Richard:  And yesterday afternoon I ................................ (4) bored. I ................................ (5)

to town for a few hours – you know round the centre. I ................................ (6)

the shopping – everything on your list – and I ................................ (7) all my

homework ...

Mother:  I ........................ (8) for an hour when the car ........................ (9) ...

**4** Look at your answers to Exercise 3 and answer these questions.

1  Look at answers 1, 2 and 3. Did 3 happen before or after 1 and 2? ..............................

What tenses does Richard use? ..................................................................

2  Look at answers 4, 5, 6 and 7. Did 4 happen before or after 5, 6 and 7? ..............................

What tenses does Richard use? ..................................................................

3  Look at answers 8 and 9. Which happened first? ..................................................................

What tenses does Richard's mother use? ..................................................................

26

## B Grammar

### 1 Past perfect simple

| + | *had* + past participle | *He'd **painted** the ceiling.* |
|---|---|---|
| – | *had not* + past participle | *He **hadn't painted** the ceiling.* |
| ? | *had ... + past participle?* | ***Had** he **painted** the ceiling?* |

We use the **past perfect simple**:

◆ when we are already talking about the past and want to make it clear that we are referring back to an even earlier time:
*Yesterday afternoon I **was** bored. I**'d been** to town, I**'d done** the shopping and I**'d finished** all my homework so I **decided** to paint my room.*

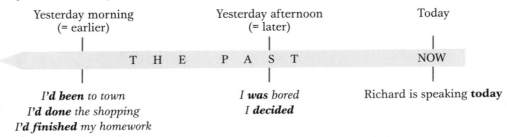

Yesterday morning (= earlier)

Yesterday afternoon (= later)

Today

T H E   P A S T   NOW

*I'd **been** to town*
*I'd **done** the shopping*
*I'd **finished** my homework*

*I **was** bored*
*I **decided***

Richard is speaking **today**

◆ in some sentences with time expressions (*when, after, by the time, as soon as*) when one event happened before the other:
***By the time** Richard's mother **got** home, he**'d finished** painting the room.*
*I**'d painted** one wall **when I ran out** of paint.*

◆ with the adverbs *just, already, ever* and *never*. They go between the auxiliary and the main verb (➢ see also Unit 8):
*He**'d just finished** painting when his mother came in.*
*When she got home he**'d already finished** painting the room.*
*Until last weekend he**'d never painted** a room.*

We don't use the past perfect:

◆ if one action happens at the same time as another:
*When Richard's mother **saw** the room, she **was** horrified.* (**not** ~~When Richard's mother had seen~~ ...)

◆ if one action comes immediately after the other and is connected to it:
*When Jill **heard** the baby cry, she **ran** to pick him up.* (**not** ~~When Jill had heard~~ ...)

**⚠** Notice the difference in meaning between these two sentences:
*When Richard's mother came into the room, he **stopped** painting.*
(= she came in, then he stopped)
*When Richard's mother came into the room, he'**d stopped** painting.*
(= he stopped, then she came in)

## 2 Past perfect continuous

| | | |
|---|---|---|
| **+** | *had been* + verb + *-ing* | **I'd been working** *hard.* |
| **–** | *had not been* + verb + *-ing* | *She **hadn't been working** hard.* |
| **?** | *had ... been* + verb + *-ing?* | ***Had** you **been working** hard?* |

We use the **past perfect continuous**:

♦ to focus on the earlier activity itself or on how long it continued:
*He had a headache because he'**d been playing** computer games for hours.*

♦ when we talk about how long something happened up to a point in the past:
*How long **had** you **been driving** when the car broke down?*
*By the time she arrived I'**d been waiting** for two hours.*

We use the **past perfect simple**:

♦ when we do not need to emphasise the activity or the period of time:
*He'**d played** all of the computer games and wanted to do something different.*

♦ when we talk about how many or how often up to a point in the past:
*I'**d driven** six kilometres when the car broke down.*
*By the time I was 18 I'**d visited** Australia six times.*

State verbs (➢ see Unit 1) are not usually used in the past perfect continuous:
*I'**d known** her since she was four years old.* (**not** ~~I'd been knowing her~~ ...)

# C Grammar exercises

**1** Fill in the gaps with suitable verbs in the past perfect continuous.

1 The phone ............*had been ringing*............ for several minutes before I heard it.

2 Katya ............................................... (*not*) German with Mr Fauser for very long when he retired.

3 Liz didn't know about the surprise party which her parents ............................................... for weeks.

4 I was very pleased when the bus finally arrived because I ............................................... that I would be late for work.

5 When the doctor eventually called my name I ............................................... for 40 minutes.

6 My brother lost his job because he ............................................... jokes to everyone in the office by email.

7 The band ............................................... (*not*) for long when the lights went out.

8 We ............................................... our money to buy a car but we decided to go to Australia instead.

9 How long ............................................... (*they*) for their keys when they found them in the boot of the car?

**2** All these sentences have a verb in the past perfect simple. Is it possible to replace it with the past perfect continuous?

1 I'd worked for the engineering company for three months before I realised my neighbour also worked there. *Yes: I'd been working*...............

2 As soon as George had finished the race, he drank three glasses of water. ...............

3 Everything was white because it had snowed all night. ...............

4 My parents were delighted when I qualified because they had always wanted me to be a doctor. ...............

5 She was exhausted when she got out of the pool because she'd swum three kilometres. ...............

6 We'd only just sat down when the waitress came to take our order. ...............

7 I could tell from their faces that they had argued about something. ...............

8 Our dinner wasn't cooked because I'd forgotten to switch the oven on. ...............

**4**

**3** Fill in the gaps with the past simple, the past perfect or the past perfect continuous of the verb in brackets.

1  I'd never ridden (*never ride*) a bike until I ...........went........... (*go*) to live in Amsterdam.

2  When Martin ................................ (*come*) into the room, his mother nearly ................................ (*faint*) because she ................................ (*see*) him for nearly 20 years.

3  We were held up in a traffic jam so the concert ................................ (*begin*) by the time we ................................ (*arrive*).

4  How long ................................ (*you applying*) for jobs when you ................................ (*get*) this one?

5  ................................ (*you ever do*) any carpentry before you ................................ (*build*) that cupboard?

6  I ................................ (*not see*) Lisa when I went round last night because she ................................ (*go*) to stay with her grandmother.

7  As soon as I ................................ (*sit*) down on the train, I realised that I ................................ (*leave*) my passport at home.

8  I ................................ (*drive*) for about four hours when I ................................ (*realize*) that I was completely lost.

9  When I ................................ (*go*) into the room, everyone ................................ (*stop*) talking and ................................ (*look*) at me.

10  After he ................................ (*wash*) his clothes, he ................................ (*hang*) them outside to dry.

11  The manager was shocked when he ................................ (*discover*) that Jane was a thief. Up until then, he ................................ (*believe*) that she was completely honest.

**4** Fill in the gaps with the past simple, the past perfect or the past perfect continuous of the verbs in the box.

~~agree~~    arrange    arrive    bang    come    forget    go    have
move    not answer    not hear    phone    play    practise

# THE BAND PLAYED ON ...

I had a rather embarrassing experience last year. At that time I played in a band with some friends of mine and, rather nervously, we'd agreed .................... (1) to play at a friend's wedding. We .................... (2) together for about three months and it was the first booking we .................... (*ever*) (3) so we .................... (4) really hard for weeks.

The wedding was on a Saturday. The day before the wedding I had moved to a new flat so I .................... (5) furniture all day and .................... (6) to bed exhausted. At nine o'clock on the Saturday morning the rest of the band met, as we .................... (7), to practise. They kept phoning me but I .................... (8). So in the end one of them .................... (9) round and .................... (10) on the door for fifteen minutes until I woke up. He told me that they .................... (11) me all morning. I .................... (12) anything and I nearly missed the wedding. When I finally .................... (13) at the wedding, I realised that I .................... (14) my guitar.

## Reading

You are going to read an article about a travel competition. For questions **1–6**, choose the answer (**A**, **B**, **C** or **D**) which you think fits best according to the text.

# OBSERVER NEWSPAPER YOUNG TRAVEL WRITER COMPETITION

*As we launch our 13th annual competition, Max Wooldridge, our first winner in 1988, writes about the award's significance and the excitement of being flung into a new world.*

THE greatest buzz I've felt during the past five years was one afternoon on the seventh floor of the car park at Hong Kong's old Kai Tak airport. It was a warm Friday a few weeks before the airport closed in 1998. I'd been writing a feature article about the new airport for the last few days and had just sent it off to a newspaper so I had a free afternoon. I couldn't afford to go shopping – when you're freelance you never have any money – and I'd heard about the locals who regularly gathered in the car park to watch the infamous landings as jumbo jets made a 90-degree turn before flying in, almost brushing the tops of the neighbouring flats.

The group of locals welcomed me into their world, warmly applauding some of the landings and being less complimentary about others who got into trouble with crosswinds or came in too fast. The only things missing were scorecards, ice-skating style. While today's increasingly superficial culture may unkindly label these people as dull, they were local heroes to me; animated, cheerful souls passionate about their beloved airport.

It was a ground-breaking trip from which I sold many stories. And it was about this time that my life finally started to come together, too. Once again, Hong Kong had worked its magic. My life always changes there, turns a corner as steep as the turn made by the pilots approaching Kai Tak. Ten years earlier, as a result of my first visit, I'd won the *Observer*'s first Young Travel Writer award. There are few better places to send budding travel writers. If you have nothing to say about Hong Kong, you should consider a career in soft furnishings instead.

I would probably have gone into writing anyway, sneaking in through the back door, but much, much later. Winning the *Observer* award threw me through the reception window. It was an official recommendation saying, 'you've got a talent, use it'. I was 21 when I won, a cheeky young man falling in and out of love and jobs every five minutes. Suddenly I'd won this great award, but was too young to know what to do with it. I realised I could write but knew nothing about the travel business or writing markets. Instead I retreated into a lonely existence, working through the night on bad novels that couldn't possibly sell. I had a lot of growing up to do.

For many years that followed I was a piece of driftwood, floating on an ocean of uncertainty, writing occasional travel pieces here and there, but still playing at writing, not really focused. It didn't help having a father who is a well-known sports writer, and the BBC's South Asia correspondent as a cousin. With such giants lurking in the background, it's hard to ignore the pressure to succeed.

It wasn't an easy decade. I had a brief but enjoyable spell on a local newspaper and then too many years on company newspapers. My low-flying career ended just as my dad embarked on a round-the-world assignment for the *Daily Mail*. Each article he wrote was headlined: 'Where's Wooldridge Now?' I mention **this** only because a similar question was asked most mornings concerning my whereabouts in the office. The money was good, the people were nice, the chair just got too comfortable.

It was ten years after the award before I felt like a proper writer, eventually cashing in on my success. Regular commissions arrived and editors phoned me. Writing is a pain, but there's nothing as enjoyable. The desire to write is a bug you can't shake. It's scary, precarious, and a nervous existence. You may get two commissions the same day, then never work again. And while it's never easy, it's hugely rewarding. You never know what's around the next corner, but that's life.

**1** Max spent the afternoon at the old Kai Tak airport because he
   **A** wanted to write a report about it for a newspaper.
   **B** wanted to visit it before it finally closed.
   **C** was looking for a way of passing the time.
   **D** had always wanted to watch the jumbo jets landing there.

> **1**

**2** What did Max think of the people he met at the airport?
   **A** He admired their enthusiasm.
   **B** He found them boring.
   **C** He thought they were brave.
   **D** He thought they were wasting their time.

> **2**

**3** What does Max say about Hong Kong in the third paragraph?
   **A** He enjoys reading the many things written about it.
   **B** He always finds it an inspiring place to visit.
   **C** He found it hard to get used to being there at first.
   **D** It is difficult for him to find anything new to write about it.

> **3**

**4** How did Max react when he realised he had won an award?
   **A** He didn't know how to take advantage of the opportunity.
   **B** He was unsure whether he really deserved it.
   **C** He became more determined to succeed as a travel writer.
   **D** He found out as much as he could about the travel business.

> **4**

**5** What does 'this' refer to in paragraph 6?
   **A** his low-flying career
   **B** his father's trip
   **C** the office where he worked
   **D** the headline of his father's articles

> **5**

**6** What does Max say about journalism as a career?
   **A** It gets easier the longer you do it.
   **B** It can make you unwell if you accept too many commissions.
   **C** It is advisable to think carefully before agreeing to a job.
   **D** It is difficult to earn a regular income.

> **6**

This is an extract from the text. Without looking back at the text, fill in the gaps with the correct form of the verbs in the box.

| ~~be~~ | be | gather | have | hear | send | write |
|---|---|---|---|---|---|---|

The greatest buzz I've felt during the past five years ............... *was* ............... (1) one afternoon on the seventh floor of the car park at Hong Kong's old Kai Tak airport. It ............................. (2) a warm Friday a few weeks before the airport closed in 1998. I ............................. (3) a feature article about the new airport for the last few days and ............................. (4) (*just*) it off to a newspaper so I ............................. (5) a free afternoon. I couldn't afford to go shopping – when you're freelance you never have any money – and I ............................. (6) about the locals who regularly ............................. (7) in the car park to watch the infamous landings as jumbo jets made a 90-degree turn before flying in, almost brushing the tops of the neighbouring flats.

## Writing

You have decided to enter a short story competition. The competition rules say that the story must begin with the following words:

*I pushed open the door. The house was empty but I could see that someone had been there and had only just left.*

Write your **story** for the competition in **120–180** words.

This task gives you a chance to practise:
using the past perfect (simple and continuous) when writing stories.

Study the opening sentence of the story carefully before you begin.

**Useful words and expressions**
*to hold one's breath, to look round, to tiptoe, nervously, suddenly, to my surprise*

## A  Context listening

**1**  You are going to hear a man called Tom having four different conversations.
Before you listen, look at the pictures. What do you think Tom's job is? .......................................

a

b

c

d

**2**  🎧 **5a** Listen and check if you were right. As you listen, match the conversations
to the pictures. 1 .......    2 .......    3 .......    4 .......

**3** 🎧 **5a** Listen to conversation 1 again and fill in the gaps.

    1 Tom's plane ....*leaves*.... at 11.05.

    2 The conference ..................... on Wednesday at 9.30.

    3 The main speaker .................... on Tuesday afternoon.

    Listen to conversation 2 again and fill in the gaps.

    4 Steve says: I ........................................ badminton in a few minutes with Paul.

    5 Tom says: I ........................................ to a conference in Amsterdam tomorrow morning.

    6 Tom says: I ........................................ my eyes tested on Saturday afternoon.

    Listen to conversation 3 again and fill in the gaps.

    Tom says:

    7 I probably ........................................ back in time.

    8 I think I ........................................ a meal in town.

    9 I ........................................ breakfast in my room.

    Listen to conversation 4 again and fill in the gaps.

    Tom says:

    10 ... in a hundred years' time, the world ........................................ a very different place.

    11 ... there ........................................ much oil available for energy.

    12 ... people ........................................ much longer.

**4** Look at your answers to Exercise 3 and answer answer these questions.

    1 Which sentences are about events fixed by a timetable? ........................................
    What tense is used? ........................................

    2 Which sentences are about actions being decided or still not certain? ........................................
    What tense is used? ........................................

    3 Which sentences are about arrangements people have made? ........................................
    What tense is used? ........................................

    4 Which sentences are about general predictions about the future? ........................................
    What tense is used? ........................................

## B Grammar

In English, several different tenses are used to talk about the future: the present simple, the present continuous, *will / shall*, the future continuous and *going to* (➢ see Unit 6 for *going to*).

### 1 Present simple

We use the **present simple** for scheduled events with a future meaning:

◆ for timetables (planes, buses etc. leaving and arriving):
*My plane **leaves** Edinburgh on Tuesday at 11.05.*
*My plane **arrives** at Amsterdam airport at 13.40.*

◆ for programmes (when a conference, a course, a football match, a film etc. begins and ends):
*The conference **starts** on Wednesday at 9.30.*

◆ for people if their plans are fixed by a timetable:
*The main speaker **arrives** on Tuesday afternoon.*

### 2 Present continuous

We use the **present continuous**:

◆ for plans which have already been arranged:
*People **are travelling** from all over the world.*
*What **are** you **doing** tomorrow evening? I'm **flying** to a conference in Amsterdam.* (= already arranged)
*I'm **having** my eyes tested on Saturday afternoon.* (= I have an appointment)

### 3 *Will*-future

| | | |
|---|---|---|
| + | *will* + verb | *They'll **arrive** soon.* |
| – | *will not* + verb | *They **won't arrive** today.* |
| ? | *will* ... + verb? | ***Will** they **arrive** soon?* |

In formal English, *shall* is occasionally used with *I / we* instead of *will*.
➢ For the use of *shall* with offers and suggestions, see Unit 13, parts 3–4.

We use *will*:

◆ for decisions made at the moment of speaking:
*I'll **have** breakfast in my room.*
*I'll **ring** them now.*

◆ for anything which is uncertain, especially with *probably*, *maybe*, *I think*, *I expect* and *I hope*:
*I **probably won't be** back in time.*
*I **think I'll** get a meal in town.*

◆ for situations that we predict will happen but which are not definitely decided or arranged:
*In 100 years the world **will be** a very different place. There**'ll be** millions more people but there **won't be** as much oil available for energy.*
(= nobody knows definitely what the world will be like in 100 years)

⚠ Compare:
*I**'m taking** my History exam again tomorrow.* (arranged)
*I**'ll get** higher marks this time.* (not something which is arranged or decided in advance − a hopeful prediction)

◆ for something in the future which doesn't depend on a decision by the speaker:
*I**'ll be** 23 on my next birthday.* (= I can't change this, it will just happen)
*There**'ll be** a full moon tomorrow.*

## 4 Future continuous

| + | will be + verb + -ing | She**'ll be working** at 7.30. |
|---|---|---|
| − | will not be + verb + -ing | She **won't be working** at 7.30. |
| ? | will ... be + verb + -ing? | Will she **be working** at 7.30? |

We use the future continuous for an event which is going on at a particular time in the future or over a period of time in the future:
*I**'ll be working** at seven o'clock.* (= I will start before seven and I will continue after seven)
*By the time you read this letter I**'ll be sailing** towards Australia.*

⚠ Compare:
*I**'ll be interviewing** him at 6.30.* (= the interview begins before 6.30 and continues afterwards)
*I**'m interviewing** him at 6.30.* (= the interview is arranged to begin at 6.30)

## C Grammar exercises

**1** Underline the most suitable form of the verbs.

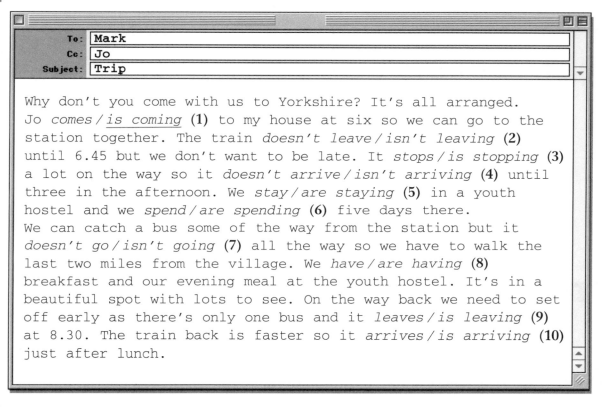

Why don't you come with us to Yorkshire? It's all arranged.
Jo *comes / is coming* (**1**) to my house at six so we can go to the
station together. The train *doesn't leave / isn't leaving* (**2**)
until 6.45 but we don't want to be late. It *stops / is stopping* (**3**)
a lot on the way so it *doesn't arrive / isn't arriving* (**4**) until
three in the afternoon. We *stay / are staying* (**5**) in a youth
hostel and we *spend / are spending* (**6**) five days there.
We can catch a bus some of the way from the station but it
*doesn't go / isn't going* (**7**) all the way so we have to walk the
last two miles from the village. We *have / are having* (**8**)
breakfast and our evening meal at the youth hostel. It's in a
beautiful spot with lots to see. On the way back we need to set
off early as there's only one bus and it *leaves / is leaving* (**9**)
at 8.30. The train back is faster so it *arrives / is arriving* (**10**)
just after lunch.

**2** Fill in the gaps with the present continuous or the *will*-future of the verb in brackets.

1 Tim: Where are you going?

  Julie: To the cinema.

  Tim: Wait for me. I think I .'ll come............................ (*come*) with you.

2 From next week all enquiries should be sent to Mary because Frances
.................................................. (*leave*) on Friday.

3 Rachel: I .................................................. (*give*) Sophie a CD for her birthday. What
.................................................. (*you give*) her?

  Fiona: I .................................................. (*probably get*) her a new purse. She keeps losing
money from her old one.

4 John: I need to finish packing today because we .................................................. (*move*)
tomorrow and there's still lots to do.

  Peter: Don't worry. I .................................................. (*come*) round tonight and help you.

5 The government hopes that the national strike ......................................... (*not continue*) after next week's meeting, otherwise the economy ......................................... (*not recover*) for years.

6 James: Never walk under a ladder or you ......................................... (*have*) ten years' bad luck.

Kay: Rubbish!

7 Details of the president's visit are now confirmed. He ......................................... (*stay*) at the Castle Hotel for two days.

8 Assistant: We have milk chocolate, plain chocolate, with nuts, with fruit.

Man: Er ... what a lot of choice. I ......................................... (*have*) a bar of milk chocolate, please.

9 Sarah: ......................................... (*you do*) anything special next Saturday?

Lee: Yes, I am. My cousin ......................................... (*arrive*) from Italy so I ......................................... (*drive*) to the airport in the afternoon to meet him.

10 Carol: Have you finished that book I lent you?

Sam: Oh sorry. I forgot all about it. I ......................................... (*get*) it now.

**3** Read the following situations. Write about what you think will happen.

1 Anna has two cousins called Rebecca Smith and Rebecca Jones. Anna gets on very well with Rebecca Smith but she doesn't like Rebecca Jones. She has received letters from her cousins asking her if they can visit. She replies to them both. She wants to see Rebecca Smith but not Rebecca Jones. Unfortunately she puts the letters in the wrong envelopes.

How will her cousins feel when they receive her letters? ....................................................

What will happen? ....................................................

....................................................

How will Anna feel when she finds out? ....................................................

**Example:** Rebecca Smith won't understand why Anna doesn't want her to visit.

2 A tour guide has just arrived in a foreign city with a group of 30 teenagers and their teachers at the end of a long journey. They don't know it yet but when they get to the hotel where they have booked rooms they will find that their rooms have been given to a group of elderly tourists who are already asleep in the rooms.

What will happen? ....................................................

What will the hotel manager do? ....................................................

....................................................

How will the teenagers and their teachers feel? ....................................................

**4** Look at the pictures and fill in the gaps with suitable verbs in the present continuous, the *will*-future, the present simple or the future continuous.

1  I expect my parents
   <u>will give me books</u> again for
   my birthday.

6  At midday tomorrow I
   ........................................... over
   the Atlantic.

2  Sam ........................................ tomorrow
   morning at ten o'clock.

7  The sale ........................................
   on Friday.

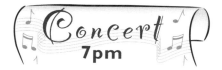

3  My grandfather ........................................
   on his next birthday.

8  This time next week we
   ........................................ in Austria.

4  The concert ........................................ at
   seven pm.

9  We ........................................ to Ireland by
   ferry this summer.

5  I think I ........................................ when I
   grow up.

10  Maybe my father ........................................
    the money I need.

41

# 5

## D  Exam practice

### Listening

🎧 **5b** You will hear a tour guide talking to a group of tourists about a day out.
For questions **1–10**, fill in the missing information.

---

## NOTES

**Meals**   Breakfast in the [_____ **1**_] from 6.45 to 9.15.

[_____ **2**_] your lunch from reception.

Meet for dinner at [_____ **3**_] .

*Any difficulties with the hotel, see the [_____ **4**_] .

## TOUR OF SOUTH WALES VALLEYS

**AM**   First visit a beautiful [_____ **5**_]

and see the remains of a [_____ **6**_] .

Then visit a museum on the site of a [_____ **7**_] .

The souvenir shop sells special [_____ **8**_] .

**Lunch**

**PM**   Go for a walk or try [_____ **9**_] .

Bring a coat, wear [_____ **10**_] , and remember your camera.

---

## Grammar focus task

**1** 🎧 **5c** Listen to the second part of the recording again and fill in the gaps.

1 ... the coach ......*is picking*...... us up ...

2 ... we ............................ back there today to have a better look ...

3 ... then we ............................ a bit further up the valley ...

4 ... we ............................ our lunch up there ...

5 ... then we ............................ our way back south ...

6 ... there ............................ time for a walk ...

7 ... we ............................ do those today ...

8 ... we ............................ at a café ...

9 ... you ............................ a coat ...

**2** Which verbs are in the present continuous and why? ............................................
..................................................................................................................

## Writing

Your college is holding an open day next month and wants to invite pupils from local schools to attend. You have been asked to write a letter to persuade them to attend. Read the programme of events and the notes about what you need to include. Then write the letter remembering to make the day sound as interesting and attractive as you can. Write a **letter** in **120–180** words in an appropriate style. Do not write any addresses.

---

# OPEN DAY PROGRAMME
## Saturday 7 April
✳—✳—✳—✳—✳—✳—✳—✳

**10.00** College open
Tours of college every 20 minutes by students

✳—✳—✳—✳—✳—✳—✳—✳

| Morning | Afternoon |
|---|---|
| Coffee available in canteen | Rock concert by students in hall |
| Gymnastic display | Tea available in canteen |
| on sports field | Drama by students in hall |
| **12.00–1.30** lunch | **4.30** Questions to principal |

*Don't forget to mention:*
*Art room displays - all day*
*Gardens open*
*Visitors can try sports facilities*

---

**Writing hints**

This task gives you a chance to practise:
using the present continuous for definite arrangements.
using the present simple for when things begin and end.
using the *will*-future.

**Useful words and expressions**
*to enjoy, to hold an open day, to look forward to, to perform, activities, to welcome*

## A  Context listening

**1**  You are going to hear a man called Simon Trite talking to a group of people on the remote and uninhabited island of Wildrock in the North Atlantic earlier this year. They went there as an experiment in survival. Simon has just come to the island.

Before you listen to the recording, look at the picture. Why has Simon come to the island? ...........................................

.......................................................................................

What do you think it is like to live on the island? ...................................

.......................................................................................

**2**  🎧 6  Listen and check if you were right.

**3**  🎧 6  Listen again and answer these questions. Stop the recording when you need to.

1  How long were they going to stay on Wildrock? <u>For at least a year.</u>

2  Why are the people going to leave Wildrock? .....................................

.......................................................................................

3  When are they going to leave? ...................................................

4  By the end of this week, what will they have achieved? ..........................

.......................................................................................

5  By the end of this week, how long will they have been living on Wildrock? .......

6  When are they going to eat a big hot meal? ......................................

7  Who is going to stay on the island? Why? .......................................

**4**  Look at Exercise 3 and answer these questions.

1  Which questions are about future actions which have already been decided?

.......................................................................................

2  Which questions are about things happening before a point of time in the future?

.......................................................................................

3  Which question is about people's plans in the past? .............................

**6**

## B Grammar

### 1 *Going to*

| + | am/is/are going to + verb | *I'm going to leave.* |
|---|---|---|
| − | am/is/are not going to + verb | *They're not going to leave.* |
| ? | am/is/are ... going to + verb? | *Are you going to leave?* |

Pronunciation note: *going to* is often pronounced *gonna*. You may see it spelt this way in comic books and pop songs.

It is often possible to use *going to* to express the future instead of the present continuous or *will* (➢ see Unit 5). *Going to* is used extremely often in everyday speech. In formal and written English *will* and the present tenses are used more often than *going to*.

We use ***going to***:

◆ for future actions which we have already decided about.
  Compare:
  *We're going to pack up our stuff, we're going to send a message to the mainland and we're going to leave.* (= they already have a clear plan)
  *We'll pack up our stuff ...* etc. (= she might be deciding as she speaks or it might be a simple statement of fact, not a planned action)
  (➢ see Unit 5).

◆ to predict something, when we already see evidence for our prediction:
  *It's going to rain soon.* (= the speaker knows it's going to rain because he can see the clouds)

There are many situations when either *going to* or *will* can be used with no real difference in meaning.

### 2 Present tenses in future clauses

In clauses referring to future time and beginning with *when, until, before, after, as soon as*, we use:

◆ a present tense (for actions at the same time as the other verb):
  *Everyone's going to be very surprised **when** you **arrive**.*

◆ the present perfect (for actions completed before the other verb):
  *And we're not going to talk to any reporters **until** we've had a long sleep.*

Sometimes we can use either a present or present perfect tense with the same meaning:
*We're going to eat a big hot meal **as soon as** we **find** a restaurant.*
*We're going to eat a big hot meal **as soon as** we've **found** a restaurant.*

## 3 Future in the past (*was / were going to*)

We use *was / were going to*:

◆ to talk about something which was planned but did not or will not happen:
*You **were going to stay** here for at least a year.* (= but now you have changed your mind)

◆ to show that we don't mind changing our plans:
Boy: *Are you busy this evening?*
Girl: *Well, I **was going to write** some letters.* (= she may forget about the letters if he has a more interesting idea)

## 4 Future perfect simple and future perfect continuous

| + | will have + past participle | *I'll **have finished** by six o'clock.* |
|---|---|---|
| − | will not have + past participle | *He **won't have finished** by six o'clock.* |
| ? | will ... have + past participle? | ***Will** you **have finished** by six o'clock?* |

We use the **future perfect simple** for an action which will be complete at a point of time in the future. It is usual to mention the point in time:
*By the end of this week we'll **have survived** longer than anyone else.*

| + | will have been + verb + -ing | *By one o'clock, I'll **have been waiting** for three hours.* |
|---|---|---|
| − | will not have been + verb + -ing | *She **won't have been waiting** for long.* |
| ? | will ... have been + verb + -ing? | ***Will** they **have been waiting** for a long time?* |

We use the **future perfect continuous** to emphasise how long an action will have lasted up to a point in the future. It is usually necessary to mention the point of time and the length of time:
*By the end of this week, we'll **have been living** here for six months.*

State verbs (➢ see Unit 1) are not used in the future perfect continuous.

## 5 *To be about to*

| + | am / is / are about to + verb | *I'm **about to go** out.* |
|---|---|---|
| − | am / is / are not about to + verb | *He **isn't about to go** out.* |
| ? | am / is / are ... about to + verb? | *Are you **about to go** out?* |

We use *to be about to* to talk about something which is going to happen very soon and for which we are already preparing:
*Actually, we're **about to leave**.*

⚠ In the negative, *to be about to* often means 'do not intend to' do something:
*We **aren't about to change** the rules just because you don't like them.*
(= we refuse to change the rules just because you don't like them)

---
**47**

## C Grammar exercises

**1** Look at these pictures and predict what is going to happen. Complete the sentences using *going to*.

1 She's going to fall asleep.

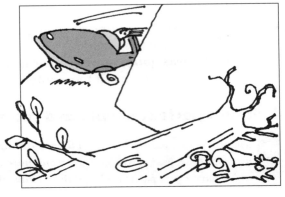

2 It ................................................................

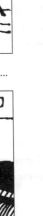

3 They ................................................................

4 She ................................................................

5 He ................................................................

6 It ................................................................

**2** These are a researcher's notes, with her predictions about how the world will have changed by the year 2100. Use the notes to write sentences in the future perfect simple.

> By the year 2100 …
> 1 human beings / travel / to Mars
> 2 the world's population / double
> 3 computers / replace / most manual workers
> 4 we / use / all the oil resources on Earth
> 5 doctors / discover / a cure for AIDS
> 6 scientists / invent / new sources of energy
> 7 sea temperatures / rise / by several degrees

1 Human beings will have travelled to Mars.

2 ............................................................................................................................

3 ............................................................................................................................

4 ............................................................................................................................

5 ............................................................................................................................

6 ............................................................................................................................

7 ............................................................................................................................

Write three predictions of your own, using the future perfect simple.

8 ............................................................................................................................

9 ............................................................................................................................

10 ............................................................................................................................

**3** In five of these sentences there is a verb in the wrong tense. Underline each mistake and write the correction.

1 I'm not going to pay you until <u>you'll have cleaned</u> up all this mess! ............... *you have cleaned* ...............

2 Before we're going to get on the train, I'm going to check that we have all our luggage.
................................................

3 As soon as the guests have unpacked, you can show them round the college.
................................................

4 Paul will probably arrive after all the others will have started work. ................................................

5 When you'll see David, will you ask him if he wants to come to the cinema with us?
................................................

6 I'll collect your things from the cleaners when I'm in town. ................................................

7 Margaret's going to phone as soon as she'll have found out what the tickets will cost.
................................................

**4** These people work in a hotel. It's now twelve o'clock. How long will they have been working by two o'clock? Write a sentence about each person, using the future perfect continuous.

1 chef / cook meals (started work at eight o'clock)
*The chef will have been cooking meals for six hours.*

2 secretary / type letters (started work at ten o'clock)
................................................

3 manager / interview new staff (started work at eight-thirty)
................................................

4 waitress / stand in the dining-room (started work at eleven o'clock)
................................................

5 cleaner / vacuum floors (started work at seven o'clock)
................................................

**5** Fill in the gaps with the correct form of the verbs in brackets. Use *going to*,
future in the past, the present simple, *about to* or the future perfect.

a John: What are your plans for the weekend?

   Sue: Well, we've just changed our plans, actually. ....We..were..going..to..have........
(*have*) **(1)** a barbecue on Sunday. But the weather forecast says it
................................................ (*be*) **(2)** cold and windy, so we
................................................ (*stay*) **(3)** indoors and watch a video.

b Beth: Is it all right for you to use the boss's office while he's on holiday?

   Nick: Oh, I'm sure he won't mind when he ................................................
(*find out*) **(4)** how many cars I've sold this week.

c Terry: Are you very busy this afternoon?

   Eddy: Well, that depends on why you're asking. I ................................................
(*wash*) **(5)** the car. Do you have a better idea?

   Terry: Yes. I ................................................ (*look round*) **(6)** the new sports club.
Do you want to come? You can wash the car tomorrow.

   Eddy: Sure. Let's go.

d Ben: Hurry up! We ................................................ (*miss*) **(7)** the beginning of
the concert.

   Mary: Don't be silly. We've got plenty of time.

   Ben: But it starts at nine. I want to arrive before the hall
................................................ (*get*) **(8)** full, otherwise other people
................................................ (*take*) **(9)** all the good seats by the time
we're there.

e Laura: Do you have a moment to discuss this letter?

   Bill: Well, I ................................................ (*have*) **(10)** something to eat, and
then I ................................................ (*write*) **(11)** a report. Is it urgent?

   Laura: Well, we ................................................ (*talk*) **(12)** about it yesterday, but
you were too busy then. I must reply to it today and I need your
opinion.

   Bill: OK. I ................................................ (*finish*) **(13)** my lunch by twenty past
one. Can you come back then?

f Chloe: By next Friday I ................................................ (*work*) **(14)** in this office
for three years. Nobody has ever thanked me for anything I've done, so
I ................................................ (*start*) **(15)** looking for another job!

## Reading

You are going to read a magazine feature about what people do during the time between school and university. For questions **1–15**, choose from the people (**A–E**). Some of the people may be chosen more than once. When more than one answer is required, these may be given in any order. There is an example at the beginning.

**Of which person or people are the following stated?**

She is going to have a holiday abroad with friends.

| **0** | A |

She is confident that she will be able to find work after her holiday.

| **1** | |

She is about to start a job.

| **2** | | **3** | |

She intends to find a job as soon as she can.

| **4** | |

She plans to spend time preparing for her course after a holiday.

| **5** | |

Her parents are very happy about her academic success.

| **6** | | **7** | |

She has no holiday plans for this summer.

| **8** | |

Her parents do not want her to spend her money on a holiday.

| **9** | |

She believes it will be hard for her to earn money over the summer.

| **10** | |

She wants to spend time with her friends at home before going to university.

| **11** | |

She intends to have a good time at university.

| **12** | |

She thinks earning money will make a good change from studying.

| **13** | |

She does not know where she will be at the start of the summer.

| **14** | |

She will have a job similar to one she's done before.

| **15** | |

# SCHOOL'S OUT

You've finished school, passed those vital exams and got a place waiting for you at university in the autumn. What are you going to do for the next ten weeks? Prize magazine asked five girls who've just finished school about their plans for the summer.

**A** Angie Hook has got it all sorted. 'I'm going to be pretty busy. First I've got to get some money, because I know I won't have enough when I'm a student, and the course I'm going to follow is really demanding, so I won't be able to take a part-time job in term time. So I've signed up with a company as a temporary secretary for most of the summer. Luckily, I'm good on a word processor and I did the same sort of thing in previous years, so I've got a bit of experience behind me, which is a big help. I am going to have a break though. Just before the university term starts I'm going to have a fortnight in Spain with some of the people who've just left school with me. My mum and dad are giving me the money for that as a reward for doing well in my exams, so I won't have to use up my savings, which is really nice of them, because I know it means they'll have less to spend on their own holiday.'

**B** Sally Price is less certain about her plans. 'I'm definitely going to have to work before I do anything else, because I'm so short of cash. I want to go away for a holiday somewhere by the sea, and I'll have to earn enough for that, so I've got to look for a temporary job first. I think I'll find something fairly quickly. After that, it'll be too late to find any more work I expect, because other people will have taken all the jobs by then, so I'll just have a month hanging about at home, messing around with my friends and things, spending time with my parents. That'll be good really, because I'm going to be a long way from home when I'm at university and I won't see them much.'

**C** Tracy Chadwick says she has little choice about what to do. 'I have to spend the last month of the summer break getting ready for my course. I've got a job in a shop for the first month until I go on my holiday. That will give my brain a rest and pay for the holiday. But I've already had this enormous reading list from the university, so as soon as I've had a couple of weeks' holiday, I'm going to settle down and get on with studying, because I don't want to be behind at the beginning of term.'

**D** Polly Targett would like to work. 'But the thing is, we live such a long way from town and I don't have my own car yet – I'm going to get one next year, for my birthday, but it's rather difficult to get anywhere at the moment. Well, there's a bus, early in the morning and I think there's one in the evening, but to be honest it's much easier to stay at home. I doubt whether I'll go away, because I've already been on holiday with my parents earlier in the year and anyway I'll have to do some studying before the term starts, because otherwise I'll just have to work so hard when I get to university there won't be time to enjoy myself with my friends.'

**E** Hilary Lee is going to start with a break. 'I'm really exhausted after all our school exams and stuff and so I'm going to have a fortnight with my parents, just relaxing completely. We're going somewhere abroad, but I don't know where, it's a surprise, a sort of present, because I've done well. I know it'll be lovely. Then I'll find a job, it doesn't matter what, just so that I can have some pocket money for the rest of the year. It won't be hard to get something, in a hotel or whatever, summer's the high season for businesses in this area. Then I'll spend a couple of weeks doing nothing much, I hope, perhaps I'll paint my bedroom or something. And that'll be it – summer'll be over. I'll be a university student.'

This is an extract from the text. Without looking back at the text, fill in the gaps with the correct form of the verbs in brackets.

1  I've got to get some money, because I won't have enough when I
   .............*am*............. (*be*) a student.

2  Just before the university term ................................... (*start*) I'm going to have a
   fortnight in Spain.

3  I'm definitely going to have to work before I ................................... (*do*) anything else.

4  It'll be too late to find any more work because other people ...................................
   (*take*) all the jobs by then.

5  I'm going to be a long way from home when I ................................... (*be*) at university.

6  I've got a job in a shop for the first month until I ................................... (*go*) on my
   holiday.

7  As soon as I ................................... (*have*) a couple of weeks' holiday, I'm going to
   settle down.

8  Otherwise I'll just have to work so hard when I ................................... (*get*) to
   university there won't be time to enjoy myself.

# Writing

You are planning a weekend trip with a group of friends. A week before you go, one of the group has to go into hospital. You decide to invite another friend to join you instead.

Look at the leaflet about the place where you are going to stay. You've added some notes about your group's plans. Write to your friend explaining your plans, say why this invitation is so sudden, and ask him / her to join you.

---

# WOODLANDS HOSTEL

**Telephone message**
*Bad news - Robin's in hospital - can we invite someone else to come with us??*

An affordable base for walkers, climbers and other visitors to Woodlands Hill Nature Reserve only 3 km from the world famous Woodlands Waterfall.

For £15 per person per night you get: *- great value*
- a bed in a room with three others
- good showers and bathrooms
- cooking facilities, including barbecue *- Saturday evening*
- food storage space *- need to take plenty!*

In return, we expect our visitors to
- provide their own sleeping bag / bedclothes *- I can lend, if necessary*
- give 30 minutes per day to help keep the building clean and tidy *- can't be avoided*

*Our plan*
- *train 5.45 pm Friday*
- *Saturday am walk to waterfall, picnic?*
- *climb in afternoon???*
- *Sunday afternoon train, home by 8 pm*

Write a **letter** in **120–180** words in an appropriate style. Do not write any addresses.

## Writing hints

**This task gives you a chance to practise:**
using *going to* for talking about plans you have made.

**Useful words and expressions**
*to book, to charge, to catch (a train), to have a great time, let me know, I'm sorry to say, as soon as possible, in the morning / afternoon / evening, instead, sudden*

# Adjectives

**comparative and superlative adjectives; position; order;
adjectives ending in -ing and -ed**

## A Context listening

**1** You are going to hear some advertisements. Before you listen, look at the
pictures and guess what will be advertised.

1 ................................. 2 ................................. 3 ................................. 4 .................................

**2** 🎧 7 Listen and check if you were right.

**3** 🎧 7 Listen again and answer these questions. Stop the recording when you need to.

1 What sort of person can you become, according to the first advertisement? ........................

......................................................................................................................................

2 What is said about the animals in the second advertisement? ..........................................

......................................................................................................................................

3 Why might someone phone Sparklers? .............................................................................

4 Why does the Music Store offer something for everyone, according to the fourth
advertisement? ................................................................................................................

**4** 🎧 7 Listen again and fill in the gaps with the words that describe these people and
things. Stop the recording when you need to.

1 _professional_ advisers ..................... route ..................... welcome ..................... facilities

2 ..................... day out ..................... wildlife park ..................... brochure ..................... offers

3 ..................... carpets ..................... sinks and surfaces ..................... finger marks
..................... prices

4 ..................... bargains ..................... rock and pop ..................... jazz
..................... classical music

## B Grammar

Adjectives are words which describe nouns (things and people).
≻ Compare with adverbs in Unit 8.

## 1 Comparative and superlative adjectives

We make comparative and superlative forms of adjectives in the
following ways:

| Adjective | Comparative | Superlative |
|---|---|---|
| one syllable<br>*strong*<br>*great* | add *-er*<br>*stronger* | add *-est*<br>*the strongest* |
| | *You can become **stronger** at Transformers Fitness Centre.*<br>*The Music Store's got **the greatest** variety of CDs ever!* | |
| two syllables, ending in *-y*<br>*tidy*<br>*funny* | drop *-y* and add *-ier*<br>*tidier* | drop *-y* and add *-iest*<br>*the tidiest* |
| | *Their flat is **tidier** than ours.*<br>*They're **the funniest** monkeys you've ever seen.* | |
| two/three/four syllables<br>*famous*<br>*beautiful*<br>*self-confident* | *more ...*<br>*more beautiful* | *the most ...*<br>*the most beautiful* |
| | *You can become a **more self-confident** person.*<br>*He is **the most famous** actor in the film.* | |

A few two-syllable adjectives (e.g. *quiet, pleasant, common, polite*) sometimes
also use *-er* or *-est*:
*It's **quieter** than any garden I've visited before.*

Two-syllable adjectives ending in *-ow, -er* and *-le* can usually add *-er* or *-est*:
*cleverer; the narrowest*

Most adjectives ending in a vowel and *-b, -d, -g, -n, -p* or *-t* double the last
letter before adding *-er* or *-est*:
*bigger; the saddest*

A few adjectives have irregular comparative and superlative forms:
*good → better → best*
*bad → worse → worst*
*far → farther → farthest*

## 2 Comparative structures

We can use comparative structures to say that:

◆ things are **more**:
*Our prices are **better than** any of our rivals.*
*We have a **more interesting** range of music **than** you'll see anywhere else.*

◆ things are **less**:
*Cassettes usually aren't **as / so expensive as** CDs.*
*The CDs in the sale are much **less expensive than** usual.*

◆ or things are **equal**:
*Classical music is **as popular as** rock music with our customers.*

## 3 Adjective position

Adjectives in English usually go in front of the word they describe:

*We visited an **old** house.*
*We saw some **beautiful** paintings and some **elegant** furniture.*

Adjectives can also follow some verbs (such as *be, get, become, look, seem, appear, sound, taste, smell, feel*):

*Everything **seemed pleasant** when we started.*
*The flowers **smelt beautiful** and the gardens **looked wonderful**.*
*But the weather **got very hot** and we all **felt exhausted** by the end of the day.*

⚠ There are many nouns in English which are used as adjectives:

*a **diamond** ring; a **library** book; a **seaside** hotel; **folk** music; **strawberry** jam*

## 4 Adjective order

When we use more than one adjective, we usually put them in a certain order. We say:

*a **strange old wooden** chair* (**not** *a ~~wooden old strange~~ chair*)

We usually begin with adjectives which give an opinion or general impression:

*a **dangerous** old car; a **delicate** oval tray; a **valuable** silver spoon*

Adjectives which give factual information usually follow the opinion / impression adjective. They go in this order:

|    | Size     | Age     | Shape | Colour | Origin | Material | Purpose |        |
|----|----------|---------|-------|--------|--------|----------|---------|--------|
| an | enormous | old     |       | red    |        |          |         | car    |
| a  | small    |         | oval  |        | French |          |         | mirror |
| an |          | antique |       |        |        | silver   | soup    | spoon  |

Two colour adjectives are separated by *and*:

*a **black and white** photograph*

When we put more than one adjective after a verb, we use *and* to separate the last one:

*The day was **hot and tiring**.*
*Lord Byron was described as **mad**, **bad and dangerous** to know.*

## 5 Adjectives ending in *-ing* and *-ed*

Some common adjectives are formed from verbs and have both *-ing* and *-ed* forms.

We use the **-ed form** to describe our feelings:

*I'm **tired**.* (= a description of how I feel: I've used up all my energy so I need a rest)

We use the **-ing form** to describe the things which make us feel like this:

*This work is **tiring**.* (= a description of the work: it takes a lot of energy to do it)

Compare these sentences:

*It's a **boring** film.*
(= there's no action in it)

*The visitors are **bored**.*
(= they have nothing to do)

*We had a **relaxing** holiday.*
(= the atmosphere was restful)

*Good driving instructors always have a **relaxed** manner.*
(= they don't seem nervous)

*That was a very **satisfying** meal.*
(= there was plenty to eat)

*The airline has many **satisfied** customers.*
(= the customers feel happy)

## C Grammar exercises

**1** Look at this designer's sketch of a costume for a film and complete the notes. Fill in the gaps with adjectives for each part of the costume.

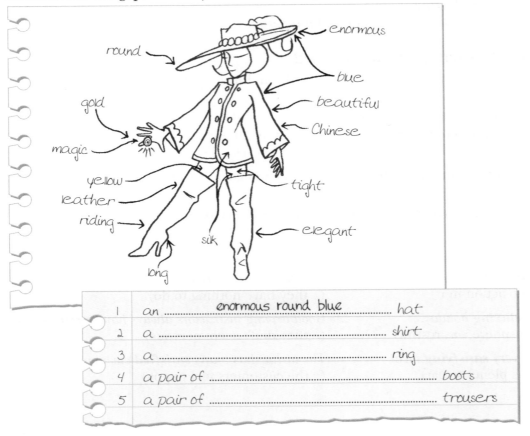

round

enormous

gold

blue

beautiful

magic

Chinese

yellow

leather

riding

tight

silk

elegant

long

| | | | |
|---|---|---|---|
| 1 | an | enormous round blue | hat |
| 2 | a | | shirt |
| 3 | a | | ring |
| 4 | a pair of | | boots |
| 5 | a pair of | | trousers |

**2** Underline the correct adjectives.

1 James told us some *fascinating* / *fascinated* stories about the music business.

2 Why are you looking so *depressing* / *depressed*? What's wrong?

3 Sarah's got an *amazing* / *amazed* collection of rock CDs.

4 Felix has this really *annoying* / *annoyed* habit of reading my letters.

5 The *boring* / *bored* students started causing trouble in class.

6 I watched the show for a while, but it wasn't really *interesting* / *interested*, so I left.

7 As the football team came out onto the pitch, their *exciting* / *excited* fans went wild.

8 The food in this canteen is absolutely *disgusting* / *disgusted*.

9 The astronaut gave a *relaxing* / *relaxed* wave and entered the space capsule.

**3** In nine of these sentences there is a mistake in the use of adjectives.
Underline each mistake and write the correction.

1 That was the <u>worse</u> film I've ever seen! ............... worst ...............

2 If you need a suitcase, I've got a leather old lovely one that you can borrow.
...............

3 He should catch a more earlier train if he wants to get to London by five.
...............

4 This is one of the commonest mistakes made by new students. ...............

5 Clothes aren't cheap here; in fact, these jeans are so expensive as the ones you bought back home.
...............

6 The peaches rotten looked so I didn't have any. ...............

7 Our last holiday wasn't so enjoyable than this one. ...............

8 My home town is small pretty peaceful. ...............

9 Which of the students lives most far from the school? ...............

10 I'm really boring with this exercise. Let's go and have a coffee. ...............

**4** Complete this letter with comparative or superlative forms of the adjectives given and any other words (e.g. *more, the, as*) that are needed.

Dear Lily,

Well, we've moved at last! When we got here, the flat seemed ............ larger ............ (large) **(1)** than we remembered, because it was empty, but now it's got our furniture in it, it doesn't feel ............... (spacious) **(2)** before. We've got to do some decorating, and that will be ............... (expensive) **(3)** we expected because the walls are in a ............... (bad) **(4)** condition than we thought. But we'll manage somehow, and soon we'll have ............... (smart) **(5)** house in the town. And if your Uncle Bob has his way, we'll have ............... (lovely) **(6)** garden as well. We'll also be ............... (poor) **(7)** and ............... (exhausted) **(8)** householders in the country, but never mind. We still think moving here is ............... (good) **(9)** thing we've done for years. We can't imagine now why we didn't do it when we were ............... (young) **(10)**. Come and see us soon. Catch a train if you can, because it's almost ............... (cheap) **(11)** the bus, and the railway station is ............... (near) **(12)** our end of town.

Love from us both,
Auntie Rosie

# 7

## D Exam practice

### Use of English

For questions **1–15**, read the text below and decide which answer (**A, B, C** or **D**) best fits each space. There is an example at the beginning (**0**).

> ⚠ This task tests grammar from the rest of the book as well as the grammar in this unit.

**0**    **A** over    (**B**) from    **C** of    **D** by

---

My wife Penny and I are recovering (**0**) ..B.. weekend visitors. Don't misunderstand me – we enjoy company and love to (**1**) ........ our friends and relatives. But not this time. Fred and Kate were old friends from our college (**2**) ........ . So you would think we would have a fairly (**3**) ........ idea what sort of people they were, even though we hadn't seen them for (**4**) ........ years.

We soon discovered, unfortunately, that our lives had (**5**) ........ very different directions. Penny and I have two small children. Delightful but (**6**) ........ , they dictate the style of our life. (**7**) ........ many other young couples, we find weekends are a matter of trying to snatch a few moments of relaxation in between catching up with all the (**8**) ........ .

Kate and Fred (**9**) ........ more money than us, they work longer hours, and they (**10**) ........ their leisure time to be just that, leisure. The (**11**) ........ tiring thing Fred does on a Sunday is to walk up the road to the (**12**) ........ newsagent. To be (**13**) ........ , Kate wasn't as bad as Fred. But she wasn't much better.

By the time they left, Penny and I were exhausted. We'd cooked, served and cleared up six meals without a (**14**) ........ offer of help. We didn't know whether to laugh or cry. Luckily, we (**15**) ........ to laugh.

|    |                |                   |              |               |
|----|----------------|-------------------|--------------|---------------|
| **1**  | **A** entertain  | **B** visit         | **C** receive  | **D** host      |
| **2**  | **A** terms      | **B** days          | **C** times    | **D** ages      |
| **3**  | **A** fine       | **B** strong        | **C** good     | **D** right     |
| **4**  | **A** numerous   | **B** plenty        | **C** passing  | **D** several   |
| **5**  | **A** taken      | **B** left          | **C** chosen   | **D** had       |
| **6**  | **A** tired      | **B** tiring        | **C** amused   | **D** amusing   |
| **7**  | **A** As         | **B** Like          | **C** Similar  | **D** Same      |
| **8**  | **A** homework   | **B** housekeeping  | **C** household| **D** housework |
| **9**  | **A** gain       | **B** fetch         | **C** earn     | **D** bring     |
| **10** | **A** intend     | **B** expect        | **C** insist   | **D** rely      |
| **11** | **A** more       | **B** very          | **C** most     | **D** almost    |
| **12** | **A** near       | **B** neighbouring  | **C** local    | **D** district  |
| **13** | **A** fair       | **B** true          | **C** real     | **D** straight  |
| **14** | **A** lonely     | **B** unique        | **C** alone    | **D** single    |
| **15** | **A** achieved   | **B** succeeded     | **C** reached  | **D** managed   |

The adjectives in the box are from the text. Without looking back at the text, fill in the gaps with the adjectives which describe each noun in the text.

> college   different   good   leisure   local
> longer   old   small   ~~weekend~~   young

1 ..weekend.. visitors   2 ................ friends   3 ................ days   4 ................ idea
5 ................ directions   6 ................ children   7 ................ couples   8 ................ hours
9 ................ time   10 ................ newsagent

# Writing

You see this competition in a design magazine.

> # WIN **one of these fabulous prizes!**
>
> ❖ a set of bedroom furniture ❖
> ❖ *or* a personal computer ❖
> ❖ *or* a new carpet and curtains ❖
>
> *All you have to do is write a short article describing YOUR ROOM.*
> *Say what's good about it and how it could be improved.*

Write your **article** in **120–180** words.

This task gives you a chance to practise:
using adjectives.

**Useful words and expressions**
*to display, to keep, to share*
*carpet, cupboard, noticeboard, poster, shelf, space*
*boring, exciting, expensive, favourite, giant, (im)possible, tiny*
*in one corner, near the door, under the window*
*the best improvement would be ..., what I like best is ..., what I'd really like to change is ...*

# 8 Adverbs

formation; adverbs and adjectives easily confused; comparative
and superlative adverbs; modifiers; position

## A Context listening

**1** You are going to hear the beginning of a radio commentary on a football
match. Before you listen, think about what you can see and hear at a match.
Tick the words you think you might hear.

- ☐ ball
- ☐ chair
- ☐ goal
- ☐ ground
- ☐ helmet
- ☐ loudly
- ☐ peacefully
- ☐ quickly
- ☐ racket
- ☐ scored
- ☐ shyly
- ☐ stadium
- ☐ spectators
- ☐ whistle

**2** 🎧 8 Listen and check if you were right. Number the words in the order you
hear them and cross out the ones you don't hear.

**3** 🎧 8 Listen again and fill in the gaps. Stop the recording when you need to.

1 And ....*finally*.... the players are coming onto the pitch.

2 There were such terrible traffic jams ................................................................................
that the match is starting ..................... .

3 ... the spectators have been waiting .............................................................. since two o'clock ...

4 ... they're cheering ......................................... .

5 Rossi ... is running ..................... down the pitch ...

6 ... he's fallen .............................................................................. .

7 He's so experienced in these kinds of conditions that
he ..................... falls.

8 Now Parker is running ..................... towards the goal ...

9 Parker is playing incredibly ..................... .

10 ......................................... he scored the winning goal ...

11 It's ..................... Parker who shoots that important goal.

**4** All the words you have filled in are adverbs or adverb phrases.
They tell us about when, where, how or how often something happened.
Put each of your answers to Exercise 3 in the correct column below.

| When? | Where? | How? | How often? |
|---|---|---|---|
| finally | in the city | patiently | rarely |
| | | | |
| | | | |
| | | | |
| | | | |

64

## B Grammar

### 1 Formation of adverbs

Adjectives (*happy, beautiful*) tell us about a noun. Adverbs (*happily, beautifully*) tell us about a verb, an adjective or another adverb. They give us information about time (when?), place (where?), manner (how?) and frequency (how often?):

*Today I feel **happy** because the weather is **beautiful**. Some children are playing **happily** in the street and a blackbird is singing **beautifully** in a tree outside.*

Some adverbs are phrases:

*He's arriving **on Tuesday**, so we're meeting him **at the station**.*

Most adverbs are formed by adding *-ly* to an adjective:

*sad → sadly; clear → clearly*

This table shows spelling rules for these adverbs:

| Adjective | | Adverb | |
|---|---|---|---|
| ending in a vowel and -*l* | *beautiful* | add -*ly* | *beautifully* |
| ending in -*y* | *angry* | drop -*y* and add -*ily* | *angrily* |
| ending in -*le* | *miserable* | drop -*e* and add -*y* | *miserably* |
| ending in -*e* | *extreme* | keep -*e* and add -*ly* | *extremely* |

An adjective ending in -*ly* (e.g. *friendly, likely, lively, lonely, lovely, silly, ugly*) cannot be made into an adverb. We have to use a phrase instead:

*She started the interview **in a friendly manner**.*
*He laughed **in a silly way**.*

### 2 Adverbs and adjectives easily confused

Some adjectives and adverbs have the same form. Some common ones are: *fast, early, hard, late, daily, weekly, monthly*:

| **Adjectives** | **Adverbs** |
|---|---|
| *He caught the **fast** train.* | *He ran **fast** to catch the train.* |
| *He caught the **early** train.* | *He always arrives **early**.* |
| *She's a **hard** worker.* | *She works **hard**.* |
| *The bus is always **late**.* | *I arrived home **late**.* |
| *My **daily** newspaper costs 50p.* | *I swim **daily**.* |

*Hard* and *hardly* are both adverbs but they have different meanings. *Hardly* means 'almost not'. It can go in various positions in the sentence:

*She **hardly** noticed when he came into the room.* (= she almost didn't notice)
*I had **hardly** finished my breakfast when they arrived.* (= only just)
*They **hardly** ever go on holiday.* (= almost never)

*Hardly* is often used with *any*:

*There was **hardly** anyone in the cinema.* (= almost nobody)
***Hardly** any of the children could read.* (= almost none of them)

*Late* and *lately* are both adverbs but they have different meanings.
*Lately* means 'recently':
*I haven't read any good books **lately**.*

The adverb for *good* is *well*:
*It was a **good** concert. The musicians played **well**.*

But *well* is also an adjective which means the opposite of *ill*:
*I had a bad headache yesterday but I'm **well** today.*

⚠ Some verbs are followed by adjectives, not adverbs (➢ see Unit 7, Grammar, part 3).

## 3  Comparative and superlative adverbs

Most adverbs use *more* or *less* to make comparatives and *the most* or *the least* to make superlatives:

*My brother speaks Italian **more fluently than** I do.*
*I speak Italian **less fluently than** my brother does.*
*Out of all the students, Maria speaks English **the most fluently**.*

Adverbs without *-ly* make comparatives and superlatives in the same way as short adjectives (➢ see Unit 8):

*hard → harder → hardest   high → higher → highest   late → later → latest*
*I work **hard**, my sister works **harder** than I do but Alex works **the hardest**.*

⚠ Note also: *early → earlier → earliest* (**not** ~~more early/the most early~~)
Some comparative and superlative adverbs are irregular:

*well → better → best   badly → worse → worst   far → farther → farthest*
*I did **better** than him in the test.*
*None of the students lives very near the school, but Darren lives **farthest** away.*

Adverbs use the same comparative structures as adjectives:

*He shouted **as loudly as** she did.*
*I can't add up **as quickly as** you can.*
*They arrived **later than** we did.*

## 4  Modifying adverbs and adjectives

Some adverbs are used to change the strength of adjectives or adverbs.
Here are some common ones:

*incredibly   extremely   really   very   rather   fairly   quite   slightly*
← stronger                                                      weaker →

*He dances **extremely** well.*
*The weather was **very** hot.*
*He spoke to her **rather** fiercely.*
*The house was **quite** old.*

Some adjectives (e.g. *perfect, impossible, excellent*) can only be strengthened with adverbs like *completely, absolutely, totally, entirely*. We can say:
*This crossword puzzle is **completely** impossible.* (**not** ... *is very impossible.*)

## 5  Adverb position

Adverbs which tell us:

◆ **how, where** and **when** something happens usually go at the end ('**end-position**'):
*The meeting took place **suddenly**. (how?)*
*The meeting took place **in the Town Hall**. (where?)*
*The meeting took place **last Tuesday**. (when?)*

If there are several end-position adverbs, we put them in this order:
how?        where?            when?
*The meeting took place **suddenly in the Town Hall last Tuesday**.*

Adverbs which tell us:

◆ **how often** something happens usually go in the middle ('**mid-position**') before a single word verb:
*I **usually** travel by train.*

but after *am/is/are/was/were*:
*I am **often** late.*

If the verb has two or more parts, the adverb usually goes after the first part:
*I have **never** been to this part of town before.*

◆ **when** something happens can go at the beginning for emphasis ('**front-position**'):
***Yesterday** he painted the kitchen.*

We can put other adverbs in front-position for emphasis:
***Angrily**, she stormed out of the room.*
***Suddenly**, she burst into tears.*

◆ **how** something happens can sometimes go in all three positions:
***Carefully**, he packed his suitcase.*
*He **carefully** packed his suitcase.*
*He packed his suitcase **carefully**.*

An adverb does not usually go between a verb and its object:
*She held his hand **tightly**. (**not** She held tightly his hand.)*

## C  Grammar exercises

**1** Use the adjectives in brackets to make adverbs and fill in the gaps.

1 She picked up the sleeping baby ....gently.... . (*gentle*)

2 When she handed him his lost wallet, he smiled at her ..................... . (*grateful*)

3 She couldn't see her son anywhere and called his name ..................... . (*anxious*)

4 They followed the directions to the hotel ..................... . (*easy*)

5 He admitted his mistake and apologised ..................... . (*sincere*)

**2** Underline the correct words.

1 She stepped *confident* / *confidently* onto the stage to begin her talk.

2 The meeting at lunchtime was a *complete* / *completely* waste of time.

3 She did *good* / *well* in the exam and she won a prize.

4 Max tried *hard* / *hardly* to make the hotel receptionist understand him, but his Spanish wasn't *fluent* / *fluently* enough.

5 After looking at the computer screen all day I had an *awful* / *awfully* headache.

6 Even though Deborah did the job *efficient* / *efficiently*, they sacked her after two months.

7 The doctor couldn't understand why Carol felt so hot because her temperature was *normal* / *normally*.

8 The boy behaved *bad* / *badly* on a school trip so the school refused to take him on any more.

**3** Rewrite each sentence with the adverbs in brackets in suitable positions.

1 She plays the guitar well for her age. (*incredibly*)
She plays the guitar incredibly well for her age.

2 They eat steak because it is so expensive. (*rarely, nowadays*)
...........................................................................................................

3 My grandfather used to take us swimming. (*in the summer holidays, in the lake*)
...........................................................................................................

4 There is a good film on TV. (*usually, on Sunday evenings*)
...........................................................................................................

5 My mother insisted that good manners are important. (*terribly, always*)
...........................................................................................................

**4** Use one word from the box to fill each gap.

| always | earlier | hardly | now | rather |
|--------|---------|--------|-----|--------|
| ~~silently~~ | skilfully | stiffly | very | warmly |

She shut the door ..silently.. **(1)** after her. Her father wasn't expecting her — she had arrived ............ **(2)** than she had said. He was sitting where he ............ **(3)** sat, in his favourite armchair by the window. It was ............ **(4)** old but had been repaired ............ **(5)** so that he could continue using it. The room had been redecorated since her last visit and was looking ............ **(6)** elegant. On the shelves were all the books which her father ............ **(7)** ever looked at any more. She called her father's name. He stood up and she noticed that he moved very ............ **(8)**. He smiled and held out his arms to her. She hadn't been in touch with him for five years but ............ **(9)** he welcomed her as ............ **(10)** as he always had.

**5** In eight of these sentences there is a mistake. Underline each mistake and write the correction.

1 The child spread <u>thickly the jam</u> on the piece of bread. ........the jam thickly........
2 I used to see Sharon at the gym every week but I haven't seen her lately. ............
3 My grandmother drives less careful than she used to. ............
4 I never have bought anything from that expensive shop over there. ............
5 Paul is extremely careless – he loses something nearly every day. ............
6 At Tony's garage I always have my car repaired. ............
7 You must return the book by next Friday to the library. ............
8 My uncle speaks very well Spanish because he lived in Peru for a while. ............
9 My sister doesn't make friends as easily than I do. ............
10 Jon can't go out much at the moment as he has to study hardly for his degree. ............

## D Exam practice

⚠ This task tests grammar from the rest of the book as well as the grammar in this unit.

### Use of English

For questions **1–10**, read the text below. Use the word given in capitals at the end of each line to form a word that fits in the space in the same line. There is an example at the beginning (**0**).

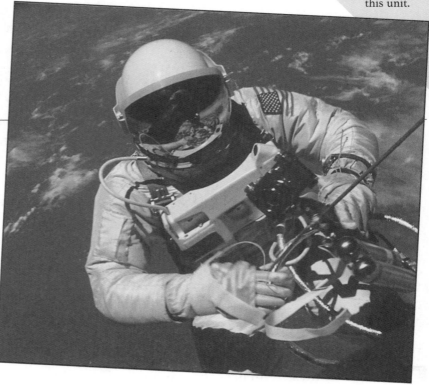

### ASTRONAUTS

There are two types of astronaut – **(0)** _commanders_ who fly the spacecraft and   **COMMAND**
carefully trained specialists who conduct **(1)** ............... experiments and carry   **SCIENCE**
out spacewalks to repair damaged **(2)** ............... .   **EQUIP**

  Astronauts have to pass a medical and have **(3)** ............... in a relevant subject.   **QUALIFY**
They have to be willing to live in an **(4)** ............... small space and work well   **EXTREME**
with other people. Experiments can go **(5)** ............... wrong, risking the lives of   **DANGER**
astronauts. They have to be able to react **(6)** ............... in a difficult situation as   **CALM**
well as be prepared to work hard.

  The first British astronaut was, **(7)** ............... , a woman – most astronauts are   **USUAL**
male. Helen Sharman got the job after hearing an **(8)** ............... on the radio.   **ANNOUNCE**
There were 18,000 applicants and, **(9)** ............... for Helen, she was chosen. She   **LUCK**
said that the most **(10)** ............... thing for her was seeing the earth from 120   **AMAZE**
miles into space.

Find eight adverbs in the text (including the gaps). Write the adverb and the adjective which it comes from.

1  carefully , careful      2  .................. , ..................      3  .................. , ..................

4  .................. , ..................      5  .................. , ..................      6  .................. , ..................

7  .................. , ..................      8  .................. , ..................

## Writing

Schools and colleges in your area have recently held a music and drama festival. You have been asked to write a report for your school magazine describing some of the most interesting events of the day. Write your **report** in **120–180** words.

This task gives you a chance to practise:
using adverbs, especially those which tell us how something happened.
using comparative adverbs (you could compare some of the events).

**Useful words and expressions**
*to entertain, to impress, group, performance, orchestra, beautifully, extremely well*

# 9 Questions

*yes / no* questions; short answers; question words;
question tags; agreeing

## A Context listening

**1** You are going to hear a telephone conversation between Peter and his girlfriend Molly. Before you listen, look at the picture. Why do you think Peter is unhappy?

..............................................................

..............................................................

**2** 🎧 9a Listen and check if you were right.

**3** 🎧 9a Listen again and answer these questions.

1 Who went out? Molly.......................................................

2 How many times did Peter phone Molly and get no answer? ..........3............................

3 Who had a change of plan? ..........Molly....................................

4 Who is sorry? .........Peter..........................................

5 Where are they meeting tomorrow? ......college....gate..................

**4** 🎧 9a Listen again for these replies. Write down the question when you hear each reply.

| | | |
|---|---|---|
| 1 | Are you home at last? | Yes, I am. |
| 2 | Have you been checking up on me? | No, I haven't. |
| 3 | ....................................................... | Yes, I did. |
| 4 | You know I love, don't you? | Of course I do. |
| 5 | And you love me? | You know I do. |
| 6 | And you'll always love me, won't you? | Of course I will. |
| 7 | Yes let's meet at college gate, shall we? | Yes, let's. |

Underline the verbs in the replies and in the questions which they refer to.

72

## B Grammar

### 1 Making *yes* / *no* questions

To make questions:

◆ which can be answered with *yes* or *no*, we put the auxiliary verb before its subject:
**You're going** on holiday soon. → **Are you going** on holiday soon?
**He's packed** his case.     → **Has he packed** his case?

◆ in the present simple or past simple (➤ see Units 1 and 2), we use the auxiliary verb *do(es)* or *did* to make the question:
**I like** Italy.         → **Do you like** Italy?
**She prefers** Greece.      → **Does she prefer** Greece?
                  (**not** ~~Does she prefers Greece?~~)
**They went** to Corsica.     → **Did they go** to Corsica?

◆ with the verb *to be*, we put *to be* before the subject:
**They're** in Madrid today.   → **Are they** in Madrid today?

◆ with modal verbs, we put the modal verb before the subject:
**We can stay** here.      → **Can we stay** here?

We make negative questions in the same way:
**They like** big cities.    → **Don't they like** big cities?
**She can't stay** here.     → **Can't she stay** here?

These questions often express surprise:
**Don't they like** big cities? (= I thought they liked big cities. Am I wrong?)
**Can't she stay** here? (= I thought she could stay here. Is that impossible?)

### 2 Short answers

We answer a *yes*/*no* question using the same auxiliary or modal verb as in the question.
If we agree with a positive question, the answer is *yes*:
**Are** you going to Greece?    **Yes, I am.**
**Did** you like the hotel?    **Yes, I did.**

If we agree with a negative question, the answer is *no*:
**Aren't** you going to Greece?   **No, I'm not.**
**Didn't** you like the hotel?   **No, I didn't.**

If we disagree with a positive question, the answer is *no*:
**Are** you going to Greece?    **No, I'm not.**
**Did** you like the hotel?    **No, I didn't.**

If we disagree with a negative question, the answer is *yes*:
**Aren't** you going to Greece?   **Yes, I am.**
**Didn't** you like the hotel?   **Yes, I did.**

## 3 Making questions with question words (*who, what, where, why, how, which*)

When we use *what*, *which* or *who* to make questions about the **subject** of the verb we do not change the word order (unlike *yes / no* questions):

*The pool* looks too small.     → **What** looks too small?
                                  (Answer: *The pool.*)

*This hotel* offers the best view.  → **Which hotel** offers the best view?
                                      (Answer: *This hotel.*)

We make questions about all other parts of the sentence in the same way as *yes / no* questions:

*They'll be in Madrid **tomorrow**.*    → **When will they be** in Madrid?
                                          (Answer: *Tomorrow.*)

*We can't stay here **because it's full**.*  → **Why can't we stay** here?
                                              (Answer: *Because it's full.*)

*She prefers to travel **by train**.*   → **How does she prefer** to travel?
                                          (Answer: *By train.*)

Compare these **subject** and object questions:

*Molly's visiting Susan.* → **Who's** visiting Susan? **Molly**. (= subject)
                            *Who's Molly visiting? Susan.* (= object)

⚠ In a subject question, *who* is always followed by a singular verb:

**Who is** coming to your party? (**not** ~~Who are coming?~~)

unless two or more people are actually mentioned in the question:

**Who are** your favourite **singers**?

⚠ Remember the difference between these questions with *like*:

*What **does** Molly **like**?* (= what does she enjoy?) *She likes dancing.*

*What **does** Molly **look like**?* (= tell me about her appearance) *She's pretty.*

*What's Molly **like**?* (= tell me about her character and / or appearance) *She's intelligent and pretty.*

## 4 Question tags

We often make a statement into a question by adding a question tag at the end. The verb in the tag must match the form of the auxiliary verb in the statement.

If the statement is positive, the tag is negative:

   +                     –

*They'**re** going to Greece, **aren't** they?* (speaker expects the answer *yes*)

If the statement is negative, the tag is positive:

   –                    +

*You **aren't** going to Greece, **are** you?* (speaker expects the answer *no*)

We make question tags:

◆ in the present simple or past simple with *do(es)* or *did* for all verbs except *to be*:
**You like** the seaside, **don't you**?
**Molly prefers** Greece, **doesn't she**?
**Your friends aren't** in Madrid now, **are they**?

◆ with the same auxiliary or modal as in the statement:
**We can** stay here, **can't we**?
**They haven't** arrived yet, **have they**?

⚠ The question tag for *let's* is *shall we?*
**Let's go** to France, **shall we**?

⚠ The question tag for *I am* is *aren't I?*
**I am** doing the right exercise, **aren't I**?

The question tag for *I'm not* is *am I?*
**I'm not** in the right place, **am I**?

We use question tags:

◆ to check that something we have just said is true. This is not a real question so our voice does not rise at the end:

They're going to Greece, **aren't they**?

◆ to ask a question. Our voice rises at the end:

They're going to Greece, **aren't they**?

## 5 Agreeing with statements

To agree with statements we use *so* (for positive statements) and *neither* or *nor* (for negative statements) and put the verb before its subject. We can do this:

◆ with the verb *to be*:
We're lost.
**So am I**.

◆ with an auxiliary verb:
I went to Spain last year.
**So did they.**

I don't want to quarrel.
**Neither do I.**

◆ with a modal:
He can't speak French.
**Nor can I.**

## C Grammar exercises

**1** In seven of these sentences there is a mistake. Underline each mistake and write the correction.

1 Who <u>did make</u> the cake for the wedding? _____made_____
2 We haven't got to do the washing-up, <u>do we</u>? _____have we_____
3 Does your sister <u>lives</u> with your parents or has she got a flat of her own? _____live_____
4 Why <u>you can't</u> walk faster? _____can't you_____
5 You weren't planning to leave early, were you? _____
6 Which sort of music <u>prefer you</u> to listen to? _____do you prefer_____
7 You went to school in Paris, <u>haven't you</u>? _____didn't you_____
8 Were both your brothers playing in the match? _____
9 What is Julie's brother <u>look</u> like? _____does_____

**2** Write suitable questions for these answers, using the words in brackets and your own ideas.

1 _Where would you like to go on holiday?_ _____ (*go*)
   The Caribbean.

2 _Did you finish all the ice cream?_ _____ (*finish*)
   No, I didn't. There's some in the fridge.

3 _How much do you want to spend there_ _____ (*spend*)
   About an hour, usually.

4 _____ (*try*)
   No, I haven't. But I'd love to.

5 _____ (*do*)
   Sometimes I watch a film and other times I read.

6 _____ (*see*)
   About once a week. It depends how busy I am.

7 _____ (*enjoy*)
   Not really. The music wasn't good, and the people weren't very interesting.

8 _____ (*be*)
   Because I overslept.

**3** Read this article and write questions to match the answers given below.

LAST NIGHT BRIAN BAINES was celebrating his appointment as manager of Farley City Football Club. He says he is particularly happy to be going back to Farley, where he was born in 1968, after playing for a number of European teams. Baines telephoned his wife Shirley as soon as he had signed the contract. He said that she is really pleased that their three children will be able to settle at schools in the city. Their many old friends are looking forward to welcoming them back to Farley.

1 What was Brian Baines celebrating last night?

His appointment as manager of Farley City F.C.

2 Where was he born?

In Farley.

3 Who did he phone?

His wife Shirley.

4 When did he phoned his wife

As soon as he had signed the contract.

5 How many children do they have

Three.

6 Why are they pleased

Because their children will be able to settle at schools in Farley.

7 Who is looking forward to welcoming them back

Their many old friends.

**4** Add the correct question tags to these questions.

1 He always forgets his homework, ...*doesn't he*...?
2 The teachers didn't see me, ...*did they*...?
3 You would like to come with us, *wouldn't you*?
4 I've got plenty of time, *haven't I*?
5 Let's have another coffee, ...*shall we*...?
6 It couldn't possibly rain, ...*could it*...?
7 Those men played really well, *didn't they*?
8 Molly will have to tell the truth, *won't she*?
9 We can't stop here, *can we*?
10 You promise you'll never tell anyone, *won't you*?

**5** Match the statements and short answers.

1 I started learning English when I was ten. — d | a So am I.

2 I didn't find it very easy. — c | b Neither will I.

3 I was always trying to sing English songs. — h | c Neither did I.

4 But I couldn't understand the words at first. — g | d So did I.

5 I'm quite good at English now. — a | e So must I.

6 I've read a couple of novels in English. — f | f So have I.

7 I won't have many problems in England, I guess. — b | g Neither could I.

8 And I must do my homework now. — e | h So was I.

## D  Exam practice

### Listening

🎧 9b  You will hear people talking in eight different situations. For questions **1–8**, choose the best answer, **A**, **B** or **C**.

___

**1**  You hear a man talking to some tourists. Who is he?
  **A**  a café owner
  **B**  a tourist guide
  **C**  a street trader

**2**  You hear a woman and her friend in an airport. What has the woman lost?
  **A**  her handbag
  **B**  her passport
  **C**  her boarding pass

**3**  You hear a man talking about his holiday. Which place did he enjoy most?
  **A**  the seaside
  **B**  Bangkok
  **C**  the north

**4**  You hear a girl talking about choosing a coat. Whose advice did she follow?
  **A**  her mother's
  **B**  her sister's
  **C**  the shop assistant's

**5**  In an office, you hear a man talking on the telephone. Where is Mr Richardson?
  **A**  in a hotel
  **B**  in America
  **C**  at home

**6**  You overhear a man telling a friend about a trip to a gym. How does the man feel?
  **A**  ashamed
  **B**  determined
  **C**  angry

**7**  You hear a woman talking to a doctor's receptionist. Why does she want an early appointment?
  **A**  because she mustn't eat before she comes in
  **B**  because she's having problems eating
  **C**  because she wants to see the doctor without taking time off work

**8** You hear a man talking about selling his bicycle. How did he do it?

   **A** He paid for an advertisement in the newspaper.

   **B** He told all his friends about it.

   **C** He advertised it at work.

| C | 8 |
|---|---|

## Grammar focus task

**These sentences are from the recording. Complete the missing question tags.**

**1** Let's order some drinks, ............_shall we_............?

**2** I didn't give it to you to hold, ..._did I_............?

**3** You know the sort of thing I mean, ..._don't you_......?

**4** It looks OK, ......_doesn't it_......?

**5** It was unlucky, ...._wasn't it_......?

**6** You can do that, ......_can't you_......?

**7** I am right, ......._aren't I_....... ?

## Writing

You have just received the address of a new English penfriend called Michael Taunt. You have no information apart from his name and address. Write your first letter. Tell him a little about yourself and ask him some questions. Write a **letter** in **120–180** words to your penfriend. Do not write any addresses.

## Writing hints

**This task gives you a chance to practise:**
asking questions.
giving information about yourself.

**Useful topics**
age, appearance, occupation, hobbies, sport, pets, music, future plans

## A  Context listening

**1** You are going to hear four people talk about their jobs. Look at the
pictures and guess what jobs they do.

1 .................................................................

2 .................................................................

3 .................................................................

4 .................................................................

**2** 🎧 **10** Listen and check if you were right.

**3** 🎧 **10** Listen again and answer these questions.

*Angela*

1  What does Angela's company make? Furniture. ........................................

2  What important part of her work does she mention? ..............................

3  What does she care about? ..................................................................

4  What is not always available? ..............................................................

*Ken*

5  When does Ken get calls from drivers who don't think ahead? ...............

6  Who calls Ken after an accident? .........................................................

7  What does he say that motorists should have? ......................................

*Charlie*

   **8**  Why does Charlie deliver pizzas? ......................................................................................................

   **9**  What subject is he studying? ......................................................................................................

*Hazel*

**10**  What is terrible? ......................................................................................................

**11**  What does she have to pay for? ......................................................................................................

**12**  Why does she say she mustn't grumble? ......................................................................................................

**4**   🎧 **10** **Listen again and answer these questions.**

   **1**  What does Angela avoid eating? ......................................................................................................

   **2**  Where does Ken work? ......................................................................................................

   **3**  What does Charlie deliver? ......................................................................................................

   **4**  What does Charlie usually avoid? ......................................................................................................

   **5**  What sort of job does he want when he graduates? ......................................................................................................

   **6**  How long has Hazel been driving a taxi? ......................................................................................................

   **7**  What does Hazel say about her family? ......................................................................................................

**5**   **Look at the nouns in your answers to Exercise 3 and compare them with the nouns in your answers to Exercise 4. Can you say how they are different?**

..........................................................................................................................................................................

## B Grammar

### 1 Countable and uncountable nouns

**Countable nouns:**

♦ can be singular:
   *a company, a job, a biscuit*

♦ or plural:
   *many companies, few jobs, some biscuits*

**Uncountable nouns:**

♦ cannot be plural:
   *health, clothing,* (**not** ~~healths, clothings~~)

♦ take a singular verb:
   **Petrol is** *expensive.* **Exercise is** *good for you.*

♦ use certain other words to refer to quantity:
   *a **piece** of furniture, a **sum** of money, a **litre** of petrol* (**not** ~~a furniture, a money, a petrol~~)

⚠ Many nouns can be countable and uncountable, but with different meanings:

*These grammar **exercises** are easy!*
(= tasks for practising grammar)

*The gallery was showing **works** by several artists.*
(= paintings, sculptures, etc.)

*The French produce some wonderful **cheeses**.*
(= different types of cheese)

*Exercise is good for you.*
(= taking exercise in general)

*I don't enjoy hard **work**.*
(= tasks and activities)

*Do we have any **cheese** in the fridge?*
(= that type of food)

### 2 A(n), the and no article

| | Means: | Introduces: | Use it with: |
|---|---|---|---|
| *A(n)* | one of many | a new item of information | singular countable nouns |
| *The* | the only one(s) **or** the particular one(s) | items we have mentioned before **or** when the speaker and listener know which items we are talking about | countable **and** uncountable nouns |
| **No article** | all **or** that quantity is uncertain or unimportant | things in a general sense | uncountable nouns **and** plural countable nouns |

Compare the use of articles in these sentences:

*There's **a supermarket** in most towns nowadays.* (= one of many that exist)
*We buy most of our food from **the local supermarket**.* (= one particular supermarket near our house)

*Have you got **a pen**?* (= one of many that exist)
***The pen** is by the phone.* (= the only pen here)

*I don't like **the music** my brother plays.* (= that particular music)
***Music** helps me to concentrate when I'm working.* (= any music)

*We planted **the trees** in our garden five years ago.* (= the particular trees in our garden)
***Trees** are easily damaged by **pollution**.* (= all trees; any pollution)

***The cheese** is in **the fridge**.* (= the cheese you need; the only fridge here)
*Help yourself to **cheese** and **biscuits**.* (= as much cheese and as many biscuits as you want)

***People** used to believe **the moon** was **a goddess**.* (= people in general; the moon that goes round this planet; one of many goddesses)

## 3 Special uses of articles

Look out for special uses of articles. Here are some common examples:

**Places**
We use *the* with:

◆ oceans, seas and rivers: *the Black Sea, the Danube*

◆ regions: *the Far East, the Midlands*

◆ groups of islands: *the Philippines*

◆ names of countries that include a word such as *Republic, Kingdom, States* or *Emirates*: *the United States, the People's Republic of China*

◆ deserts and mountain ranges: *the Kalahari, the Alps*

We say:
*the sea, the coast, the seaside, the country, the mountains, the hills.*
*My parents spend their holidays by **the coast**, but I prefer walking in **the mountains**.*

We do not use *the* with:
◆ lakes: *Lake Garda*

◆ continents, most countries, states, cities, towns and villages: *Europe, France, Florida, Rome*
⚠ but we say: *the Netherlands, The Hague*

◆ buildings and locations that use the name of their town in the name: *Manchester Airport, Birmingham City Art Gallery, Cardiff station, Edinburgh Castle, Durham University, Chelmsford High School*

## Jobs

We use *a(n)* to say what job someone does:

*I'm **a doctor**.* (**not** ~~I'm doctor.~~)

## Definitions

We use *a(n)* to give a definition of something:

*A **department store** is a shop which sells a wide range of goods.*
(**not** ~~Department store~~ *is a shop which sells a wide range of goods.*)

## Exclamations

We use *a(n)* with exclamations:

*What **an exciting film**!* (**not** ~~What exciting film!~~)

## Fixed expressions

Some fixed expressions use *the* and some use no article:

*We travel **by train / bus**.* (**not** ~~by the train / bus~~)
*We **have lunch / dinner** at one.* (**not** ~~the lunch / dinner~~)
*We listen to **the radio**.* but *We watch **television**.*
*We play **the guitar**.* (a musical instrument) but *We play **tennis**.* (a sport)
*We go to **the cinema**, **the theatre** etc.*

We say:

*My mother is **at work**.*

but:

*My mother is **at the office**.* (= the office where she works)

⚠ We use *the* or no article before some places, with a difference in meaning:

*The children are **at school** now.* (= they are students there)
*My father is **at the school** now.* (= he is visiting it)
*Peter spent a lot of time **in hospital** as a child.* (= he was a patient)
*Dr Dibble has an office **in the hospital** and another at home.*
(= she works there)

This rule also applies to *at church, in prison, at college* and *at university*.

# 10

## C Grammar exercises

**1** a Complete each phrase with a noun from the uncountable or the countable box. Use your dictionary if necessary. Can any of the phrases be used with more than one of the nouns?

| Uncountable: | glass | ~~luggage~~ | meat | paper | rice |

| Countable: | books | cards | clothes | shoppers | tools |

1 an item of ...luggage......    2 a pack of ..........................    3 a sheet of ..........................
4 a crowd of ..........................    5 a pane of ..........................    6 a slice of ..........................
7 a set of ..........................    8 a bundle of ..........................    9 a grain of ..........................
10 a pile of ..........................

b Use your dictionary to find words to use with these uncountables. There may be more than one possible answer for each.

1 a .......................... of bread    2 a .......................... of ice    3 a .......................... of oil
4 a .......................... of wood    5 a .......................... of dust

Remember to make a note of other words like these when you meet them.

**2** Complete the diagram with the words that belong in each group. Use your dictionary if necessary.

| accommodation | advice | cheese | coffee | experience |
| experiment | glass | ~~hair~~ | hobby | homework |
| information | journey | leisure | luck | ~~luggage~~ |
| meat | scenery | time | traffic | ~~vegetable~~ |

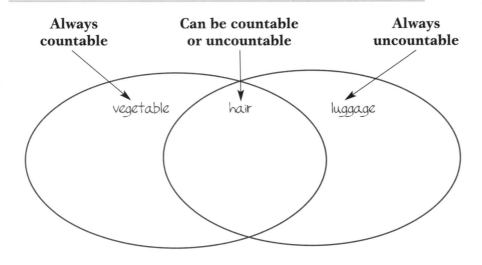

Always countable

Can be countable or uncountable

Always uncountable

vegetable

hair

luggage

**3** Fill in the gaps with *a*, *an*, *the*, or – (for no article).

# Pancake recipe

You need 100 grams of flour, ......*an*...... (1)
egg, a little milk, and a spoonful of butter.
Beat .................... (2) egg with .................... (3)
flour. Add .................... (4) milk until the
mixture is runny. Heat .................... (5)
butter in .................... (6) frying pan. Pour
.................... (7) spoonful of ....................
(8) mixture into .................... (9) pan. Cook
for one minute. Turn .................... (10)
pancake over and cook a little longer.
Serve hot, with .................... (11) sugar
and .................... (12) lemon juice.

**4** Fill in the gaps with the words in brackets. Add *a* or *the* if necessary.

1 We've got some important visitors flying in from ...*the West Indies*... next week.
Can you meet them at ............................................ ? (*West Indies*, *Birmingham Airport*)

2 Ferdinand spent his holiday sailing across ................................ from ................................
to ................................ . (*Mediterranean*, *Naples*, *Corsica*)

3 My brother's idea of a holiday is trekking across ................................ or exploring
................................ . Personally, I'd rather explore ................................ and do some
shopping! (*Sahara*, *Andes*, *Paris*)

4 Have you met Cora's new boyfriend? He's ................................ from ................................ .
(*ski instructor*, *Switzerland*)

5 What................................! Our train broke down near Ely and we had to get a
bus from there to ................................ and then wait hours for the next train.
(*terrible journey*, *Peterborough station*)

10

**5** Correct the mistakes in this letter.

Dear Monique,

We had a great trip to the France last weekend. We went to little hotel that you recommended and it was very pleasant. Foods at the hotel weren't so good, as you warned us, but we strolled down to city centre on Saturday evening and had lovely meal there. In fact, we ate so much for the dinner that we didn't want a breakfast on Sunday!

Thanks again for the advice and informations. Now I must unpack and do the washings.

See you soon.

Love, Freda

88

## D Exam practice

⚠ This task tests grammar from the rest of the book as well as the grammar in this unit.

### Use of English

For questions **1–15**, read the text below and look carefully at each line. Some of the lines are correct, and some have a word which should not be there, If a line is correct, put a tick (✓). If a line has a word which should not be there, write the word. There are two examples at the beginning, (**0** and **00**).

### CLEANER AIR

**0** <u>they</u> The government has recently announced some plans which they

**00** ✓ should help to protect the environment. Firstly, the tax system

**1** ........ could be changed, so that anyone who drives a big car which

**2** ........ consumes a lot of the petrol will pay more taxes than people who

**3** ........ drive smaller cars. In an addition, company car parks may

**4** ........ be taxed so that companies who will encourage their employees

**5** ........ to travel to work by the train or bus. There will also be money

**6** ........ available to build more cycle tracks, which allow people to cycle

**7** ........ safely, and reducing the need for so many car journeys. Lastly,

**8** ........ the government wants to reduce down the number of heavy

**9** ........ lorries on the roads and they persuade manufacturers to

**10** ........ use a rail transport instead. These ideas are good, but they do

**11** ........ not go far enough. Too many people live so far away from the

**12** ........ place where they have work or study that they cannot be

**13** ........ expected to walk or cycle to there regularly. Few modern

**14** ........ factories are so unpleasant to live near that they must be far away

**15** ........ from houses. If small factories and offices were closer to people's

homes, we would save money and reduce pollution.

**Which of these nouns from the text are countable (C) and which are uncountable (U)? Can any of them be both (B)? Use your dictionary if you want to.**

1 bus ..C..        2 government ........        3 money ........        4 petrol ........
5 place ........        6 pollution ........        7 train ........        8 transport ........

## Writing

Write an answer to the question below in **120–180** words in an appropriate style.

You see this competition in a student magazine:

# "Eat well, stay healthy."

What's your advice to your fellow students?

Win a free meal for two in this week's competition by describing a diet which is both healthy and enjoyable.

Send your article to the editor by the end of the month.

The winning entry will be printed in our next issue.

Write your **article** for the magazine.

**This task gives you a chance to practise:** writing about food and diet.

**Useful words and expressions**
*to cook, to go on a diet, to prepare, to put on / lose weight, to serve*
*delicious, fresh, frozen, good for you, instant, tinned*
*a balanced diet, dish, fast food, healthy eating, meal*

# Pronouns and determiners

possessives; reflexive pronouns; *each other* etc.; *there* and *it*;
*someone* etc.; *all*, *most* and *some*; *each* and *every*; *both*, *neither* etc.

11

## A  Context listening

**1** You are going to hear a female travel agent and a male customer having a conversation. Before you listen, look at the pictures below. Which place do you think the woman went on holiday to last year? ...................................................
Which place do you think the man would prefer to go to?

...................................................

a

b

c

d

**2** 🎧 **11** Listen and check if you were right.

**3** 🎧 **11** Listen again and fill in the gaps. Stop the recording when you need to.

1  Have you looked at any of our brochures? Do ........*help yourself*........ .

2  I went to this place ........................................... last year with some friends ........................................... .

3  ........................................... of those would suit me.

4  Are you going on your own?
   Yes, ........................................... .

5  That's better because you get to know ........................................... really well.

6  All I want is ........................................... quiet.

7  ........................................... of the holidays look enjoyable at all.

## B  Grammar

### 1  Possessive 's and *of*

The position of the apostrophe is important:
*my brother's friends* (= one brother)
*my brothers' friends* (= more than one brother)

When we speak we sometimes omit the second noun:
*I stayed at **Simon's**.* (*house* is omitted)
*I went to the **dentist's**.* (*surgery* is omitted)
*I stopped at the **newsagent's**.* (*shop* is omitted)

We use 's with people, countries and animals:
*The girl's clothes were very dirty.* (**not** ~~the clothes of the girl~~)
*Britain's roads get more crowded every year.*
*I tripped over the dog's tail.*

and with time expressions:
*I want to go on a **week's** holiday.*
*That's last **year's** brochure.*

but we usually use *of* instead of 's with things:
*What's the price **of** that holiday?* (**not** ~~the holiday's price~~)

### 2  Reflexive pronouns

| myself   yourself   himself   herself   itself   ourselves   themselves |
| --- |

We use a reflexive pronoun:

◆ to make it clear that we are talking about the subject of the verb:
  *Tim hurt **himself** when he fell off his bike.* but *Sam cried when Tim hurt **him**.*
  (= Tim hurt Sam)

  *Amy blamed **herself** for what had happened.* but *Amy blamed **her** for what
  had happened.* (= Amy blamed another person, not herself)

◆ for emphasis:
  *I went to this place **myself** to see what it was really like.*

◆ with a number of common expressions like *by (your)self, enjoy (your)self,
  behave (your)self, help (your)self, make (your)self at home*:
  ***Help yourself** to some brochures.*
  *It's got everything you need to **enjoy yourself**.*

⚠ We don't usually use a reflexive pronoun after *wash, shave* and *dress* but
we can for emphasis:
*She dressed quickly.* but *The little girl managed to dress **herself** quickly.*
(= it was difficult for her)

---

## 3  Possessive pronouns and adjectives

| Possessive pronouns: | mine | yours | his | hers | ours | theirs |
|---|---|---|---|---|---|---|
| Possessive adjectives: | my | your | his | her | its | our | their |

Possessive adjectives are used before a noun:
*I went with **my** friends.*

We always use them with parts of the body and clothes:
*My father broke **his** leg.*
*They washed **their** clothes in the river.*

We can say:
*my friends* or *some friends **of mine** / **yours** / **Tim's*** etc. (**not** ~~friends of me~~)

We use a possessive adjective + *own* to emphasise possession:
*I'd rather have **my own** apartment.* (= just for me) or *I'd rather have an apartment **of my own**.*

*On (your) own* means 'alone' and can be used instead of *by (your)self*:
*I'm going **on my own**.* or *I'm going by **myself**.*

*Own* can be used for emphasis in the same way as *myself*:
*I make my **own** clothes.* or *I make my clothes **myself**.*

## 4  *Each other, one another* and *someone else*

There is a difference between the reflexive pronouns and *each other / one another*:
*The two boys hurt **themselves**.* (= each boy was hurt)
*The two boys hurt **each other / one another**.* (= when they had a fight)
*The two boys hurt **someone else**.* (= together they hurt a third person)

There is also a possessive form of *each other / one another*:
*They borrow **each other's / one another's** shoes because they take the same size.*

## 5  *There* and *it* + the verb *to be*

We use *there* + the verb *to be*:
◆ to say that somebody / something exists (or not) especially when we refer to somebody / something for the first time:
   ***There are** some lovely apartments.*
   ***There's** a tour guide.*
   ⚠ Note that the verb after *there* agrees with the noun which follows.

We use *it* + the verb *to be*:
◆ to refer to a particular thing, action, situation or place already mentioned:
   ***There's** a hotel by the sea. **It's** quite old.*

- to introduce information about time, weather and distance:
  **It's** *twenty past five and* **it's sunny** *here in New York.*
  **It's** *only a few metres from the beach.*

- to avoid using a phrase with *-ing* or *to* infinitive as the subject:
  **It's** *surprising to see you here.* (= *To see you here is surprising.*)
  **It's** *a waste of time coming here.* (= *Coming here is a waste of time.*)

## 6 *Someone, anywhere, everybody* etc.

Words like *someone, anywhere* etc. follow the same rules as *some* and *any*:
*Some* is used in positive sentences:
*I want to go* **somewhere** *sunny.*

*Any* is used in questions and negative sentences:
*Are you interested in* **anywhere** *in particular?*
*I haven't got* **anything** *as cheap as that this year.*

*Any* is also used in positive statements to show 'it doesn't matter which':
**Anywhere** *quiet will be fine.*

⚠ Words like *someone, everybody* etc. are followed by a singular verb:
**Everyone's** *going there this year.* but **Nobody wants** *to go to that hotel.*

## 7 *All, most* and *some*

We use *all, most* and *some* followed by the noun without *the* when the meaning
is general:
**All** *hotels have bedrooms.* (= hotels throughout the world)
**Most** *hotels have a restaurant.*
**Some** *hotels have a private beach.*
But when we refer to a particular group we use *all / most / some of the*:
**All (of) the** *hotels (in this street) have a restaurant.*
**Most of the** *hotels (in this town) are expensive.*
**Some of the** *hotels (in the brochure) have a swimming pool.*
⚠ Note that we can omit *of* after *all* but not after *some* or *most*.

With a pronoun we use *all / most / some (+ of)*:
**All / Most / Some (of them)** *have a private beach.* (**not** *All them have* ...)

We use *all* for emphasis:
*They are* **all** *near the airport.*

*All* can also stand alone:
**All** *I want is somewhere quiet.* (= the only thing)

*Whole* is used instead of *all* before a singular noun:
*The* **whole trip** *was spoilt by the weather.*
but we use *all* with a plural noun:
**All the hotels** *were booked.*

## 8 *Each* and *every*

*Each* and *every* can be used with the same meaning:
***Every / Each*** *apartment has a balcony.*

but sometimes they have different meanings:

◆ *Each* is used for individual things or people in a group:
***Each*** *child drew a picture of her own parents.*
*The customs officer checked* ***each*** *passport in turn.*

◆ *Every* emphasises that all the people or things in a group are included:
***Every*** *brochure you've shown me ...*

*Each* (but not *every*) can be followed by *of* + a plural noun or pronoun:
***Each*** *apartment /* ***Each of*** *the apartments /* ***Each of them*** *has a balcony.*
(**not** ~~Every of the apartments / every of them~~)

⚠ Notice the difference between *every* and *all*:
*He sat by the river* ***every*** *morning.* (= regularly)
*He sat by the river* ***all*** *morning.* (= one complete morning)

## 9 *Both, neither, either* and *none*

We use *both, neither* and *either* when we refer to two items:
***Both*** *places are too noisy.* or ***Both (of)*** *the places ...* or ***Both of*** *them ...*
***Either / Neither*** *place suits me.* or ***Either /Neither of*** *the places ...* or
***Either / Neither of*** *them ...*
⚠ Note that with plurals we can omit *of* after *both* but not after *either*
or *neither*.

We can use *both / neither / either* alone:
*Which holiday would you prefer?* ***Either. / Neither.***
*Which holiday did you enjoy?* ***Both.***

We use *both ... and / neither ... nor / either ... or* to connect two things or
actions:
***Both*** *the Hotel Flora* ***and*** *the Hotel Princess* ***have*** *a good restaurant.*
***Neither*** *the Hotel Flora* ***nor*** *the Hotel Princess* ***has*** *a restaurant.*
*I'd like to stay at* ***either*** *the Hotel Flora* ***or*** *the Hotel Princess.*

*None* means 'not any' and is usually followed by a singular verb, but a plural
is also sometimes possible:
***None*** *of the apartments* ***has / have*** *a balcony.*
***None of them has / have*** *a balcony.*

## C  Grammar exercises

**1** Fill in the gaps with *it is*, *there is* or *there are*.

Sometimes I dream of a place where I'd like to live. ........It is........ **(1)** at the top of a mountain and on the south-facing side

..................................... **(2)** a little house.

..................................... **(3)** very pretty and

..................................... **(4)** flowers all around it.

..................................... **(5)** no other houses nearby but ..................................... **(6)** lots of sheep and goats and wonderful vegetables growing.

..................................... **(7)** always sunny and warm and it only rains at night. ..................................... **(8)** not far from a little village where

..................................... **(9)** a restaurant which serves my favourite food. Unfortunately

..................................... **(10)** just a dream!

**2** In seven of these sentences there is a mistake. Underline each mistake and write the correction.

1  Why are you reading that? It's <u>yesterdays'</u> newspaper. ..........yesterday's..........

2  The cat's fur was soaking wet because it had been sitting in the wet grass. .....................

3  My violin lesson was cancelled because the car of my teacher wouldn't start.

.....................................

4  Nobody wanted to come to the cinema with me so I went on myself. .....................

5  We really enjoyed us when we went to the fair last weekend. .....................

6  My mothers' job is really interesting – she works as a fashion designer. .....................

7  When I saw him fall I really thought he had broken the leg. .....................

8  My cousin never behaves himself when he goes to other people's houses. .....................

9  Simon asked some friends of him to help him move house. .....................

10  The college decided to publish the students' results in the newspaper because they had all done so well. .....................

**3** Underline the most suitable words.

I'm going to tell you about a party game you might want to play. It's a game _most_ / _most of_ (1) people would enjoy and it's a good way for people to get to know _each other_ / _themselves_ (2) when they first arrive. There is a pile of cards and _all_ / _every_ (3) card has the name of a famous person on it. _Every_ / _Each_ (4) of the famous people has a partner, for example, Romeo's partner is Juliet. It's important that they're people that _all_ / _everyone_ (5) has heard of. _Everyone_ / _Someone_ (6) has one of these cards pinned to their back and they have to find out who they are by questioning _every_ / _all the_ (7) other people in the room. The first pair to find _one another_ / _the other_ (8) gets a prize. _The whole_ / _All the_ (9) game takes about twenty minutes and by the end _nobody_ / _anybody_ (10) is feeling shy any longer.

**4** Complete these sentences describing the three brothers, Peter, John and Rob. Use the words in the box.

| bald | beard | earring | ~~fair hair~~ | glasses | moustache | short hair |

Pete    John    Rob

1 Both ......_John_...... and _Rob have fair hair._
2 Both ................... and ...................
3 Neither ................... nor ...................
4 All of them ...................
5 They all ...................
6 None of them ...................

Write sentences about your own family or three of your friends.

7 Both ................... and ...................
8 Neither my ................... nor my ...................
9 All my family / friends ...................
10 None ...................

## D Exam practice

⚠ This task tests grammar from the rest of the book as well as the grammar in this unit.

### Use of English

For questions **1–15**, read the text below and think of the word which best fits each space. Use only **one** word in each space. There is an example at the beginning (**0**).

**NAMES**

If, like me, you are called John Smith and you live in England, you have the same name
(**0**) ......*as*...... thousands of other people. When I was a child, I thought that
(**1**) .................... in the world had a different name and I had a name of my (**2**) ...................., 
but as (**3**) .................... as I went to school I realised that I was wrong because I found
(**4**) .................... were two other boys with my name. In fact, one of them became a close
friend of (**5**) .................... .

When I meet someone for (**6**) .................... first time, they often think that they have met
me before somewhere, but then they realise that in fact they are thinking of somebody
(**7**) .................... – another John Smith. If I say my name in a hotel or a bank, the
receptionist often looks at me suspiciously as (**8**) .................... is a name which people
use (**9**) .................... they have to invent one quickly.

Having met people (**10**) .................... all kinds of names, I have decided it is better to have
a common name rather (**11**) .................... a very unusual one. (**12**) .................... parent
chooses a name they like but when I recently met two people called Honey Moon and
Holly Bush I wondered (**13**) .................... their parents were thinking of. (**14**) .................... of
them appeared to mind having unusual names although they (**15**) .................... agreed that
people sometimes did not take them seriously.

Look at these phrases and find expressions in the text which mean the same.

1 all the people = ............................ *everyone* ............................

2 My name was unique to me = ..........................................................

3 one of my best friends = ..........................................................

4 a different person = ..........................................................

5 every sort of = ..........................................................

6 both of them seemed happy = ..........................................................

7 two people said the same thing = ..........................................................

## Writing

Your class has recently been discussing the advantages and disadvantages of the growth of international travel both for travellers and for the countries they visit. Your teacher has now asked you to write a composition in **120–180** words, giving your own views on the following statement:

*International travel is becoming easier, faster and cheaper for many people. Is this good?*

Write your **composition**.

This task gives you a chance to practise:
using *all, most* and *some, anywhere* etc., *both, each* and *every, neither* and *none, someone, there* and *it.*

Useful words and expressions
*to benefit, to damage, to get to know, to improve, to increase, to spoil*
*abroad, economy, environment, tourism, trade*
*on the one hand, on the other hand*

# 12 Modals 1
## use of modals; obligation; necessity

## A Context listening

**1** You are going to hear a conversation between Chris and a girl called Alice. Look at the picture of Chris. What is his job? ........................................

**2** 🎧 12 Listen and check if you were right.

**3** 🎧 12 Listen again and answer these questions.

1 Why isn't Alice at school? <u>She's left school.</u> .......................................................................

2 How many rich and famous people does Chris meet? .......................................................

3 Why isn't Chris at work today? .............................................................................................

4 How is this job different from Chris's last job? ...................................................................

5 What does Chris offer to do? .................................................................................................

**4** 🎧 12 Listen again and match the beginnings and endings of these phrases. Stop the recording when you need to.

| | |
|---|---|
| 1 ... you need ..<u>e</u>.. | a think about the hotel kitchen today. |
| 2 Chefs have ........ | b to work every day except Monday. |
| 3 I needn't ........ | c to spend their time in the kitchen. |
| 4 You don't have ........ | d come to the hotel one day. |
| 5 I need ........ | e to talk to me ... |
| 6 I have ........ | f to work longer hours. |
| 7 I had ........ | g to work all day ... |
| 8 I'll have ........ | h go now. |
| 9 I must ........ | i to get up early. |
| 10 You must ........ | j to stay until all the food is cooked and served ... |

**5** Look at your answers to Exercise 4. Which verbs aren't followed by *to*? .........................................

**100**

## B Grammar

### 1 Use of modals

The modal verbs *can, could, may, might, must, ought to, shall, should, will* and *would*:

◆ are always used before another verb:
*He **can** swim.*

◆ never change – they do not add *-s* or *-ed* or *-ing*.

◆ are followed by a verb in its infinitive form without *to*:
*You **should** get up earlier.* (**not** ~~You should to get up earlier.~~)
but notice that we say:
*You **ought to** get up earlier.*

◆ are immediately followed by *not* in the negative:
*You **should not** (or **shouldn't**) be late for college.*
but notice that we say:
*You **ought not to** be late for college.*

◆ go immediately before the subject in a question:
***Could you** wake me up?*

*Need* can be a modal verb as well as a main verb (▷ See Grammar, part 3).

### 2 Obligation
#### Must and have to

| + | *must* + verb | *We **must leave** now.* |
|---|---|---|
| ? | *must ... + verb?* | ***Must** we **leave** now?* |

| + | *have to / has to* + verb | *He **has to leave** now.* |
|---|---|---|
| ? | *do / does ... + have to + verb?* | ***Do** we **have to leave** now?* |

For obligation, we can often use *must* or *have to*:
*I **must** go now or I'll miss the bus.* or *I **have to** go now or I'll miss the bus.*

We use *must* to give orders or strong advice, including to ourselves:
*You **must** tell me everything.* (= I feel strongly about this)
*She **must** be home by midnight.* (= these are my instructions)
*You **must** come to the hotel one day.* (= I strongly advise you to)
*I **must** go now.* (= I have decided to do this)

When there is a rule or where the obligation does not come from the speaker, *must* is possible but *have to* is more usual:
*You **have to** pay to park your car here.* (= this is a rule)
*I **have to** stay until the food is cooked.* (= this is part of my job)

We usually use *have to* for habits:
*I **have to** get up early to cook breakfast.*
*He **has to** practise the piano for twenty minutes a day.*

---

**101**

We only use *must* in the present tense. In all other tenses, we use *have to*:

*I **had to** work every day.* (past simple)
*I'll **(will) have to** work longer hours.* (future)
*I avoided **having to** speak to him by crossing the street.* (verb + -ing)
*If I got the job, I'd **(would) have to** buy a car.* (conditional)

## Mustn't and *don't have to*

| | |
|---|---|
| *must not* + verb | *We **mustn't be** late.* |
| *do / does not have to* + verb | *We **don't have to be** early.* |

Although *must* and *have to* both express obligation, *mustn't* and *don't have to* have different meanings. *Mustn't* means 'don't do it' and *don't have to* means 'it's not necessary to do it':

*I **mustn't** wear jeans at work.* (= it is wrong to do this, it isn't allowed)
*You **don't have to** stay at school until you're 18.* (= you are not obliged to but you can if you want)

## Should

When we are talking about the right thing to do, we use *should*:

*He **should** take more care when he's cycling.* (= it's a good idea but he doesn't)
*I **shouldn't** spend so much time watching TV.* (= it's a bad idea but I still do)

To talk about the past, we use *should have* + past participle:

*I **should have** told the truth.* (= it was a good idea but I didn't)
*We **shouldn't have** lent her that money.* (= it was a bad idea but we still did)

(> See also Unit 13, Grammar, part 5)

## 3 Necessity

We can use *need* like a normal main verb in all the tenses, but it can also be a modal verb in questions and in the negative:

***Need I** come with you?* (= ***Do I need to** come with you?*)
*I **needn't** come.* (if I don't want to) (= *I **don't need to** come. / I **don't have to** come.*)

In positive statements, we say:
*I **need** to come.* (**not** *I need come.*)

To talk about the past, we say:
*He **needed** to buy some food.* (= it was necessary because he didn't have any)
*He **didn't need to** buy any food.* (= he didn't buy any food as it wasn't necessary)

⚠ *Needn't have* has a different meaning:
*He **needn't have** bought any food.* (= he bought food but it wasn't necessary)

## C  Grammar exercises

**1**  Fill in the gaps with the correct form of *have to* or *must*.

1  Most students in Britain ..........*have to*.......... pay at least part of their university fees.

2  Joe ............................................. get up early on Fridays as he has no lectures in the morning.

3  You ........................................ talk during the film because other people will get annoyed.

4  These library books are overdue so I ........................................ pay a fine when I return them.

5  Jeremy ................................................ drive to work because the bus gets there too late.

6  Because she could already play the piano, she ................................ practise much when she learnt to play the organ.

7  You ........................................ borrow this video – you'll enjoy watching it.

8  ........................................ (*you*) work every Saturday in your new job?

9  Non-swimmers ........................................ go into the deep end of the pool.

10  You ........................................ come to the rehearsal tomorrow if you want to be in the play.

11  When I was a child, I ........................................ change schools seven times because my parents moved house a lot.

12  Every morning the children ........................................ feed their rabbit before school.

13  I ........................................ stop eating so much chocolate or none of my clothes will fit.

14  They've promised to lend me a tennis racket so I ........................................ take mine.

**2**  Match the beginnings and endings of these sentences.

1  I shouldn't ...g...          a  wear a helmet when he's cycling on a busy road.

2  Need I .......          b  to take any money or is it free?

3  We don't need .......          c  to ask his boss before he leaves the office.

4  They needn't .......          d  take sandwiches with them because Jenny's cooking lunch.

5  He should .......          e  to send them our new address because they already have it.

6  Should you .......          f  fill in my application form now? I'm busy at the moment.

7  He needs .......          g  spend so much time playing computer games.

8  Do they need .......          h  carry that suitcase with your bad back?

**3** Read this article about a pop star.

# The diary column

Popstar Lee Divine travelled from London to New York yesterday by plane. Lee had visited his hairdresser before he went to the airport and wore his latest designer clothes, as he likes to look his best in photos. Press photographers usually follow him wherever he goes but the weather was very bad yesterday and, to Lee's obvious disappointment, there were no photographers at the airport. Because he is famous, he didn't stand in the queue and his bodyguard carried his luggage for him. Although most people have to walk from the car park, Lee has a driver who drove him right to the door. Even this did not seem to make him happy. Lee got angry with his driver on the way because he said she wasn't driving fast enough. Of course, they arrived at the airport in plenty of time.

**Write six sentences about Lee Divine.**

1 He needn't have _visited his hairdresser._ .................................................................

2 He needn't have ..................................................................................................

3 He didn't need to ...............................................................................................

4 He didn't need to ...............................................................................................

5 He didn't need to ...............................................................................................

6 He needn't have .................................................................................................

**4** Rewrite these sentences using the correct form of *must*, *need*, *should* or *have to*.

1 It's her fault that she's lost her watch because she didn't look after it.
   She *should have looked after her watch.*

2 I don't expect you to phone me before you come.
   You ...........................................................................................................................................

3 It is essential for students to buy a good dictionary.
   Students ...................................................................................................................................

4 It was wrong of you to take money from my purse without asking.
   You ...........................................................................................................................................

5 I was getting ready to drive to the station to pick up my sister when she arrived in a taxi.
   I ...............................................................................................................................................

6 It's not fair that I do the washing-up on my own.
   You ...........................................................................................................................................

7 Students aren't allowed to smoke in the canteen.
   Students ...................................................................................................................................

8 She turned the music down to avoid disturbing her neighbours but they'd gone out.
   She ...........................................................................................................................................

9 I think she's wrong to make promises which she doesn't keep.
   She ...........................................................................................................................................

10 You can give the tour guide a tip but it is not necessary.
   You ...........................................................................................................................................

## D  Exam practice

### Reading

You are going to read a magazine article about working in offices. Choose the most suitable heading from the list **A–I** for each part (**1–7**) of the article. There is one extra heading which you do not need to use. There is an example at the beginning (**0**).

---

**A**  A problem often overlooked

**B**  Get regular rest

**C**  Managing your meals

**D**  More than just keeping fit

**E**  Changing your mind

**F**  Effects on others

**G**  A variety of health problems that can be solved

**H**  Learning to enjoy exercise

**I**  A modern problem

# Find your energy again

**0** | I

The offices that most of us work in aren't the most healthy places in the world. If you work in a building that is more than 50 years old, it may not be perfectly designed for the office environment but it is probably healthier than one built recently. Even the best designed of today's offices represent an artificial environment where it can be difficult to stay positive and bursting with energy.

**1**

Complaints about feeling tired, no energy, no interest in food, headaches and backache are commonplace. Office workers often say that these health problems are the inevitable consequences of working in an office. However, this is not the case. While there may be little you can do about the ever-ringing phones or the tempers of your colleagues, you needn't feel unwell. There is plenty you can do to restore those energy levels and feelings of well-being.

**2**

The first thing you must address is tiredness. If at the weekend you stay up all night dancing or going to dinner parties and sleep all the following morning, you can't expect your body to adjust on a Monday morning to a completely different routine. Some people seem to keep this lifestyle up without any trouble but for most of us it isn't a good idea.

**3**

Our diets are another way we mistreat ourselves. Many office workers say they don't have breakfast – but you really should eat something, however small, before you leave the house. And if you're busy over lunch or have to go shopping, it's possible to forget that too. So you get to the evening and suddenly realise how hungry you are. This is a disastrous way to manage (or not manage) your diet. Nothing is more important than eating and drinking regularly.

**4**

You should also do a session of exercise once or twice a week in the evenings. This will help you to get to sleep and wake up refreshed in the morning. Recent American research has established that regular, vigorous exercise is a good way of improving your mood and that the effects last far longer than the session itself. It does have to be vigorous though – walking or tennis have to be kept up for at least an hour to have a positive effect.

**5**

All the advice on exercise says that you should choose something which you like doing. To this, many people reply: but I don't like doing any form of exercise! Most people start off with the intention of exercising but soon lose interest. The answer here is you must do it until you get so used to doing it that you miss it when you don't do it. In order to motivate yourself, you need to keep reminding yourself of the advantages.

**6**

If you're working in an office with no natural light, you should go out for a walk for at least half an hour a day, even when the weather is dull and rainy. The importance of spending some time in daylight is often ignored. We now know that lack of sunlight can cause depression. It is, however, something that needn't happen because it can easily be overcome.

**7**

You may be bothered by some of your colleagues' bad temper or lateness. Think about how their behaviour influences your own state of mind and remember that you don't need to behave in the same way. You are much more likely to enjoy your evening or weekend if you leave work feeling positive and it's the same for your colleagues.

**Grammar focus task**

Look at these sentences and find expressions in the text which mean the same.

1 It is not necessary for you to feel ill. *You needn't feel unwell.*

2 It is essential first of all for you to deal with tiredness. ...........................

3 It is important that you exercise at least once a week after work. ...........................

4 It is essential to walk or play tennis for at least an hour. ...........................

5 It is important that you do a form of exercise that you enjoy. ...........................

6 It is essential that you continue until it is a habit. ...........................

7 It is necessary that you don't forget the positive things. ...........................

8 It is not necessary for you to behave like them. ...........................

# Writing

You have been studying at a college in Britain for the last year. You live in a room in the college hostel. A friend of yours is coming to stay in the same college and has written you a letter asking you about the hostel. Read the letter, the college rules and the notes you have made. Answer your friend's questions. You may add any relevant ideas of your own.

Write a **letter** in **120–180** words in an appropriate style. Do not write any addresses.

I really want to know about the college hostel. Are there many rules about what we have to do? What do I need to bring with me? Can you reply soon as I am leaving in two weeks.

See you soon.
Chris

## Rules

Pay rent in advance
Order meals 24 hours before
Hostel locked at midnight
No music after midnight
No smoking

Necessary
Swimming things
Warm clothes (hostel cold)

Not necessary
Towels
Sheets
Coffee maker

## Writing hints

**This task gives you a chance to practise:**
using modal verbs to talk about obligation (rules) and necessity (what do you need).

**Useful words and expressions**
*although, because, in advance, otherwise, so, warden*

## A    Context listening

**1**  You are going to hear a teenage girl called Sophie asking her mother to do five things for her. What do you think Sophie might ask? .....................................
.....................................................................
.....................................................................
.....................................................................
.....................................................................

**2**  🎧 **13a** Listen and write Sophie's questions. Were any of your guesses right?

Sophie says:                                          Her mother agrees (✓) or
                                                      doesn't agree (✗):

1  Will you lend me ten pounds? .......................................          ✓
2  ..................................................................................          ........
3  ..................................................................................          ........
4  ..................................................................................          ........
5  ..................................................................................          ........

**3**  🎧 **13a** Listen again and put a tick (✓) in Exercise 2 if Sophie's mother agrees to do something and a cross (✗) if she doesn't agree.

**4**  🎧 **13a** Listen again. Sophie asks her mother two things for a second time at the end of the conversation. What does she say? Why does she ask differently the second time?
..................................................................................................................................
..................................................................................................................................

## B Grammar

### 1 Asking for and giving permission

We can ask for permission by saying: *Can I? Could I?* or *May I?*
**Can I** *leave my bag here while I look round the museum?* (= a simple request which expects the answer *yes*)
**Could I** *borrow your car for a few days?* (= more polite or a request which is less sure of the answer being *yes*)
**May I** *sit here?* (= a more formal request, particularly to a stranger)

We usually answer by saying:
*Of course (you can). / OK. / Certainly.*
*I'm afraid not.* (= polite) / *No, you can't.* (= not very polite)

*May* is often used in written notices to say what is or is not allowed:
*You **may** borrow six books from the library.*
*You **may not** keep any book for longer than three weeks.*

### 2 Making requests

We use *Can you?* and *Will you?* to ask someone else to do something:
**Can you** *pass me the bread?*
**Will you** *get me some stamps from the post office?*

To be more polite, we use *Could you?* and *Would you?*:
**Could you** *tell me where the station is?*
**Would you** *lend me your camera?*

We usually answer by saying:
*Of course (I **can** / **will**).* or *OK.*
*I'm sorry I **can't**.* (**not** ~~No, I won't~~, which sounds rude)

⚠ We never use *May you?* to ask someone to do something.
(**not** ~~May you give me a lift?~~)

### 3 Making offers

There are several ways of offering help to someone else:
**Can I / we** *help you to cook dinner?*
**Shall I / we** *clean the car for you?*
**I can / I could / I'll** *lend you some money.*
**Why don't I** *carry that bag for you?*

## 4 Making suggestions

To make a suggestion, we can use all the following expressions:

| *Shall I / we*<br>*Why don't I / we* | *go by bicycle today?* |
|---|---|
| *Let's* | *go by bicycle today?* |
| *How about*<br>*What about* | *going by bicycle today?* |

If we are less sure of what we are suggesting, we can say:
*We could go by bicycle today.*

## 5 Giving orders and advice

To give orders and advice, we use:

*must    had better    ought to/should    could*

←———————————————————————→
strong                          less strong

*You really* **must** *start looking for a job.* (= an order – I am telling you to do this, or this is my opinion which I feel very strongly about)
*You***'d better** *start looking for a job.* (= advice – otherwise you may regret it)
*You* **should / ought to** *start looking for a job.* (= advice)
*You* **could** *start looking for a job.* (= this is only a suggestion)

In the negative we use *had better not* and *oughtn't to / shouldn't*:
*You***'d better not** *forget to post that application form.*
*You* **shouldn't / ought not to** *wear those clothes for the interview.*

⚠ We don't use *mustn't* or *couldn't* when giving advice.

To talk about the past we say:
*You* **should have / ought to have** *accepted that job.* (= it was a good idea to accept but you didn't)

In the negative we say:
*You* **shouldn't have / ought not to have** *worn those clothes.* (= you wore them but it wasn't a good idea)

We can use all these verbs to talk about the right thing to do:
*I* **must** *try harder not to be late.*
*She* **should / ought to** *be more thoughtful.*
*He***'d better** *go and say sorry.*
*I***'d better not** *upset her today.*
*They* **shouldn't / ought not to** *talk so much.*

To talk about the right thing to do in the past we say:
*They* **shouldn't have / ought not to have** *talked so much.*

(➤ See also Unit 12, Grammar, part 2)

## C Grammar exercises

**1** Fill in the gaps in these sentences.

1 ......_Can_...... I change traveller's cheques here?

2 I'm sorry to bother you. ..................... I look at your timetable, please?

3 ..................... cycling to town today for a change? It will be good for us.

4 We ..................... ask Paula if she'd like to come riding with us. What do you think? I know she'll enjoy it.

5 ..................... you get that tin down from the shelf for me, Dad? I can't quite reach.

6 I ..................... post your parcel on my way to work if you want.

7 We haven't got any plans this weekend so ..................... we go sailing? The weather's going to be fine.

8 Excuse me, ..................... you tell me where the nearest tube station is?

9 A: '..................... I take this bag onto the plane?'

   B: 'No, I'm afraid not.'

10 ..................... you turn that television down? I need to use the phone.

**2** Daniel runs his own business. He isn't very tidy. Tomorrow an important client is coming to visit him in his office. Give him some advice, using at least four different structures and the words in the box.

| coat    cups    ~~desk~~    filing cabinet
lampshade    telephone
wastepaper bin    window |

1 _You'd better tidy the desk._

2 ..................................................................

3 ..................................................................

4 ..................................................................

5 ..................................................................

6 ..................................................................

7 ..................................................................

8 ..................................................................

**13**

**3** Fill in the gaps with the phrases in the box.

> Can I do    ~~Can I help~~    Could I see    I'm afraid
> Shall I ask    Would you exchange    You can't have
> You could give    You'd better not    You should ask
> You shouldn't have done

Assistant: .............Can I help............ **(1)** you?

Laura: I'd like to have a refund on a CD which I was given as a present.
.................................................... **(2)** that here?

Assistant: Yes you can. I'll do it for you. .................................................... **(3)** the receipt, please?

Laura: .................................................... **(4)** not. I haven't got one, you see, because it was a present.

Assistant: .................................................... **(5)** a refund without the receipt. Those are the rules, I'm afraid.

Laura: .................................................... **(6)** it for something else then?

Assistant: What CD is it? Oh, but you've taken it out of its wrapping.
.................................................... **(7)** that if you wanted to return it.

Laura: Christabel did it before she gave it to me.

Assistant: Did you say Christabel? Does she work here at weekends?

Laura: I don't know. She's got dark hair and glasses.

Assistant: .................................................... **(8)** her where she got this. She was probably given it free because it has no wrapping. .................................................... **(9)** the manager what he thinks?

Laura: .................................................... **(10)** do that. I don't want to get her into trouble.

Assistant: .................................................... **(11)** it to someone else for their birthday, I suppose.

**4** **What you would say in the following situations? Write sentences.**

1 You have just started work in a new office and you want to know how the coffee machine works. Ask someone.

*Excuse me, could you tell me how the coffee machine works, please?*

2 Your sister has just moved into a new flat and you offer to help her clean it.

.................................................................................................................................

3 Your friend is trying to decide what to buy her mother for her birthday. Give her some suggestions.

.................................................................................................................................

4 Your brother puts lots of salt onto his food. You don't think this is a good idea because too much salt is bad for you. What do you say?

.................................................................................................................................

5 You want a book which you can't find in the bookshop. Ask the assistant to order it.

.................................................................................................................................

6 You are buying something in a shop and you want to pay by credit card. Ask the assistant if this is possible.

.................................................................................................................................

7 Your friend is always late because he doesn't have a watch although he can afford to buy one. What advice do you give him?

.................................................................................................................................

8 You have been at a party at a friend's house and the kitchen is in a terrible mess. Offer to help clear up.

.................................................................................................................................

9 Your sister is going shopping. You need a new film for your camera. Ask her to get one for you.

.................................................................................................................................

10 You need a lift home. Your friend has a car but lives in the other direction. Ask him politely for a lift.

.................................................................................................................................

## D Exam practice

### 🎧 13b Listening

You will hear five different people giving advice. For Speakers **1–5**, choose from the list **A–F** who is speaking. Use the letters only once. There is one extra letter which you do not need to use.

**A** a neighbour

Speaker 1 [ ] **1**

**B** a teacher

Speaker 2 [ ] **2**

**C** a parent

Speaker 3 [ ] **3**

**D** a tour guide

Speaker 4 [ ] **4**

**E** a colleague

Speaker 5 [ ] **5**

**F** a shop assistant

Grammar focus task

These extracts are from the recording. Which ones make offers? Which ones give advice? Which ones give orders or strong advice? Write *F* for offers, *A* for advice, and *O* for orders or strong opinion.

1 Shall I leave you to think about it ... ?   ..F..

2 You must bring something warm ........

3 You'd better all go and get a pullover ........

4 ... I could lend it to you ... ........

5 Why don't I pop across the road and get it? ........

6 ... you must bring one of those wonderful shirts back. ........

7 You ought to take things for the daytime. ........

8 ... you'd better not spend all your money in the airport shop ... ........

## Writing

Every term your evening class goes on a day-trip to a place of interest. Last term you were responsible for the arrangements. Your teacher has asked you to write a report on the trip, giving suggestions and advice for the person who will organise the next one. Write your **report** in **120–180** words.

Writing hints

This task gives you a chance to practise:
using modal verbs to make suggestions and give advice.

**Useful words and expressions**
*to check, to make sure, to remind*
*castle, museum, gallery, traffic, delay, disaster, problem*
*luckily, interesting*

117

## Modals 3
ability; deduction: certainty and possibility; expectations

**1** You are going to hear two college students called Clare and Fiona talking about a boy called Danny. Before you listen, look at the picture. Do you think Danny is sitting with his sister, his girlfriend or his mother? ...........................

...........................................................

**2** 🎧 14 Listen and check if you were right.

**3** 🎧 14 Listen again and answer these questions.

1 Who does Clare think Danny is with at first? ........................................................................................

2 Fiona doesn't agree. Why not? ............................................................................................................

3 What do the two girls decide to do? ...................................................................................................

4 Why doesn't Fiona want to say hello? ...............................................................................................

5 What do you think Fiona really feels about Danny? ........................................................................

**4** 🎧 14 Listen again and fill in the gaps.

1 Clare:  It ..........*might be*.......... Danny.

2 Clare:  She ............................. his mother.

3 Fiona:  She ............................. his mother.

4 Fiona:  He ............................. me.

5 Fiona:  She ............................. his new girlfriend.

**5** Look at the sentences in Exercise 4. In which sentences does the speaker:

1 seem sure that something is true? ......................................................................................................

2 think something is possible, but isn't sure? .....................................................................................

## B  Grammar

### 1  Ability

#### *Can* and *be able to* – present

| + | *can* + verb | *I **can** swim.* |
| – | *can't* + verb | *She **can't** swim.* |
| ? | *can ... + verb?* | ***Can** you swim?* |

| + | *am/is/are able to* + verb | *I**'m able to** swim.* |
| – | *am/is/are not able to* + verb | *He**'s not able to** swim.* |
| ? | *am/is/are ... able to* + verb? | ***Are** you **able to** swim?* |

We use *can* or *be able to* to say that someone has an ability:
*James **can** / **is able to** play chess but he **can't** / **isn't able to** ride a bicycle.*

#### *Can* and *be able to* – past

| + | *could* + verb | *I **could** swim.* |
| – | *couldn't* + verb | *She **couldn't** swim.* |
| ? | *could ... + verb?* | ***Could** you swim?* |

| + | *was/were able to* + verb | *I **was able to** swim.* |
| – | *was/were not able to* + verb | *I **wasn't able to** swim.* |
| ? | *was/were ... able to* + verb? | ***Were** you **able to** swim?* |

We use *could* or *was able to* to say that someone had an ability in the past:
*He **could** / **was able to** read when he was three but he **couldn't** / **wasn't able to** catch a ball when he started school.*

⚠ We do not use *could* to talk about one occasion in the past, but we can use *couldn't*:
*She **was able to** (**not** ~~could~~) come to the meeting but she **couldn't** / **wasn't able to** stay for lunch.*
*They **were able to** (**not** ~~could~~) see the match because they had a day off.*

#### *Be able to* – other tenses

*Can* is only used in the present tense and *could* is only used in the past.
In all other tenses we use *be able to*:
*I **will be able to** give you a lift on my way to college.* (future)
*They **haven't been able to** contact Mary because of the storms.*
(present perfect)
*If you saved enough money, you **would be able to** visit me in New Zealand.* (conditional)
*They hope **to be able to** visit me next year.* (infinitive)

## 2 Deduction: certainty and possibility

### Talking about the present

**Certainty**

We use:

- *must* when we are sure something is true:
  It **must be** *from Steven because he's in Australia.*
  (= I am certain it is from Steven ...)

- *can't / couldn't* when we are sure something
  is not true:
  It **can't be / couldn't be** *from Steven because that's
  not his writing.* (= I am certain it's not from Steven ...)

**Possibility**

We use:

- *might / may / could* when we think something
  is possibly true:
  The letter **might be / may be / could be** *from Dad's friend, Tony, because he
  moved to Australia recently.* (= I know Tony lives there and it is possible, not
  certain, that the letter is from him)

- *might not / may not* when we think something is possibly not true:
  It **may not be / might not be** *from anyone that we know.* (= it is possible
  that it is not)

Susie is looking at a letter with an Australian
stamp which has just arrived for her father.

| Present | True | Not true |
|---|---|---|
| Certainty | *must* + infinitive without *to* | *can't/couldn't* + infinitive without *to* |
| Possibility | *might/may/could* + infinitive without *to* | *might not/may not* + infinitive without *to* |

⚠ Notice that *could* means the same as *might* and *may*,
but *couldn't* is different from *might not* and *may not*.
All the verbs in the box above can also be followed by
*be* + verb + *-ing*:
*Steven* **might be travelling** *home at this moment.*

### Talking about the past

**Certainty**

We use:

- *must have* when we are sure something is true:
  *Steven* **must have arrived** *in Perth by now.*
  (= I am certain he has arrived ...)

- *can't / couldn't have* when we are sure something is
  not true:
  He **can't / couldn't have got** *there yet because it will
  take at least two weeks.* (= I am certain he hasn't
  got there ...)

Steven is making a journey across Australia by
car from Sydney to Perth.

## Possibility

We use:

◆ *might have / may have / could have* when we think something is possibly true:

He **might / may / could have stopped** *for a few days on the way.*
(= it is possible)

◆ *might not have / may not have* when we think something is possibly not true:

He **might / may not have had** *time to do everything he wanted.* (= it is possible he didn't)

| Past | True | Not true |
|---|---|---|
| **Certainty** | *must have* + past participle | *can't have/couldn't have* + past participle |
| **Possibility** | *might have/may have/could have* + past participle | *might not have/may not have* + past participle |

Notice that *could have* means the same as *might have* and *may have*, but *couldn't have* is different from *might not have* and *may not have*.

## Talking about the future

We also use *might (not)*, *may (not)* and *could* when we are not certain about the future:

*James* **might** *go out to see Steven in Australia next month.*

## 3  Expectations

When we expect something will happen, we use *should (not)* + infinitive without *to*:

*Steven* **should write** *to us soon.* (= I expect he will write ...)
*It* **shouldn't be** *too long before we hear from Steven.* (= I expect it will not be too long ...)

We also use *should* when we discover that a situation is not as we expected:

*This letter is from Melbourne. Steven* **should be** *in Sydney.* (= he is in Melbourne but I'm surprised because I expected him to be in Sydney)

When we talk about a past situation, we use *should (not) have* + past participle:

*He* **should have left** *Alice Springs several days ago.* (= I expect he left Alice Springs ...)
*He* **shouldn't have had** *any trouble finding places to stay.* (= I expect he didn't have any trouble ...)

## C  Grammar exercises

**1**  Fill in the gaps with *can('t)*, *could(n't)*, or the correct form of *be able to*.
Sometimes there are two possible answers.

### The maths genius

**Ryan Kennedy speaks to Nick Evans about his amazing talent.**

'One day when I was four years old, my father was telling my mother how much money he'd spent and while he was talking I added it all up. They didn't believe that I _could / was able to_ **(1)** do that because I ........................... **(2)** read or write. I'm now at university and I ........................... **(3)** still add up complicated sums in my head. I did a maths exam once which I finished so quickly I ........................... **(4)** eat a meal in the canteen before the others had finished. Next year we have to write essays and I'm not sure whether I ........................... **(5)** do that because I ........................... (never) **(6)** spell very well. I would like ........................... **(7)** use my mathematical skill in a job but I haven't decided what yet. I ........................... **(8)** be a maths teacher – I'd enjoy the maths but I'm not sure about the children! I entered a maths quiz show on TV once but when they asked me the questions I ........................... **(9)** think of the answers because I was just too nervous. So I ........................... **(10)** imagine myself as a TV star. I ........................... **(11)** always get work in the supermarket when the tills break down, I suppose!'

**2**  Complete the sentences about the man in the picture with some of the words and phrases in the box.

| ~~famous~~   a film star   fit   Greek |
| married   rich   a schoolboy   Spanish |
| a tennis champion   45 years old |

1  He might be ............ *famous* ............ .
2  He must be ........................... .
3  He might be ........................... .
4  He may be ........................... .
5  He can't be ........................... .
6  He could be ........................... .
7  He couldn't be ........................... .
8  He must be ........................... .

**3** Read about what has happened on a camping trip.

> Two boys are camping with their families near a lake. One day they find an old boat and decide to row out to an uninhabited island. They explore the island until suddenly they realise it's getting dark. They run to find the boat, but it's gone.

Here are some of the things their families say when they don't come back.

1 There can't be much to eat on the island.
2 Someone may have noticed them rowing across the lake.
3 They could be stuck there for days.
4 A fishing boat might see them.
5 They must have forgotten how late it was.
6 They must be getting scared.
7 There may be a cave or hut they can shelter in.
8 The boat could have sunk.
9 Someone may have taken the boat.
10 They can't have tied the boat up properly.

Write the number of the sentences with their meanings, a or b.

a I feel certain about this. 1 ................................................................................
b I think this is possible. ................................................................................

**4** Fill in the gaps with a modal verb and the correct form of the verb in brackets.

1 Jenny's brother ............ *can't be* ............ (*be*) a doctor because he's only 18.
2 Samantha said she'd go for a swim as soon as she reached the seaside so she
   ................................................ (*swim*) in the sea right now.
3 I don't seem to have my wallet. I ................................................ (*leave*) it at home
   because I paid for my train ticket.
4 A: I left Camilla a message on her answerphone but she hasn't rung yet.
   B: She ................................................ (*not listen*) to it yet. She usually has a shower
   as soon as she gets home from work.
5 A: I found this watch in the changing rooms.
   B: It ................................................ (*be*) Peter's. I think he's got one like that.
6 I can't make the video recorder work. I ................................................ (*do*)
   something wrong. Where are the instructions?
7 I can't think what's happened to Annie. She left home hours ago so she
   ................................................ (*be*) here by now.
8 These football boots don't fit me any more. My feet ................................................ (*grow*).

9 He remembers when there were fields here instead of houses so he
.......................................................... (*be*) very old.

10 A: I don't really like James. Why did you invite him?

B: Don't worry. He .............................................................. (*not come*) anyway. He said he wasn't sure what his plans were.

**5** **Read this police report about a stolen painting.**

A very small but valuable painting has been stolen from Sidcombe art gallery.
We know it was stolen between 6.00 and 7.30 on Friday evening.
There are several suspects. They all have keys to the art gallery:

**The caretaker, Sam Willis**
Sam, who has worked at the gallery for 32 years, locked up at 6.30 as usual after the cleaners had left.

**A student, Daniel Foreman**
When the gallery shut at 5.30 Daniel begged the caretaker to let him stay a bit longer to finish his work. The caretaker saw him coming out of the toilets at 6.30 and told him to leave. He bought an expensive car on Saturday.

**A cleaner, Sandra Thompson**
Sandra cleaned the offices and the galleries with two other cleaners. They finished at 6.00 and had a chat in the cloakroom before leaving together at 6.15. She says the picture was still there at 6.00.

**The shop manager, Sophie Christie**
Sophie closed the museum shop at 5.30 but had to stay and wait for a delivery. The driver got delayed in the traffic and arrived at 6.05. He left straight away and Sophie said she left at about 6.15 but nobody saw her leave the building.

**The director, William Rees**
William was on the phone in his office between 6.00 and 7.00. He says he left the gallery at 7.15 but nobody saw him leave.

**The cloakroom attendant, Josie McCartney**
The cloakroom closed at 5.30 and Josie tidied up. She was just leaving when the cleaners arrived and she stopped to have a chat with them. They all left together at 6.15.

Who had the opportunity to steal the painting? Complete these sentences using *must have, can't have, couldn't have, might have, may have* and *could have*. Use each structure once.

1 Sam Willis ...... *might have stolen* ...... the painting because *he was there until 6.30.*

2 Sandra Thompson .............................................. the painting because .............................................

3 William Rees .............................................. the painting because .............................................

4 Daniel Foreman .............................................. the painting because .............................................

5 Sophie Christie .............................................. the painting because .............................................

6 Josie McCartney .............................................. the painting because .............................................

# D Exam practice

## Use of English

For questions **1–10**, read the text below. Use the word given in capitals at the end of each line to form a word that fits in the space in the same line. There is an example at the beginning (**0**).

> ⚠ This task tests grammar from the rest of the book as well as the grammar in this unit.

**THE WOMAN ON THE HILL**

| | |
|---|---|
| A woman has lived in complete (**0**) *isolation* in a large house on a hill in north | **ISOLATE** |
| Yorkshire for the last fifty years. She (**1**) .................... visits the nearby village to order | **OCCASION** |
| food. She walks (**2**) .................... down the main street but she only speaks to the | **CONFIDENCE** |
| different shop (**3**) .................... in order to ask for something. Apart from that, she | **ASSIST** |
| doesn't speak to anyone at all. She receives a (**4**) .................... of wood once a year for | **DELIVER** |
| her fire but the van driver has (**5**) .................... to leave it on the doorstep and go away. | **INSTRUCT** |
| She must have been very (**6**) .................... when she was young and her clothes were | **ATTRACT** |
| probably (**7**) .................... 50 years ago. She must be about 70 years old now. | **FASHION** |
| She gives the (**8**) .................... from the way she behaves that she might have been | **IMPRESS** |
| an (**9**) .................... once. But nobody in the village knows who she is and they are | **ACT** |
| (**10**) .................... to find out unless she tells them. | **LIKE** |

**What do you think the villagers say about the woman on the hill? Complete the sentences using *must, might (not), may (not), could(n't)* or *can't*.**

1 ......*She might be*...... shy.          4 ................................................ any family nearby.

2 ................................................ happy.          5 ................................................ rich.

3 ................................................ lonely.          6 ................................................ an interesting background.

## Writing

You have just moved house. In the attic you find a pile of letters written about 100 years ago. You read the letters and decide to send an article to the local newspaper saying what you have guessed about the writer's life. You hope someone who reads your article might know who wrote the letters. Write your **article** in **120–180** words.

**This task gives you a chance to practise:**
using modal verbs: *can't have, couldn't have, may have, might have, must have.*

**Useful words and expressions**
*to hide, to hope, important, rich, romantic, unhappy, servant*

## A Context listening

**1** You are going to hear a radio news bulletin. Before you listen, look at the pictures and decide what happened. Put the pictures in order.

1 ...d... 2 ...a... 3 ...b... 4 ...c...

**2** 🎧 **15** Listen and check if you were right.

**3** Read this newspaper article.

## BURGLARS' 'LUCK' WAS WELL PLANNED

**FOUR BURGLARS** have escaped from custody only hours after ......*being*...... **(1)** sentenced to ten years in prison. They ...*were being*...... **(2)** transferred from the law courts in Manchester to Strangeways Prison. They ...*have been*...... **(3)** found guilty of stealing electrical goods and money from shops in the Manchester area. It ......*is*...... **(4)** thought that they were all members of the same gang. They escaped from the van in which they ...*were being*...... **(5)** transported, when the driver ......*was*...... **(6)** forced to stop because of a tree across the road. It ......*is*...... **(7)** believed that the tree ......*was*...... **(8)** placed there by other members of the gang, who ...*would been*...... **(9)** informed of the route ...*to be*...... **(10)** taken by the van. A full investigation of the events leading to the escape ...*has been*...... **(11)** ordered and anyone with information ......*is*...... **(12)** asked to contact the police to help with their enquiries.

🎧 **15** Listen again and fill the gaps. Stop the recording when you need to.

**4** How many of the verbs you completed in Exercise 3 are in the passive? ...*all of them*...

## B Grammar

### 1 The passive
#### How the passive is formed
We form the passive by using the verb *to be* followed by the past participle:

Active:

*The police officer **saw** <u>the robber</u> at the airport.*
*She's **following** <u>him</u>.*
*She'll **catch** <u>him</u> soon.*

Passive:

*<u>The robber</u> **was seen** at the airport.*
*<u>He</u>'s **being followed**.*
*<u>He</u>'ll **be caught** soon.*

| Active | | Passive |
|---|---|---|
| *to catch* | → | *to be caught* |
| *to have caught* | → | *to have been caught* |
| *catching* | → | *being caught* |
| *having caught* | → | *having been caught* |
| *am / are / is catching* | → | *am / are / is being caught* |
| *catch(es)* | → | *am / are / is caught* |
| *will catch* | → | *will be caught* |
| *am / are / is going to catch* | → | *am / are / is going to be caught* |
| *has / have caught* | → | *has / have been caught* |
| *caught* | → | *was / were caught* |
| *was catching* | → | *was being caught* |
| *had caught* | → | *had been caught* |
| *would catch* | → | *would be caught* |
| *would have caught* | → | *would have been caught* |

## When the passive is used

The passive is used quite often in English, both in speech and writing.
We use the passive when:

◆ we don't know who or what did something:
  *My bicycle's **been stolen**. (= Someone has stolen my bicycle.)*
  *The first tools **were made** in Africa two million years ago. (= People made the first tools ...)*

◆ the action is more important than who did it:
  *Income tax **was introduced** in England in 1798.*

◆ it is obvious who or what did something:
  *The thief's **been arrested**.*

We can use *by* + person / thing to show who does the action if this information is important:
*The robber was seen **by the police officer**. (= **The police officer** saw the robber.)*

## Verbs with two objects

Sometimes an active verb (e.g. *give*) has two objects:
*A witness gave **the police some information**.*
or *A witness gave **some information** to **the police**.*

Either object can be the subject of a passive sentence:
***The police** were given some information by a witness.*
or ***Some information** was given to the police by a witness.*

## 2  To have something done

When we ask someone else to do something for us, we often use the structure *to have something done*. It is not usually necessary to say who did the action:
*The president **had** the car **taken** to the airport (by his driver).*
*(= The president's driver **took** the car to the airport.)*

*I **had** my hair **cut**. (= The hairdresser **cut** my hair.)*
*I'm **having** my kitchen **painted**. (= The decorator **is painting** my kitchen.)*
*They want **to have** their car **fixed**. (= They want the garage **to fix** their car.)*

In informal speech, we sometimes use *get* instead of *have*:
*I **got** my hair **cut**. (= I **had** my hair **cut**.)*

## C Grammar exercises

**1** In five of these sentences there is a mistake in a verb form. Underline each mistake and write the correction.

1 The children wanted <u>to be allow</u> to stay up late and see the fireworks. ....<u>to be allowed</u>........
   ~~ed~~

2 Our flight was delaying by fog and we missed our connection. ...................................

3 Lauren was sulking because she hadn't been invited to Ralph's party. ...................................

4 By the time we arrived at the market, the best fruit had be sold. ...................................
   *en*

5 While the meal was being prepare we had a drink on the terrace. ...................................
   *d*

6 The new library will be opened by the Mayor next Saturday. ...................................

7 I can't see any coffee in this cupboard. Was it all been finished? ...................................
   *has*

**2** Fill in the gaps with the correct passive form of the verb in brackets.

1 A government minister .........*was found*......... (*find*) guilty of fraud yesterday.

2 It was a lovely surprise to find all the washing-up .....*had been done*..... (*do*) while I was asleep.

3 These souvenirs .....*were made*..... (*make*) by children from the local school.

4 I didn't come here in order .....*to be made*..... (*make*) a fool of!

5 The votes .....*are being counted*..... (*count*) right now and we should know the result before midnight.

6 This parcel appears .....*to have opened*..... (*open*) before it .....*was delivered*..... (*delivered*).

7 As he .....*had been sacked*..... (*sack*) from his previous job, he found it hard to get another.

8 The judges still have to decide which design .....*will be awarded*..... (*award*) the top prize.

**3** Read this report in the *Cybernian News*.

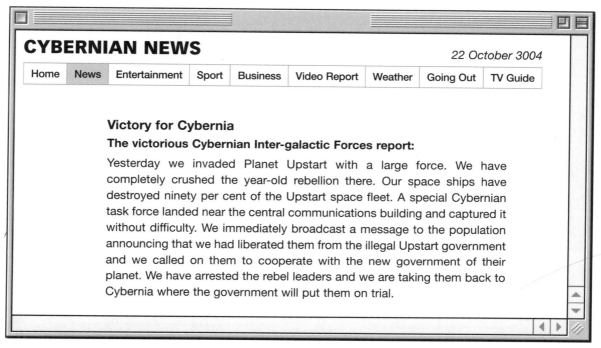

Fill in the gaps below with the passive form of the verbs in the *Cybernian News* above.

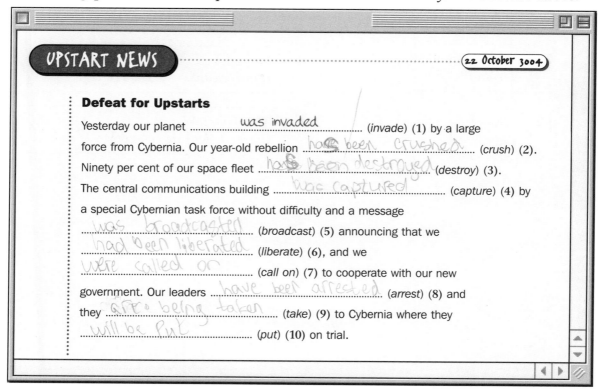

# 15

**4** Match the two halves of the conversations and fill in the gaps with the correct form of the verbs in brackets.

1 ( I thought those chairs were broken. ) _e_    a ( I have _had coloured it_ (*have / colour*). )

2 ( Your bike's got a flat tyre! ) _c_    b ( Yes, you need _have taken to in them_ (*have / take in*). )

3 ( This carpet's filthy. ) _g_    c ( I can _have fixed it_ (*have / fix*) at the cycle shop. )

4 ( What's happened to your hair? ) _a_    d ( I agree – we should _have re decorated it_ (*have / redecorate*). )

5 ( I don't like this room. It's too dark. ) _d_    e ( I've _had them mended_ (*have / mend*). )

6 ( These jeans are much too loose. ) _b_    f ( At the garage. We _have serviced it_ (*have / service*) before we go away. )

7 ( What a beautiful garden! ) _h_    g ( We must _have it cleaned_ (*have / clean*). )

8 ( Where's the car? ) _f_    h ( Thank you. We _have designed it_ (*have / design*) by an expert. )

## D  Exam practice

### Use of English

⚠ This task tests grammar from the rest of the book as well as the grammar in this unit.

Complete the second sentence so that it has a similar meaning to the first sentence, using the word given. **Do not change the word given.** You must use between **two** and **five** words, including the word given. There is an example at the beginning (**0**).

**0** My grandfather hasn't spoken to me since Sunday.
   **spoke**
   My grandfather ............... *last spoke to me on* ............... Sunday.

**1** The students gave a concert after their exams.
   **was**
   A concert ........................................................ students after their exams.

**2** The children played football and also went swimming.
   **addition**
   The children played football ........................................................ swimming.

**3** Jane's neighbours looked after her flat while she was away.
   **by**
   Jane's ........................................................ her neighbours while she was away.

**4** Someone forgot to hand my message in to the teacher.
   **not**
   My message ........................................................ to the teacher.

**5** The teacher said Simon had cheated.
   **accused**
   Simon ........................................................ his teacher.

**6** When we were children we often used to make fires in the garden.
   **would**
   As children ........................................................ fires in the garden.

**7** He had said he'd help us so we were disappointed when he didn't come.
   **promised**
   Having ........................................................ help, we were disappointed when he didn't come.

**8** No one was able to explain how the accident happened.
   **not**
   The cause of ........................................................ explained by anyone.

**9** My computer needs to be repaired before the weekend.

**have**

I need ............................................................ before the weekend.

**10** This part of the building isn't normally open to the public.

**often**

The public ............................................................ into this part of the building.

**Which of the sentences test the passive?** ............................................................

## Writing

You see this competition in a magazine.

You decide to enter the competition. Write a composition in **120–180** words.

*Win* **two airline tickets to the country of your choice!**

Describe how your town or village celebrates any special occasion. How are the streets or houses decorated? What else can be seen? The best descriptions will be published and writers will win a free trip to see how people celebrate in other parts of the world.

**This task gives you a chance to practise:**
using the passive (for example, you can say things like *the streets are decorated* but it is not always necessary to say who does it).

**Useful words and expressions**
*to display, to march, to organise, to plan*
*atmosphere, balloons, band, costumes, flags, flowers, parade*
*bright, cheerful, colourful, loud, noisy*

# Reported speech
tense changes in reported speech; reporting in the same tense;
verbs used for reporting; reporting questions

# 16

## A  Context listening

**1** You are going to hear part
of a radio programme.
Rachel is a radio reporter
in a studio in London.
She is talking to a man
called James Baker who
is taking part in a round-
the-world yacht race.
What do you think she
is asking him? ...........................
...................................................................
...................................................................

**2** 🎧 16 Listen and check if you were right.

**3** 🎧 16  Later, Rachel tells a colleague about the conversation. Read what Rachel says,
then listen again and fill in the gaps with James's actual words.

1  Rachel: James told me he was about 100 kilometres off the coast of Australia.
   James:  'I'm about................... 100 kilometres off the coast of Australia.'

2  Rachel: He said he hadn't seen another boat for a few days.
   James:  'I ......................................... another boat for a few days.'

3  Rachel: He said he thought he might win.
   James:  'I ......................................... win.'

4  Rachel: He said there had been a terrible storm.
   James:  'There ......................................... a terrible storm.'

5  Rachel: He said he hadn't slept for three days.
   James:  'I ......................................... for three days.'

6  Rachel: He told me the sea was calm, the sun was shining.
   James:  'The sea ......................................... calm, the sun ......................................... .'

7  Rachel: He said that he could sometimes see sharks and dolphins swimming.
   James:  'I ......................................... sometimes see sharks and dolphins swimming.'

8 Rachel: He said he would spend two hours in a hot bath.
  James:  'I ............................................. two hours in a hot bath.'

9 Rachel: He said he had to get his hair cut.
  James:  'I ............................................. hair cut.'

**4** 🎧 **16** **Listen again and complete the questions Rachel asked.**

1 Rachel: I asked him where he was.
         'Where ...........................................................?'

2 Rachel: I asked him if he thought he was going to win.
         'Do you ................................................ to win?'

3 Rachel: I asked him what the weather was like.
         'What ............................................... like?'

4 Rachel: I asked him if he could see dolphins there.
         '............................................... dolphins there?'

**5** **Can you see any pattern to the changes to the tenses in Exercises 3 and 4?**

..............................................................................................................................................

## B Grammar

### 1 Tense changes in reported speech

When we report what someone else said, we are usually reporting at a later time so we change the tenses used by the original speaker:

| | |
|---|---|
| **present simple** | → **past simple** |
| 'I'm (I am) about 100 kilometres from Australia.' | → He said (that) he **was** about 100 kilometres from Australia. |
| **present continuous** | → **past continuous** |
| 'The sun's (is) shining.' | → He said (that) the sun **was shining**. |
| **past simple** | → **past perfect** |
| 'There **was** a terrible storm.' | → He said (that) there'**d** (**had**) **been** a terrible storm. |
| **present perfect** | → **past perfect** |
| 'I **haven't** (**have not**) **seen** another boat.' | → He said (that) he **hadn't** (**had not**) **seen** another boat. |
| **past perfect** | → **past perfect** |
| 'I **hadn't** (**had not**) **expected** the storm.' | → He said (that) he **hadn't** (**had not**) **expected** the storm. |
| **am going to** | → **was going to** |
| 'I'm (I am) going to win.' | → He said (that) he **was going to** win. |
| **will** | → **would** |
| 'I'll (I will) spend two hours in a bath.' | → He said (that) he'**d** (he **would**) **spend** two hours in a bath. |
| **can** | → **could** |
| 'I **can** see sharks and dolphins.' | → He said (that) he **could** see sharks and dolphins. |
| **may** | → **might** |
| 'I **may** win.' | → He said (that) he **might** win. |
| **might** | → **might** |
| 'I **might** win.' | → He said (that) he **might** win. |
| **must** | → **had to** |
| 'I **must** get my hair cut.' | → He said (that) he **had to** get his hair cut. |

⚠ These verbs do not change when they are reported at a later time:
could, would, should, might, ought to and used to, and verbs in the past perfect.

When we report *must*, we can use either *must* or *had to* in the reported speech but *had to* is more common:
Kate: 'I **must** buy some fruit.'
→ Kate said she **must** / **had to** buy some fruit.

⚠ We use *must*, not *had to*, when we report:
◆ a negative:
Paul: 'You **mustn't** tell Sally our secret.'
→ Paul said we **mustn't** tell Sally our secret.
◆ or a deduction:
Sarah: 'Jim **must** be tired after the flight.'
→ Sarah said Jim **must** be tired after the flight.

## 2 Reporting in the same tense

If the reporting verb (e.g. *says*) is in the present tense, we use the same tenses as the original speaker:

Amy: *'I've missed the bus so I'll be a bit late.'*
→ *Amy says she's missed the bus so she'll be a bit late.*

If the reporting verb (e.g. *said*) is in the past, we sometimes use the same tenses as the original speaker if the situation is still true:

Robert: *'I have three sisters.'*
→ *Robert said he has three sisters.* or *Robert said he had three sisters.*

Carlo: *'I'm getting married in June.'*
If we report what Carlo said before June we can say:
*Carlo said he is getting married in June.* or *Carlo said he was getting married in June.*

## 3 Verbs used for reporting

We often use *say* to report what somebody said:
*He said (that) he was going to win.*

If there is an object (a noun or a pronoun), *say* must be followed by *to*:
*He said to me (that) he was going to win.* (**not** *He said me ...*)

When we use *tell* to report what someone said, it is always followed by an object without *to*:
*He told them (that) he was going to win.* (**not** *He told to them ...* ,
*He told that ...*)

We often use other reporting verbs instead of *say* and *tell*.
Some are nearly always followed by *that* and usually have no object:
*He answered that ..., He replied that ...*

Some behave like *tell*:
*He reminded me (that) ..., He persuaded me (that) ..., He informed me (that) ...*

Some are nearly always followed by *that* and sometimes have an object:
*He agreed (with me) that ..., He explained (to me) that ..., He mentioned (to me) that ...*

## 4 Reporting offers, advice and promises

After some reporting verbs the *to* infinitive is usually used:

*'I'll be a good leader.'* → *He **promised to be** a good leader.*
*'You should vote for me.'* → *He **advised us to vote** for him.*
*'We could help you.'* → *They **offered to help** me.*

The infinitive is sometimes used after *tell* and *ask* (➢ see Unit 17):

*'Be careful.'* → *I **told him to be** careful.*
*'Please don't smoke.'* → *I **asked her not to smoke**.*

## 5 Reporting questions

Questions are reported using the word order of a statement rather than a question.

Questions with question words (*who*, *what*, etc) keep these words when they are reported:

*'How do you **feel**?'*
→ *Rachel **asked James how he felt**.* (**not** *Rachel asked James how did he feel.*)

*'**What's** the weather like?'* → *Rachel **asked** James what the weather **was** like.*
(**not** *Rachel asked James what was the weather like.*)

*Yes/no* questions are reported with *if* or *whether*:

*'**Can** you hear me?'*
→ *Rachel **asked** James **if / whether** he **could** hear her.*

*'**Is** the weather good?'*
→ *Rachel **wanted to know if / whether** the weather **was** good.*

⚠ We use the same structure when we ask politely for information:
*__Can you tell me__ what time the next train **leaves**?*
*__I'd like to know if__ there's a flight to Australia next Thursday.*

## 6 References to time, place etc.

Unless we are speaking on the same day, we have to change references to time when we report what someone said:

| | |
|---|---|
| *yesterday* | → *the day before* |
| *today* | → *that day* |
| *tomorrow* | → *the next / following day* |
| *next week* | → *the following week* |
| *now* | → *then* |

Other changes include:

| | |
|---|---|
| *here* | → *there* |
| *this* | → *that* |

*'I **saw** him **here yesterday**.'*
→ *She explained that she had seen him **there the day before**.*

## C Grammar exercises

**1** You talk on the phone to a friend, Luke.
This is what he says.

1 'I've given up my job.'

2 'I can easily find another one.'

3 'I'm going to travel round Africa.'

4 'I lived there as a child.'

5 'I might get a part-time job there.'

6 'I'm packing my bag.'

7 'I'm really excited.'

8 'I'll be away for a year.'

9 'I may stay longer.'

10 'You could come too.'

After Luke has left, you tell another friend what he said. Complete the sentences.

1 He said he *had given up his job.*

2 He said he .................................................................................

3 He said he .................................................................................

4 He said he .................................................................................

5 He said he .................................................................................

6 He said he .................................................................................

7 He said he .................................................................................

8 He said he .................................................................................

9 He said he .................................................................................

10 He said I .................................................................................

**2** Match the beginnings and endings of these sentences.

| | |
|---|---|
| 1 She told ..c.. | **a** I could help my neighbour mend his car. |
| 2 My sister asked ........ | **b** whether my sister could give me a lift. |
| 3 I said ........ | **c** me she couldn't afford to come to the theatre. |
| 4 My parents said ........ | **d** to me, 'You shouldn't watch so much TV.' |
| 5 I wanted to know ........ | **e** if I wanted to go on holiday with her. |
| 6 I told ........ | **f** the dentist that Thursday was the only day I was free. |

**3** You apply for a job at a children's holiday camp.
When you meet the organiser he asks the following questions:

1  Are you married?
2  How old are you?
3  Which university are you studying at?
4  Where do you come from?
5  Have you worked with children before?
6  What sports do you play?
7  Will you work for at least two months?
8  Can you start immediately?
9  Do you need accommodation?
10  Would you like any more information?

> **Work abroad**
> We are looking for enthusiastic and lively young people to work in a children's holiday camp over the summer.

A friend of yours called Miguel is also going to apply for a job at the same camp.
Complete the letter, telling him what questions you were asked.

> Dear Miguel
>
> Good luck with the job application! These are the things the organiser asked me about – he'll probably ask you the same sorts of questions.
>
> He asked me .......... *if I was married* .......... (1).
>
> He wanted to know .................................... (2),
>
> which university .................................... (3) at
>
> and where .................................... (4) . Then he asked
>
> .................................... (5) with children before
>
> and what sports .................................... (6).
>
> He wanted to know .................................... (7) for at least
>
> two months and .................................... (8) immediately.
>
> He asked .................................... (9) accommodation
>
> and wondered .................................... (10) any more
>
> information.

**4** **A teacher is talking to Andy, a student.**

> You need to work harder.

> You could do well.

> Do you study every evening?

> What time do you go to bed?

> You won't get good marks.

> You spend too much time with your friends.

> Have you decided on a career yet?

**Later, Andy tells a friend what the teacher said. Complete his sentences.**

1 He said *I needed to work harder.* .................................................................

2 He told .................................................................................................................

3 He wanted to know .............................................................................................

4 He wondered .......................................................................................................

5 He warned ...........................................................................................................

6 He complained ....................................................................................................

7 He asked ..............................................................................................................

**5** **Read what happened to Suzie the other day. Then write the conversation that she actually had.**

I travel to college on the same bus every day. The other day when I got on the bus I realised that I had left my purse at home and didn't have the money for the bus fare. But the woman sitting behind me told me not to worry because she would lend me some money. She said the same thing had happened to her the day before. I asked her what she had done. She said someone had lent her the fare and she was going to give it back that day on the bus, so she was happy to do the same for me. She told me I could give the money back to her the following day. I thanked her very much and told her I was very glad she was there.

Woman: *Don't worry. I'll lend you some money.* ................................................

.................................................................................................................

Suzie: ...................................................................................................................

Woman: ................................................................................................................

.................................................................................................................

.................................................................................................................

Suzie: ...................................................................................................................

## D   Exam practice

⚠ This task tests grammar from the rest of the book as well as the grammar in this unit.

### Use of English

Complete the second sentence so that it has a similar meaning to the first sentence, using the word given. **Do not change the word given.** You must use between **two** and **five** words, including the word given. There is an example at the beginning (**0**).

**0**  The tourist guide said to us: 'Take a map if you go walking in the hills.'
   **advised**
   The tourist guide ........... *advised us to take* ........... a map if we went walking in the hills.

**1**  Rose didn't try to be friendly to us.
   **made**
   Rose ........................................... be friendly to us.

**2**  The weatherman forecast that there would be sunshine all day.
   **shine**
   The weatherman said: 'The ........................................... all day.'

**3**  'I haven't heard from Helen for a long time,' Paul said to me.
   **told**
   Paul ........................................... heard from Helen for a long time.

**4**  How about going to the top of the tower to look at the view?
   **we**
   Why ........................................... to the top of the tower to look at the view?

**5**  'Did you book a room with a balcony?' I asked my mother.
   **if**
   I asked my mother ........................................... a room with a balcony.

**6**  The only person to be late was Lucy.
   **apart**
   Everyone ........................................... was on time.

**7**  Jack wanted to know what time they would leave the next day to catch the train.
   **we**
   Jack asked: 'What time ........................................... to catch the train?'

**8**  Hurry up, the show will be starting in a moment.
   **about**
   Hurry up, the show ........................................... start.

**9** The little boy said he could dress himself without any help.

I

The little boy said: '............................................................. without any help.'

**10** 'Are we meeting David in the morning or the afternoon?' Karen asked.

**whether**

Karen wondered ................................................................. in the morning or the afternoon.

Which of the sentences test reported speech? ....................................................................

In three of the reported sentences the verbs can be replaced with the following: *predict; insist; complain.* Write the reported sentences again using these verbs.

1 .........................................................................................................................

2 .........................................................................................................................

3 .........................................................................................................................

## Writing

Your school is thinking of starting a film club. You went to a meeting where the students talked about how the club would be organised and what it would do. Your teacher couldn't attend the meeting and wants to know the students' different opinions. He has asked you to write a report explaining what was said. Write your **report** in **120–180** words.

This task gives you a chance to practise:
using reported speech to tell the teacher what the different students said.

**Useful words and expressions**
*to agree, to check, to choose, to decide, to discuss, to suggest, committee, membership fee, review, variety, the best place, the best time*

# The *to* infinitive and *-ing*
verb + *to* infinitive; verb + infinitive without *to*; verb + *-ing*;
verb + object + *to* infinitive; verb + *that*; adjectives

17

## A   Context listening

**1** You are going to hear a TV chef telling a group of people how to cook something. Look at the picture below which shows the things he uses. Can you guess what the man is going to make? .........................................................................

**2** 🎧 **17** Listen and check if you were right.

**3** 🎧 **17** Listen again and fill in the gaps. Stop the recording when you need to.

1 *Continue* ......*doing*...... this ...

2 *Avoid* ..................... the eggs all at the same time ...

3 ... *keep* ..................... all the time.

4 ... don't *forget* ..................... the baking powder ...

5 I *recommend* ..................... sultanas and apricots ...

6 ... if you *prefer* ..................... dates or raisins, that's fine.

7 Some people *like* ..................... some nuts too ...

8 If you *decide* ..................... nuts, chop them up small.

9 *Remember* ..................... if the fruit cake is ready ...

10 I *suggest* ..................... a little lemon juice ...

11 Don't *try* ..................... the cake ...

12 ... don't *expect* ..................... much fruit cake left ...

**4** What do you notice about the forms of the verbs you have filled in? .........................................................................

.........................................................................................................................

## B Grammar

When one verb follows another, the second verb can either be the *-ing* form or the *to* infinitive. It depends on the first verb.

⚠ All the verbs in this unit marked * can also normally be followed by a *that* clause with the same meaning (➢ see Grammar, part 8).

### 1  Verb + *to* infinitive

| | | | | | | |
|---|---|---|---|---|---|---|
| *(can't) afford* | **agree* | *aim* | *appear* | **arrange* | *attempt* | |
| *choose* | **decide* | **demand* | *deserve* | *fail* | **hope* | *learn* |
| *manage* | *neglect* | *offer* | *omit* | *plan* | *prepare* | **pretend* |
| **promise* | *refuse* | *seem* | *tend* | **threaten* | *(can't) wait* | *wish* |

*If you **decide to add** nuts ...*
*Don't **expect to have** much cake left.*

Notice how the negative is formed:
*If you decide **not to ice** it ...*

The following verbs + *to* infinitive **always** have an <u>object</u>:

| | | | | |
|---|---|---|---|---|
| *dare* | *encourage* | *force* | *invite* | *order* |
| *persuade* | *remind* | *teach* | *tell* | *warn* |

*Her father **taught** <u>her</u> **to play** tennis.*
*The teacher **reminded** <u>the children</u> **to bring** their swimming things.*

The following verbs + *to* infinitive **sometimes** have an <u>object</u>:

| | | | | | |
|---|---|---|---|---|---|
| *want* | *ask* | **expect* | *beg* | *help* | **intend* |

*We **expected to be late**. or We **expected** <u>Tom</u> **to be** late.*
*We **wanted to stay** longer. or We **wanted** <u>them</u> **to stay** longer.*

⚠ *Would like, would love, would prefer* etc. are also followed by the *to* infinitive (➢ See Grammar, part 4).

### 2  Verb + infinitive without *to*

Modal verbs (*can, could, may, might, must, needn't, shall, should, will, would*), *had better* and *would rather* are followed by the infinitive without *to* (➢ see also Units 12–14):
*You **should add** them slowly.*
*You **needn't include** nuts.*

*Help* can be followed by the infinitive with or without *to*:
*We **helped** <u>them</u> **(to) start** their car.*

*Make* and *let* (always with an <u>object</u>) are followed by the infinitive without *to*:

**Let** <u>the cake</u> **cool** *for half an hour.*
*I* **made** <u>my sister</u> **help** *with the cooking.*

⚠ The passive form of *make* is followed by the *to* infinitive:
*I* **was made to do** *my homework.*

## 3 Verb + *-ing*

| | | | | | | |
|---|---|---|---|---|---|---|
| *\*admit* | *\*appreciate* | *avoid* | *can't face* | *can't help* | *can't stand* | *carry on* |
| *\*confess* | *\*consider* | *delay* | *\*deny* | *detest* | *dislike* | *enjoy*   *fancy*   *feel like* |
| *finish* | *give up* | *\*imagine* | *involve* | *\*keep / keep on* | *\*mention* | *(not) mind* |
| *miss* | *postpone* | *practise* | *put off* | *risk* | *resist* | *\*suggest* |

*I* **enjoy making** *it.*
**Avoid adding** *the eggs ...*
**Keep doing** *this ...*
*I* **suggest adding** *a little lemon juice ...*

Notice how the negative is formed:
*If you don't leave immediately, you risk* **not catching** *your plane.*
*Can you imagine* **not having** *a car nowadays?*

## 4 Verbs + *to* infinitive or *-ing* (with no difference in meaning)

| | | | | |
|---|---|---|---|---|
| *attempt* | *begin* | *can't bear* | *continue* | *hate* |
| *like* | *love* | *prefer* | *\*propose* | *start* |

**Continue adding** *the flour.* or **Continue to add** *the flour.*
*I* **prefer using** *apricots.* or *I* **prefer to use** *apricots.*
*I* **love making** *cakes.* or *I* **love to make** *cakes.*

Two *-ing* forms do not usually follow each other:
*I was* **starting to make** *a cake when the phone rang.* (**not** ~~I was starting making a cake ....~~)

*Like* + *to* infinitive has a slightly different meaning from *like* + *-ing*:
*I* **like to catch** *the early bus on Mondays.* (= this is a good plan or it's a habit, but not necessarily something I enjoy)
*I* **like dancing**. (= I enjoy it)

⚠ *Like, prefer, hate* and *love* can be followed by the *to* infinitive or *-ing*, but *would like, would prefer, would hate* and *would love* are always followed by the *to* infinitive:
*She* **would like to go out** *but we* **would prefer to stay** *in.*

## 5 Verb + *to* infinitive or *-ing* (with a difference in meaning)

The following verbs have two different meanings depending on the verb form that follows:

| *remember* | *forget* | *regret* | try | stop | mean | go on |
|---|---|---|---|---|---|---|

### Verb + *to* infinitive

**Remember to check** whether the cake is ready. (= an action which will be necessary)

Don't **forget to add** the baking powder. (= an action which will be necessary)

I **regret to inform** you that your application was unsuccessful. (= I am sorry to tell you ...)

**Try to ice** the cake quickly. (= attempt to do it quickly if you can)

She **stopped to have** a rest. (= in order to have a rest)

They don't **mean to upset** you. (= they don't intend to)

He **went on to tell** them how to make a different cake. (= the next thing he did was to tell them ...)

### Verb + *-ing*

I **remember checking** that I had my keys when I left the house. (= a memory of a past action)

I'll never **forget going** to school on my own for the first time. (= a memory of a past action)

We **regret sending** our daughter to that school. (= we wish we hadn't)

**Try adding** nuts as it will improve the flavour. (= as an experiment)

**Stop beating** when the mixture is pale and fluffy. (= finish doing it)

If you go by train that **means taking** a taxi to the station. (= it involves)

They **went on cycling** until they reached the farm. (= they continued)

## 6 Verb + object + *to* infinitive or no object + *-ing*

The following verbs are followed by the *to* infinitive when they have an object and by *-ing* when they have no object:

| *advise* | allow | forbid | permit | *recommend* |
|---|---|---|---|---|

I **recommend using** apricots. or I **recommend you to use** apricots.
I **advise adding** nuts. or I **advise you to add** nuts.

## 7 Verb + *-ing* or infinitive without *to* (with a difference in meaning)

The following verbs always have an object (these are mainly to do with the senses):

> *feel   hear   notice   see   watch*

Notice the difference in meaning between verb + *-ing* and verb + infinitive without *to*:

*I **watched** the boys **playing** football.* (= an activity continuing over a period of time)
*I **watched** the boy **kick** the football into the road.* (= short completed action)

*She **heard** her mother **singing** as she came downstairs.* (= continuing action)
*She **heard** the doorbell **ring**.* (= a short completed action)

## 8 Verb + *that* clause

All the verbs marked * in this unit can also be followed by a *that* clause with the same meaning:

*I **suggest adding** some lemon juice.* = *I **suggest (that) you add** some lemon juice.*
*I **recommend using** sultanas and apricots.* = *I **recommend (that) you use** sultanas and apricots.*
*They **agreed to leave** early.* = *They **agreed (that) they would leave** early.*

## 9 Adjectives

The following adjectives are usually followed by the *to* infinitive: *afraid, cheap, *dangerous, delighted, *difficult, *easy, expensive, happy, impossible, interesting, *nice, pleased, possible, safe, sorry, surprised*:

*I'm **surprised to see** you here.*

The adjectives marked * can sometimes also be followed by *-ing* with the same meaning.
*It's **nice meeting** friends after school.*
or *It's **nice to meet** friends after school.*

➢ See also Unit 22, Grammar, part 1 for adjectives followed by a preposition + *-ing* or a noun.

## C Grammar exercises

**1** **Complete this conversation using the verbs in brackets.**

Andy:   I've decided _to leave_ (leave) **(1)** my job next month.

Sally:   But I thought you enjoyed ..................... (work) **(2)** in an architect's office.

Andy:   Oh, I do. But I feel like ..................... (do) **(3)** something different for a while.

Sally:   Didn't you promise ..................... (stay) **(4)** there at least two years?

Andy:   Yes, I did but I just can't stand ..................... (work) **(5)** with those people. One of them refuses ..................... (stop) **(6)** talking while she works, another one keeps ..................... (sing) **(7)** to himself. And then there's a man who attempts ..................... (tell) **(8)** awful jokes all the time which he always gets wrong. I detest ..................... (work) **(9)** with all that noise around me.

Sally:   It sounds quite a cheerful place to me. Can't you manage ..................... (ignore) **(10)** them and get on with your work?

Andy:   No, I can't. I just can't carry on ..................... (go) **(11)** there every day. I'm hoping ..................... (go) **(12)** abroad for a bit.

Sally:   Well, good luck.

**2** **Underline the correct form of the verb.**

**1** I noticed the man _drop_ / _dropping_ / _to drop_ his ticket so I picked it up for him.

**2** The tour guide advised the tourists not _take_ / _taking_ / _to take_ too much money out with them.

**3** I heard the horses _come_ / _coming_ / _to come_ down the lane so I waited for them to pass before driving on.

**4** The old man said he would love _have_ / _having_ / _to have_ the chance to fly in an aeroplane again.

**5** Don't make the children _come_ / _coming_ / _to come_ with us if they don't want to.

**6** I saw the boy _jump_ / _jumping_ / _to jump_ into the lake before anyone could stop him.

**7** I recommend _phone_ / _phoning_ / _to phone_ the hotel before you set off.

**8** My father used to forbid us _play_ / _playing_ / _to play_ in those woods.

**9** The college only allows _smoke_ / _smoking_ / _to smoke_ in the common room.

**10** It was my drama teacher who encouraged me _become_ / _becoming_ / _to become_ an actor.

**3**  Fill in the gaps with a suitable verb in the correct form.

1  If I go to the wedding it will mean ....buying.... a new dress.

2  Please try ...................... to the airport in good time – I'll be nervous waiting for you.

3  Will you stop ...................... that noise? I'm trying ...................... this book.

4  I forgot ...................... a table at the restaurant and it was full when we got there.

5  The two children went on ...................... their ball against the wall although they had been told several times to stop.

6  We regret ...................... you that the course you applied for is now full.

7  Tommy says he didn't come to the party because he didn't know about it but I remember ...................... him.

8  When you go out, remember ...................... the key with your neighbour because I haven't got one.

9  Why don't you try ...................... glasses? Then you might not get so many headaches.

10  I saw Philip when I was in the park so I stopped ...................... to him.

11  I meant ...................... you a postcard but I didn't have time.

12  I regret not ...................... to Egypt with my sister because she says it was a really great trip.

13  After getting a degree in biology, my son went on ...................... a book about monkeys.

14  I shall never forget ...................... the sun come up over the mountains when I was in the Himalayas.

**4**  Tony is about to go on a trip to your home town. He knows nothing about your country. Complete these sentences giving him some advice.

1  I advise you (*visit*) ........to visit the market in Green Street.........

2  You'll enjoy (*see*) ...................................................................

3  Don't miss (*go*) .....................................................................

4  Before you go, don't forget (*buy*) ..........................................

5  While you're there, try (*eat*) ..................................................

6  You must promise ...................................................................

7  Avoid ......................................................................................

8  Remember ..............................................................................

## D  Exam practice

### Use of English

For questions **1–15**, read the text below and decide which answer
(**A**, **B**, **C** or **D**) best fits each space. There is an example at the beginning (**0**).

**0** Ⓐ round    **B** through    **C** across    **D** over

⚠ This task tests grammar from the rest of the book as well as the grammar in this unit.

### BALLOON ADVENTURE

Brian Jones is the British half of the first team to go (**0**) ...A... the world in a
balloon. He and his Swiss co-pilot have written an account of the 19-day
expedition they (**1**)........ in March 1999. It was an astonishing triumph.
Nobody (**2**)........ them to finish the voyage. They (**3**)........ with poisonous fumes,
temperatures of minus 50 degrees Celsius and an Atlantic crossing with
(**4**)........ any fuel.

Fourteen years (**5**)........ , Brian was a reasonably successful businessman,
(**6**)........ he tired of his furniture business and (**7**)........ to buy a balloon.
Before long he was one of the country's (**8**)........ balloon instructors and pilots.
Why did he risk everything for one trip? He says he was not a very confident
child: 'At seven a friend (**9**)........ me to go down a water slide. I still (**10**)........
being absolutely terrified. I couldn't swim and I have never learnt to swim
properly.' He thinks everyone should face their greatest (**11**)........ and that
is one reason why he went up in the balloon. Six of the 19 days they were
(**12**)........ the air were spent (**13**)........ at the Pacific Ocean – 8,000 miles
of water. Brian says he won't (**14**)........ to do it again because there are so
many other things he (**15**)........ to do.

| | | | | |
|---|---|---|---|---|
| **1** | **A** followed | **B** succeeded | **C** performed | **D** completed |
| **2** | **A** expected | **B** hoped | **C** intended | **D** admitted |
| **3** | **A** did away | **B** got along | **C** kept up | **D** put up |
| **4** | **A** almost | **B** hardly | **C** quite | **D** rather |
| **5** | **A** after | **B** ago | **C** since | **D** past |
| **6** | **A** but | **B** although | **C** since | **D** so |
| **7** | **A** thought | **B** considered | **C** afforded | **D** decided |

8   **A** unique        **B** preferable    **C** leading       **D** suitable

9   **A** demanded      **B** dared         **C** threatened    **D** wished

10  **A** forget        **B** remind        **C** remember      **D** regret

11  **A** fears         **B** suspicions    **C** disturbances  **D** frights

12  **A** on            **B** in            **C** by            **D** to

13  **A** watching      **B** observing     **C** seeing        **D** staring

14  **A** delay         **B** imagine       **C** attempt       **D** suggest

15  **A** wants         **B** fancies       **C** enjoys        **D** appreciates

These are some words from the exam task. Without looking back, put them into the right columns.

(can't) afford    admit    appreciate    attempt    consider
dare    decide    delay    demand    enjoy    expect    fancy
hope    imagine    suggest    threaten    want    wish

| Verbs followed by *to* infinitive | Verbs followed by *-ing* |
|---|---|
| can't afford | admit |

## Writing

Your class has recently had a discussion about how much freedom parents should allow young people to have nowadays. Your teacher has asked you to write a composition giving your own views on the following statement:

*Young people are given too much freedom nowadays by their parents.*

Write your **composition** in **120–180** words.

**This task gives you a chance to practise:**
using the structures which follow certain verbs.

**Useful words and expressions**
*admit, advise, afford, agree, allow, forbid, force, give up, order, permit, persuade, promise, suggest, tell, warn*
*clothes, drinking, driving, parties, smoking*

## A  Context listening

**1** You are going to hear a girl called Donna talking about a pop group she was in. Look at these pictures, which show what happened. Read the sentences below and put them in the correct order according to the pictures.

a  Bella, Jo and Zoe made plans without telling Donna. ☐

b  Donna had some problems. ☐

c  Donna left the group. ☐

d  Donna was in a pop group with Bella, Jo and Zoe. ☐

e  Donna had a row with the other girls. ☐

f  One night the group didn't perform. ☐

**2**  🎧 **18** Listen and check if you were right.

**3**  🎧 **18** Read the definitions 1–11. They all refer to phrasal verbs which Donna uses. Listen again and complete the phrasal verbs. Stop the recording when you need to.

1  *separate* = ....break.... up

2  *have a good relationship* = .................... on with

3  *rely on* = .................... on

4  *support* = .................... up

5  *take care of* = .................... after

6  *continue* = .................... on

7  *cancel* = .................... off

8  *meet* = .................... together

9  *discuss* = .................... over

10  *make someone leave* = .................... out

11  *surrender* = .................... in

# 18

## B Grammar

### 1 Meaning and form

The meaning of some phrasal verbs is clear:
*I **picked up** the phone.* (*picked* and *up* have their normal meanings)

Many phrasal verbs are idiomatic and you have to learn what they mean.
They may contain the same verb but have different meanings, depending
on the preposition or adverb which follows:
*He **turned back** because he had left something at home.* (= changed direction)
*He **turned down** the invitation because he was feeling tired.* (= refused)
*They **turned up** unexpectedly.* (= arrived)

Some phrasal verbs have several meanings:
*She **put on** her clothes.* (= she got dressed)
*She **put on** weight.* (= her weight increased)
*She **put on** the light.* (= she switched the light on)
*The students **put on** a play.* (= performed)

➢ See Appendix 1 for a list of phrasal verbs you should understand.

The form of phrasal verbs can vary.
Some verbs have **two parts**: a verb (e.g. *do, go*) and another word
(sometimes called a particle) which can be an adverb (e.g. *back, out*) or a
preposition (e.g. *at, into, from*).
Some verbs have **three parts**: a verb (e.g. *come*), an adverb (e.g. *up*) and a
preposition (e.g. *against*).

Phrasal verbs behave differently depending on whether they are
a verb + preposition, a verb + adverb, or a verb + adverb + preposition.

### 2 Verb + preposition

When a phrasal verb consists of a verb and a preposition:
◆ it always has an object.
◆ the <u>object</u> (noun or pronoun) always goes after the preposition (the
  verb and preposition can't be separated):
  *The rest of the group **looked after** <u>Donna</u>.* (**not** ~~looked Donna after~~)
  *I **counted on** <u>them</u>.* (**not** ~~counted them on~~)
  *They **went over** <u>their plans</u>.* (**not** ~~went their plans over~~)
  *I really **cared about** <u>them</u>.* (**not** ~~cared them about~~)

### 3 Verb + adverb

When a phrasal verb consists of a verb and its adverb:
◆ it doesn't always have an object:
  *They **got together** every Monday morning.*
  *They **carried on** without me.*

◆ the <u>object</u> (when it is a noun) can come before or after the adverb (the verb and adverb can be separated):
*They **didn't back** <u>Donna</u> **up** when she was in trouble.*
or *They **didn't back up** <u>Donna</u>.*

*They wanted to **throw** <u>Donna</u> **out** because of what she did.*
or *They wanted to **throw out** <u>Donna</u>.*

*They **called** <u>the concert</u> **off**.* or *They **called off** <u>the concert</u>.*

◆ the <u>object</u> (when it is a pronoun) must go between the verb and the adverb:
*They **backed** <u>me</u> **up**.* (**not** ~~backed up me~~)
*They wanted to **throw** <u>me</u> **out**.* (**not** ~~throw out me~~)
*They couldn't do the concert without her so they **called** <u>it</u> **off**.* (**not** ~~called off it~~)

◆ the <u>object</u> (when it is very long) is usually put after the adverb:
*They **called off** <u>the concert, which had already been postponed twice</u>.*
(**not** ~~called the concert, which had already been postponed twice, off.~~)

⚠ Some phrasal verbs have two meanings and take an object with one meaning and no object with the other meaning, e.g. *give in*:
*I won't **give in** until they pay me what they owe.*
(verb + adverb + no object = surrender)
*I **gave in** <u>my homework</u> on time.*
(verb + adverb + object = hand it to the teacher)

⚠ Some words (e.g. *down, in, off, on, past, through, up*, etc.) can be either prepositions or adverbs:
*She **picked** <u>the book</u> **up**.* or *She **picked up** <u>the book</u>.*
(verb + adverb can be separated)
*She **went up** <u>the stairs</u>.* (**not** ~~went the stairs up.~~)
(verb + preposition can't be separated)

You can check if a phrasal verb is a verb + preposition or a verb + adverb by looking in a good dictionary.

## 4 Verb + adverb + preposition

When a phrasal verb consists of three parts:
◆ it always has an object.
◆ the <u>object</u> (noun or pronoun) always goes after the phrasal verb (the three parts can't be separated):
*I always **got on with** <u>the other members of the group</u>.*
*... I **came up against** <u>some problems</u> ...*
*I **put up with** <u>this</u> for a while.*
*They're not going to **get away with** <u>it</u>.*

# 18

## C Grammar exercises

Use your dictionary to do these exercises if you need to.

**1** Complete these sentences with words from the box to make phrasal verbs with *get*.

| at | away with | by | down | on | ~~out of~~ | over | round | round to | through |
|---|---|---|---|---|---|---|---|---|---|

1 Simon always manages to get .........*out of*......... doing the washing-up because he says he has a lot of homework.

2 My grandfather got ........................................... the flu very quickly because he's such a fit man.

3 Maria's daughters must be on the phone all the time because I can never get ........................................... when I try to ring her.

4 I tried to take a message but I didn't get ........................................... everything Paula said.

5 Peter hasn't had much success with jobs so far but I'm sure he'll get ........................................... in his new one.

6 I finally got ........................................... watching the video of a film I recorded two months ago.

7 People think they need lots of money but you can get ........................................... with very little.

8 We don't keep things on the top shelf because we can't get ........................................... them without standing on the table.

9 The news of Billy and Jane's engagement got ........................................... the office very quickly.

10 I can never get ........................................... telling a lie because my face always goes bright red.

**2** Fill in the gaps with phrasal verbs from the box which mean the same as the verbs in brackets.

| ~~care for~~ | carry on | cut down | fill in | put off |
|---|---|---|---|---|
| ring up | set off | take in | turn down | turn up |

I had been doing the same job for years and I didn't really .......*care for*....... (~~like~~) (1) it any more but it was extremely well paid. Then one day I decided to look for another job, realising I would need to ........................... (*reduce*) (2) what I spent on luxuries. I ........................... (*completed*) (3) lots of forms but all my applications were ........................... (*rejected*) (4). I ........................... (*continued*) (5) looking for a job but nothing suitable ........................... (*appeared*) (6) so I booked a holiday. The day before I was due to ........................... (*leave*) (7) I was ........................... (*telephoned*) (8) by a TV company who asked me to go for an interview the next day. I ........................... (*postponed*) (9) my holiday immediately. It was the job of my dreams. I could hardly ........................... (*absorb*) (10) the news when they offered it to me. And I never went on that holiday.

**158**

**3** Fill in the gaps with the correct form of verbs in the box to make phrasal verbs.

~~break~~   come   do   fall   get   give
go   hand   look   make   turn   work

## On the Run

The film *On the Run* tells the story of three prisoners who manage to ......break...... (1) out of a jail on an island. One of the prison guards is not very honest. The prisoners .................. (2) round him by offering him money and he .................. (3) over some keys. They .................. (4) for a nearby forest and decide to wait there for a bit because they haven't had time to .................. (5) out a plan. While they .................. (6) over the possibilities, a woman who is walking through the forest .................. (7) across them and promises to bring them food each day if they help her to .................. (8) for wood. They are hungry and are not very good at .................. (9) without their dinner. She is also very beautiful so they .................. (10) in with her idea. But on the third day the woman .................. (11) up with a policeman. She .................. (12) away their secret in order to get the reward offered.

**4** **a** Look up the phrasal verbs in italics in a dictionary and decide if they are *verb + preposition* or *verb + adverb* or *verb + adverb + preposition*. Then decide if the underlined noun can go in any other place and rewrite the sentences where possible.

1 I can't *give up* <u>chocolate</u> however hard I try.
<u>Verb + adverb: I can't give chocolate up however hard I try.</u>

2 He was so angry he *broke up* <u>the sculpture</u> into small pieces.
..................................................................................................................

3 The girl *went over* <u>her work</u> several times before she was satisfied.
..................................................................................................................

4 We've *run out of* <u>biscuits</u> – could you fetch some more?
..................................................................................................................

5 I could tell from his expression that he'd *made up* <u>the excuse</u>.
..................................................................................................................

6 I can't *put up with* <u>that noise</u> any longer.

............................................................................................................

7 I *looked after* <u>the children</u> while their mother was busy.

............................................................................................................

8 Don't forget to *put out* <u>the lights</u> when you leave.

............................................................................................................

9 With her dark eyes and hair, she *takes after* <u>her father</u>.

............................................................................................................

10 That shop *puts up* <u>its prices</u> every month.

............................................................................................................

**b** Replace each of the nouns in brackets with a pronoun and rewrite the sentences with the pronoun in the correct place.

1 I can't give up (chocolate) however hard I try.
   *I can't give it up however hard I try.*

2 He was so angry he broke up (the sculpture) into small pieces.

............................................................................................................

3 The girl went over (her work) several times before she was satisfied.

............................................................................................................

4 We've run out of (biscuits) – could you fetch some more?

............................................................................................................

5 I could tell from his expression that he'd made up (the excuse).

............................................................................................................

6 I can't put up with (that noise) any longer.

............................................................................................................

7 I looked after (the children) while their mother was busy.

............................................................................................................

8 Don't forget to put out (the lights) when you leave.

............................................................................................................

9 With her dark eyes and hair, she takes after (her father).

............................................................................................................

10 That shop puts up (its prices) every month.

............................................................................................................

## D Exam practice

⚠ This task tests grammar from the rest of the book as well as the grammar in this unit.

### Use of English

Complete the second sentence so that it has a similar meaning to the first sentence, using the word given. **Do not change the word given.** You must use between **two** and **five** words, including the word given. There is an example at the beginning (**0**).

**0** It is essential that all library books are returned by July 5th.
**bring**
You ............*must bring back*............... all library books by July 5th.

**1** Maria had to go away unexpectedly so they postponed the wedding for a month.
**off**
Maria had to go away unexpectedly so they .................................................... for a month.

**2** It isn't worth asking Philip to tidy up.
**point**
There's .............................................. Philip to tidy up.

**3** They decided not to go on holiday after all because the baby was ill.
**baby's**
Because .................................................... they decided not to go on holiday after all.

**4** I suggest phoning your aunt before turning up at her house.
**you**
I suggest .................................................. your aunt before turning up at her house.

**5** When I tried to make changes to the school timetable, I was faced with a lot of opposition.
**against**
When I tried to make changes to the school timetable, I .......................................................... a lot of opposition.

**6** Dr Brown was respected by his grandchildren who all wanted to be like him.
**up**
Dr Brown's grandchildren .................................................... him and all wanted to be like him.

**7** They had just started their walk when it began to pour with rain.
**set**
They had just .................................................. their walk when it began to pour with rain.

**8** You'll miss your plane if you don't hurry a bit more.
**unless**
You'll miss your plane ...................................................... a bit more.

**9** I really can't bear to live near the railway line any longer.

**put**

I really can't ................................................................................ near the railway line any longer.

**10** Try not to make a mess while you're cooking.

**avoid**

Try ................................................................................ a mess while you're cooking.

**In which of the sentences is a phrasal verb used?** ................................................................

**Rewrite the following sentences using the phrasal verbs from the exam task.**

**1** They arrived unexpectedly while we were having dinner.

_They turned up while we were having dinner._ ................................................................

**2** By the time we started our journey it was getting dark.

................................................................................................................................

**3** I really can't bear to sit in this heat any longer.

................................................................................................................................

**4** This desk is for books which are being returned to the library.

................................................................................................................................

**5** When I'd nearly finished mending the car, I was faced with a problem I couldn't solve.

................................................................................................................................

**6** James had always respected his boss.

................................................................................................................................

**7** The play was postponed for a week because the main actor was ill.

................................................................................................................................

# Writing

You and your school-friends want to have an end-of-term party and have decided to hire a room in a hotel near the school. You have offered to organise the booking. Read the information about the hotel and the notes you have made on it. You should cover all the points in your notes. You may add relevant information of your own.

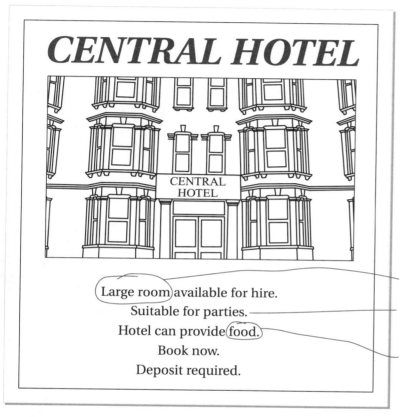

**CENTRAL HOTEL**

CENTRAL HOTEL

Large room available for hire. ———— Big enough for 50 people? How much?

Suitable for parties. ————— Reduction for students?

Hotel can provide food.

Book now. ———— Only snacks wanted – drinks?

Deposit required. Saturday 30th June – start 8pm – how late can we finish?

Ask about music – we want disco

Write a **letter** in **120–180** words in an appropriate style. Do not write any addresses.

## Writing hints

**This task gives you a chance to practise:**
using some of the following phrasal verbs: *ask for, carry on / go on, clear up, do without, get together, hand over, join in, let in, look after, look over, ring up, run out of, see about, set up, write back.*

**Useful words and expressions**
*to hire, included, crisps, noise, nuts, bar staff, dancing, soft drinks, waiter*

## A   Context listening

**1**   You are going to hear a spy, known as Double X, talking to his boss,
Mr Seymour, about a photograph which Mr Seymour gives him.
Mr Seymour is asking Double X to do something. Before you listen,
guess what he is asking. .................................................................................

**2** 🎧 **19** Listen to the beginning of the conversation and check if you were right.

**3** 🎧 **19** Listen to the whole conversation and answer these questions.
Play the recording twice if you need to.

1 What does Mr Seymour want Double X to do? <u>To follow a man and find out all about him.</u>

2 Why doesn't Mr Seymour give Double X a better photo? ...................................................

3 Who sent the photo to Mr Seymour? ...................................................

4 Why is the photo fuzzy? ...................................................

5 How is it possible to make the picture clearer? ...................................................

6 Who is in the photo? ...................................................

7 Can you guess who sent the photo to Mr Seymour, and why? ...................................................

**4** 🎧 **19** Listen again and fill in the gaps.

1 If you ............................... him, I ............................... extremely pleased.

2 If we ............... a better picture, we ............... it to you.

3 If she ............... us that, I ............................... to ask for your help.

4 It ............................... me somewhere to start if I ............... where she'd phoned from.

5 It ............... a bit clearer if you ............... at it with your eyes half closed.

**5** Look at the sentences in Exercise 4 and answer these questions.

1 Look at sentence 5. Which tense is used after *if*? ...................................................

2 Look at sentence 1. Which tense is used after *if*? ...................................................

3 Look at sentences 2 and 4. Which tense is used after *if*? ...................................................

4 Look at sentence 3. Which tense is used after *if*? ...................................................

## B  Grammar

Conditional sentences tell us a condition (*if* ...) and its consequence. The tenses we use depend on:
♦ whether the condition and its consequence are real or imaginary.
♦ whether they are generally true, or linked to a particular event.

Often the condition comes before the consequence, but sometimes the consequence comes first. When the condition comes first, it is followed by a comma. When the consequence comes first, we don't use a comma.

We can divide conditionals into four groups.

### 1  Zero conditional

| | |
|---|---|
| *If* + present tense, + present tense<br>present tense (no comma) + *if* + present tense | *If you're in love, nothing else **matters**.*<br>*Nothing else **matters** if you're in love.* |

We use this to state general truths:
*If you're in love, nothing else **matters**.*
*All the world **seems** wonderful **if** you're in love.*
*If we **heat** ice, it **melts**. = Ice **melts** if we **heat** it.*

### 2  First conditional

| | |
|---|---|
| *If* + present tense, + future tense<br>future tense (no comma) + *if* + present tense<br>imperative condition + *and* + future tense | *If you **leave** me, I'll **die** of a broken heart.*<br>*I'll **die** of a broken heart if you **leave** me.*<br>***Leave** me **and** I'll **die** of a broken heart.* |

We use this for a condition which we believe is possible:
*If you **leave** me, I'll **die** of a broken heart.* (**not** ~~If you'll leave~~)
*I'll **love** you forever **if** you **buy** me a diamond ring.* (**not** ~~If you'll buy~~)

Sometimes we use the imperative to express this kind of condition (the imperative always comes first):
***Leave** me **and** I'll **die** of a broken heart.*
***Buy** me a diamond ring **and** I'll **love** you for ever.*

### 3  Second conditional

| | |
|---|---|
| *If* + past tense, + *would* + verb<br>*would* + verb (no comma) + *if* + past tense | *If you **left** me, I **would die** of a broken heart.*<br>*I **would die** of a broken heart if you **left** me.* |

We use this for an imaginary condition, which we believe to be impossible or very improbable. We use the past tense although the speaker is thinking about the present or future:
*If you **left** me, I'd (**would**) **die** of a broken heart.* (but I believe you won't leave me, so my heart is safe)

*If you **were** in love, nothing else **would matter**.* (but I believe you're not in love, so other things are important to you)
*All the world **would seem** wonderful **if** you **were** in love.* (but the speaker believes you're not in love, so everything doesn't seem wonderful)
*I'd (would) love you for ever **if** you **bought** me a diamond ring.* (but I don't expect you will buy me one, so I may not love you for ever!)

⚠ With *I* we often use *were* instead of *was* in conditional sentences, especially when we write. It is more formal:
*If **I was** you, I wouldn't phone him.*
*If **I were** you, I would write him a letter.*

## 4  Third conditional

| *If* + past perfect tense, + *would have* + past participle | *If you **had left** me, I **would have died** of a broken heart.* |
|---|---|
| *would have* + past participle (no comma) + *if* + past perfect tense | *I **would have died** of a broken heart **if** you **had left** me.* |

We use this to talk about past events which cannot be changed, so we know that the condition is impossible and its consequence is imaginary:
*If you'd (had) left me, I'd (would) have died of a broken heart.* (but you didn't leave me, so I was all right)
*If you'd (had) been in love, nothing else **would have mattered**.* (but the speaker knows you were not in love at that time, so other things were important to you)
*All the world **would have seemed** wonderful **if** you'd (had) been in love.* (but the speaker knows you were not in love so everything didn't seem wonderful)
*I'd (would) have loved you for ever **if** you'd (had) bought me a diamond ring.* (but you didn't buy me one, so I stopped loving you!)

⚠ Other modal verbs like *might* and *could* are sometimes used instead of *would* in second and third conditional sentences:
*I **might** love you if you bought me a diamond ring.*
*I **could** have loved you for ever if you'd (had) bought me a diamond ring.*

## 5  Mixed conditionals

We sometimes meet sentences which contain a mixture of second and third conditionals because of their particular context:
*If my boyfriend **gave** me diamonds like that, I'd **have married** him by now.*
(= my boyfriend does not give me diamonds like that so I haven't married him)
*If the weather **had been** fine last week, there **would be** roses in my garden.*
(= the weather was bad last week so there are no roses in my garden now)
*Lesley **wouldn't have missed** the bus **if** she **was** better organised.*
(= Lesley missed the bus because she is a badly organised person)

## C Grammar exercises

**1** Match the beginnings and endings of these sentences.

1  If Sally opens that door, ...g...
2  If Mike had listened to his father, ........
3  I would quite like Juno ........

4  If Dave didn't work so much, ........
5  We would have arrived early ........
6  If I was as lovely as Nancy, ........
7  If teenagers want to have a party, ........
8  The house wouldn't have been such a mess ........
9  Take one look at Alan ........
10 If you were as handsome as a film star, ........

a  if she wasn't such a jealous type.
b  I'd probably have lots of boyfriends.
c  they usually wait until their parents go out.
d  and you'll never forget his face.
e  he wouldn't have got into trouble.
f  I still wouldn't love you!
g  she'll get a nasty surprise.
h  if the roads had been less busy.
i  he wouldn't get so tired.
j  if the guests hadn't been careless.

**2** Put the verbs in brackets into the correct form.

1  I won't help you with your homework if you ........don't tidy........ (*not tidy*) your bedroom.
2  You'll need a visa if you ................................ (*want*) to travel to China.
3  If he ................................ (*care*) about other people's feelings, he wouldn't behave that way.
4  She ................................ (*not be*) successful if she doesn't learn to control her temper.
5  If I'd known you were such a gossip, I ................................ (*not tell*) you my secret.
6  They would work harder if they ................................ (*not be*) so tired.
7  The boss ................................ (*be*) furious if he'd found out what you were up to.
8  If the temperature ................................ (*fall*) below freezing, water turns to ice.
9  If they ................................ (*not expect*) delays, they wouldn't have set off so early.
10 Open the envelope and we ................................ (*discover*) what John has been doing.

**3** Complete the sentences for each picture using the third conditional, to show how missing her bus one day resulted in a new job for Zoe.

1 If she hadn't missed her bus, she wouldn't <u>have gone into the café.</u>

2 If there had been a free table, she ......................................................................

3 ........................................................., she wouldn't have had to wait for her coffee.

4 ........................................................., she wouldn't have read the back of the man's paper.

5 If she hadn't noticed the advertisement, ......................................................................

**4** Complete these sentences, using your own ideas.

1 If I was incredibly good-looking <u>my friends would be jealous of me.</u>

2 I wouldn't have to study English if ......................................................................

3 If I pass First Certificate ......................................................................

4 I won't pass my exam if ......................................................................

5 If my teacher didn't ......................................................................

6 If I hadn't ......................................................................

7 If English grammar ......................................................................

8 You have to ........................................................... if ......................................................................

9 If you listen to English pop songs ......................................................................

10 If I complete this sentence quickly ......................................................................

**169**

## D Exam practice

### Reading

You are going to read a magazine article about a young woman who works in a nursery school. Seven paragraphs have been removed from the article. Choose from the paragraphs **A–H** the one which fits each gap (**1–6**). There is one extra paragraph which you do not need to use. There is an example at the beginning (**0**).

---

# CHANCES | Nursery school teacher Sarah Oliver tells how a chance meeting changed her life

I really love my job, it makes me feel good at the beginning of every week, because I love working with small children and I enjoy the challenges that arise. But I also think what I do is something worthwhile and there was a time when I thought I would never have that sort of career.

| **0** | H |
|---|---|

But in my final term I started thinking what I might do and I realised that I didn't have much to offer. If I'd worked harder, I would have had better grades, but it was too late. I just accepted that I wasn't the type to have a career.

| **1** | |
|---|---|

Their father worked abroad and their mother had some high-powered job in an insurance company. I did most of the housework and I had a lot of responsibility for the children although I was only sixteen.

| **2** | |
|---|---|

The problems began really when I agreed to live in, so that I would be there if my boss had to go out for business in the evening. What was supposed to happen was, if I had to work extra hours one week, she'd give me time off the next.

| **3** | |
|---|---|

Anyway, one Sunday, I was in the park with them, while their parents were on yet another business trip, and I met this girl Megan I used to go to school with. We weren't particularly friendly before, but she asked me what I was doing, so we got chatting.

| **4** | |
|---|---|

I thought you couldn't do courses if you didn't have all sorts of exams from school, but she persuaded me to phone the local college and they were really helpful. My experience counted for a lot and I got on a part-time course.

| **5** | |
|---|---|

But it was worth it in the end. Now I've got a full-time job. Most of the children in this school come from families where there are problems, unemployment, poor housing and so on.

| **6** | |
|---|---|

I shall always be grateful to Megan. If I hadn't bumped into her, I would have stayed on where I was, getting more and more fed up. I wish I'd realised earlier that you can have a real career, even if you aren't top of the class at school.

**A**

I had to leave my job with the family, but I got work helping out at a nursery school. I was really short of money and I even had to get an evening job as a waitress sometimes.

**B**

I find that the work we do helps in lots of ways. The children benefit, but also the parents. It gives them time to sort things out, go for training, or job interviews and so on.

**C**

But unfortunately, it didn't often work out. I was getting more and more tired and fed up, because I had too many late nights and early mornings with the little ones. I felt trapped, because if I walked out there wouldn't be anyone to look after them.

**D**

Then I thought, well, I've spent every holiday for the past five years helping my mum – I've got two little brothers and a little sister, all much younger than me. So I found myself a job as a nanny, looking after two little girls.

**E**

It wasn't too bad at first, because I was living at home and my mum gave me advice and looked after me when I got home exhausted. And it felt great to be earning.

**F**

I was telling her how I loved the kids but hated the job and she said, if you want to work with children, you ought to do a course and get a qualification.

**G**

The following year I gained a further certificate which means I could apply for the post of deputy if it became vacant, or even transfer somewhere else if I want to.

**H**

I wasn't very good at school. I mean, I didn't like studying much, so I didn't try very hard. I thought I was the sort of person who couldn't do schoolwork, I suppose. I was just impatient to leave as soon as I could.

**Without looking back at the text, match the beginnings and endings of these phrases.**

1 I thought you couldn't do courses ...g..

2 If I'd worked harder, ........

3 If I hadn't bumped into her, ........

4 I could apply for the post of deputy ........

5 ... if you want to work with children, ........

6 ... if I walked out ........

7 ... if I had to work extra hours one week, ........

a there wouldn't be anyone to look after them.

b you ought to do a course and get a qualification.

c if it became vacant ...

d she'd give me time off the next ...

e I would have stayed on where I was ...

f I would have had better grades ...

g if you hadn't done all sorts of exams at school ...

# Writing

You are going to England for a few months with a friend. You need to find somewhere to stay. You have found some information and have written some notes on it. Write to your friend giving your opinion of the different places. Say what you can do if you stay in each place. Write a **letter** in **120–180** words in an appropriate style. Do not write any addresses.

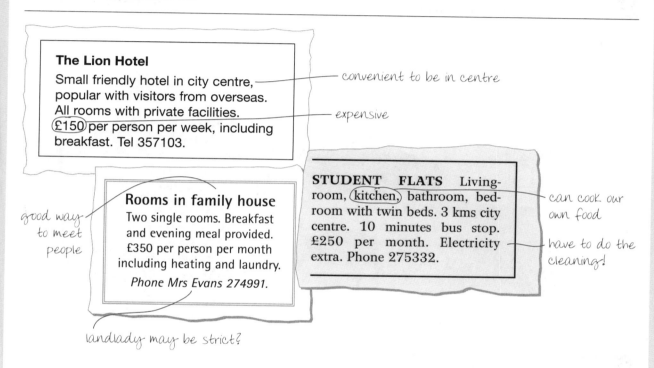

**The Lion Hotel**

Small friendly hotel in city centre, popular with visitors from overseas. All rooms with private facilities. £150 per person per week, including breakfast. Tel 357103.

— convenient to be in centre

— expensive

**Rooms in family house**

Two single rooms. Breakfast and evening meal provided. £350 per person per month including heating and laundry.

*Phone Mrs Evans 274991.*

good way to meet people

landlady may be strict?

**STUDENT FLATS** Living-room, kitchen, bathroom, bedroom with twin beds. 3 kms city centre. 10 minutes bus stop. £250 per month. Electricity extra. Phone 275332.

can cook our own food

have to do the cleaning!

## Writing hints

**This task gives you a chance to practise:**
using conditionals.
using comparatives (▷ see Unit 7).

**Useful words and expressions**
*to afford, to charge, to cost, to enjoy yourself, to get to know, to stay in / with*
*central, cheap, comfortable, convenient, expensive*
*accommodation, landlady, price, rent*

# 20

## Conditionals 2

*unless; in case; as/so long as; provided that; I wish/if only;*
*it's time; I'd rather; otherwise/or else*

## A Context listening

**1** You are going to hear a man talking to a group of people about something they are going to do the next day. Here are some of the things they will take with them. What do you think they are going to do? .................................................................................................

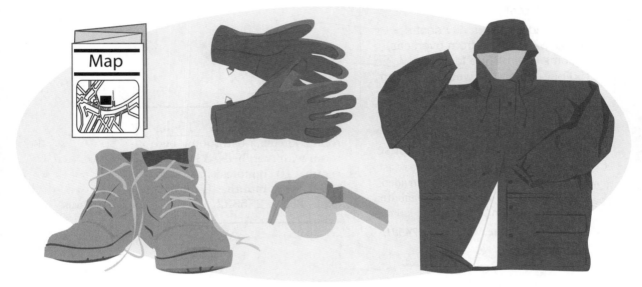

**2** 🎧 20a Listen and check if you were right.

**3** 🎧 20a Listen again and fill in the gaps. Stop the recording when you need to.

1 We're going ............*unless*............ the weather gets much worse.

2 ................................. that it doesn't snow too heavily tonight, I'll see you back here at six o'clock.

3 We won't reach the top of the mountain ................................. we set out early.

4 You need a whistle ................................. you get separated from the rest of the group.

5 ................................. you didn't bring large cameras.

6 ................................. we all stay together, we'll have a great time.

7 I ................................. you'd come a few weeks ago.

8 ................................. we had dinner now.

**4** Look at sentences 1, 2, 3, 4 and 6 in Exercise 3. What do you notice about the tense of the verbs which follow the words in the gaps? .................................................................................................

**174**

## B Grammar

### 1 Unless

*Unless* means *if not* and is used with the present tense to talk about the future (in the same way as *if*). *Unless* can usually be replaced by *if not*:
*We're going **unless** the weather **gets** much worse.* (= if the weather doesn't get much worse)
*We won't have time to reach the top of the mountain **unless** we **set** out early.* (= if we don't set out early)
***Unless** you **drive** more slowly, I'll be sick.* (= if you don't drive more slowly)

### 2 In case

*In case* shows an action is taken because of something else that might happen.
We use *in case* with the present tense to talk about something which might happen in the future:
*Take a whistle **in case** you **get** separated.* (= there's a chance you might get separated and a whistle will help us find you)
*Take my phone number **in case** you **miss** the bus.* (= I expect you'll get the bus, but if you miss it, you'll need to phone me)

We use *in case* with the past simple to explain an action:
*He took his surfboard **in case** they **went** to the beach.*
(= he took his surfboard because he thought they might go to the beach)

*In case* can also be followed by the present perfect:
*I'll buy some extra food **in case** the visitors **have** already **arrived**.*

⚠ *In case* does not mean the same as *if*. Compare:
*I'll cook a meal **in case** Sarah **comes** over tonight.* (= I'll cook a meal now because Sarah might visit me later)
*I'll cook a meal **if** Sarah **comes** over tonight.* (= I won't cook a meal now because Sarah might not visit me)

### 3 Provided / providing that and as / so long as

These expressions are used with a present tense to talk about the future. They have a similar meaning to *if*:
***As long as** we all **stay** together, we'll have a great time.*
***Provided** that it **doesn't snow** too heavily, I'll see you here at six o'clock.*

⚠ *If, unless, in case, provided / providing that* and *as / so long as* are all followed by the present tense to talk about the future. Some adverbs (*when, until, after, before, as soon as*) are also followed by the present tense to talk about the future (➢ see Unit 6).

175

## 4 *I wish* and *if only*

*I wish* means the same as *if only*. *If only* is less common and is usually stronger.

***Wish / if only* + the past simple** is used when we express a wish:

♦ about a present situation:
   *I **wish** you **loved** me.* (= but you don't love me)
   *I **wish** I **had** lots of money.* (= but I haven't got lots of money)
   ***If only** he could drive.* (= but he can't drive)
   ⚠ Notice that we use the past tense, although we are talking about now.

We can use *were* instead of *was* after *I* and *he / she / it*:
*I **wish** I **was / were** clever like you.* (= but I'm not clever)
*I **wish** the weather **wasn't / weren't** so wet here.* (= but it is wet)

***Wish / if only* + the past perfect** is used when we express a wish or regret:

♦ about the past. It's like the third conditional – the event can't be changed:
   *She **wishes** she'**d (had)** never **met** him.* (= but she did meet him)
   *I **wish** we'**d (had) come** a few weeks ago.* (= but we didn't come)
   ***If only** I **hadn't broken** his heart.* (= but I did break his heart)

***Wish / if only* + *would*** is used when we express a wish:

♦ for something to happen:
   *I **wish** the train **would arrive**.*
   ***If only** the rain **would stop**.*

♦ for someone to do something (often when we are annoyed):
   *I **wish** you **wouldn't leave** your bag in the doorway.*
   *I **wish** the waiter **would hurry up**.*

⚠ Notice the difference between *I hope + will* and *I wish + would* when talking about the future:
*I **hope** he **will phone**.* (= there's a good chance he will phone)
*I **wish** he **would phone**.* (= it's unlikely he will phone)

## 5 *It's time* and *I'd rather*

These expressions are followed by the past tense with a present meaning:
***It's time we ate** dinner now.*
***I'd rather** you **didn't bring** large cameras.*

## 6 *Otherwise* and *or else*

These words mean 'because if not' and they always go in the middle of a sentence. We use them when we feel sure about something:
*I have to go to bed early, **otherwise** I get too tired.* (= if I don't go to bed early, I get too tired)
*Carry that tray with both hands **or else** you'll drop it.* (= if you don't carry it with both hands, you'll drop it)

## C  Grammar exercises

**1** Rewrite these sentences using *unless* instead of *if not*.

1  Sam will pass his driving test if he doesn't drive too fast.
<u>Sam will pass his driving test unless he drives too fast.</u>

2  They'll be here soon if their plane isn't delayed.

3  If you're not in a hurry, you could take the bus.

4  I won't be able to come to see you tomorrow if my brother can't give me a lift.

5  If the factory doesn't increase its production, it will close down.

6  If you don't write your address down for me, I'll forget it.

7  I won't stay in that hotel if it hasn't got a good restaurant.

8  If I don't hear from you, I'll meet you at six.

**2** Fill in the gaps with *in case* or *if*.

1  Elaine will post the letters ........*if*........ she goes out.
2  I'll go for a swim ................. I finish college early.
3  I'll teach you to windsurf ................. you teach me to play golf.
4  I always leave the answerphone on when I go out ................. I miss an important phone call.
5  I'll take Tim's address with me ................. I have time to visit him while I'm in London.
6  Our team will win the match ................. our goalkeeper plays like he did last week.
7  It's a good idea to have two address books ................. you lose one of them.
8  I'll leave these videos here ................. you have time to watch them.

**3** Chloe is on holiday in a foreign city. She was so busy admiring the sights that she has got lost. What does she wish? Write sentences with *wish*.

1  I haven't got a map.

> I wish I had a map.

2  The streets all look the same.

3  I didn't bring my mobile phone.

4  I can't speak the language.

5  I didn't buy a phrase book.

6  I'm hot and thirsty.

7  I came here alone.

8  I need someone to help me.

9  I'm sorry I came here.

10  I want to be back in my hotel.

**4** Read this email. Fill in the gaps with the correct form of the verbs in the box. You need to make some of the verbs negative.

be    be    behave    bring    can    change    finish    ~~have~~    learn    know

To: JOE
From: ROBIN
Subject: PARTY!

Hi Joe

I'm having a birthday party on Saturday in my uncle's flat. I wish I ......*had*...... (1) a bigger flat but I haven't. Anyway, my uncle has offered me his flat so long as there ........................ (2) no more than thirty people and provided that the party ........................ (3) by midnight. So please come and bring a friend, but I'd rather you ........................ (4) Matthew with you because he always causes trouble. I wish he ........................ (5) to behave better. I had to work hard to persuade my uncle and unless everyone ........................ (6) well, he won't let me do it again. I'll send you a map in case you ........................ (7) the street where my uncle lives. If you ........................ (8) find it, just ring me on my mobile. So I'll see you on Saturday unless my uncle ........................ (9) his mind! By the way, has Sally changed her phone number? I can't get hold of her. I wish I ........................ (10) rude to her last week, as she's not speaking to me now.

Bye for now.

Robin

## D Exam practice

### Listening

🎧 **20b** You will hear people talking in eight different situations. For questions **1–8**, choose the best answer, **A**, **B** or **C**.

---

**1** You hear a woman telling someone about a film she has seen. What kind of film was it?
- **A** a thriller
- **B** a love story
- **C** a comedy

[ ] **1**

**2** You overhear a conversation in a restaurant. What is the man complaining about?
- **A** the food
- **B** the service
- **C** the noise

[ ] **2**

**3** You hear a woman talking to a colleague. How did the woman feel?
- **A** upset
- **B** ashamed
- **C** shocked

[ ] **3**

**4** You overhear a man talking to a friend on the phone. What was damaged?
- **A** a piece of sports equipment
- **B** a musical instrument
- **C** a piece of furniture

[ ] **4**

**5** You hear a couple planning to meet. When will the woman telephone the man?
- **A** about lunchtime
- **B** late afternoon
- **C** early evening

[ ] **5**

**6** You hear the weather forecast. What will the weather be like at the weekend?
- **A** foggy
- **B** wet
- **C** sunny

[ ] **6**

**7** Listen to a phone conversation between two women. Why is Sarah ringing Katya?
- **A** to make an apology
- **B** to offer an invitation
- **C** to make a request

[ ] **7**

**8** You overhear a woman talking to someone in a shop. Who is she talking to?

   **A**  the shop manager

   **B**  a customer

   **C**  a colleague

                                                             **8**

## Grammar focus task

**Complete these sentences about the people in the recordings.**

1 The woman says she wishes *she'd persuaded her friend to go to the cinema.*

2 The man says he won't come to the restaurant again unless ............................................................................................................................................................................................................................................

3 The woman was trying not to listen to the conversation in case ...................................................................................................................................................................................................

4 The man wishes ..................................................................................................................................................

5 The woman says they can meet that evening unless ......................................................................................................................................................................................................................

6 Next week will be sunny as long as ...................................................................................................................................

7 Katya will lend some cutlery as long as ..........................................................................................................................

8 The woman will stand up to the manager if ....................................................................................................

## Writing

You have decided to enter a short story competition. The competition rules say that the story must be called 'A missed opportunity' and it must end like this:

*I remembered what my brother had said when I was setting out. If only I'd listened to his advice!*

Write your **story** for the competition in **120–180** words.

## Writing hints

**This task gives you a chance to practise:**
joining sentences with *in case, if* and *unless*.
using *I wish* and *if only*.

**Useful words and expressions**
*although, as, disappointed, ignored, noticed, realised, suddenly, then*

## A  Context listening

**1** You are going to hear a news broadcast. Before you listen, look at the television screens and guess what the news stories are.

a .................................................................

b .................................................................

c .................................................................

d .................................................................

**2** 🎧 21 Listen and check if you were right. As you listen, put the television screens in the order you hear the stories.    1 ........    2 ........    3 ........    4 ........

**3** 🎧 21 Listen again and answer these questions. Stop the recording when you need to.

1 Where will the Prime Minister be for the next two days? *At a conference in Washington.*

2 When will he fly to Mexico? ..............................................................................................................

3 What is Cherry Pickles attempting to do? ......................................................................................

4 When does she intend to be in Chile? ..............................................................................................

5 How far do the traffic jams stretch? ...............................................................................................

6 How long will the motorway remain closed? ................................................................................

7 Where was the security man? ............................................................................................................

8 When was the manager released? ....................................................................................................

**4** Look at your answers to Exercise 3.

1 Which prepositions are used in answers about time? .................................................................

2 Which prepositions are used in answers about place? ...............................................................

## B Grammar

### 1 Prepositions of place

#### *In*, *at* and *on*

***In* is used:**

- for someone or something inside a limited area (e.g. a town, a country, a garden):
  *The Prime Minister is **in** Washington ...*
  *... she still intends to be **in** Chile ...*
  *There are some lovely trees **in** this garden.*

- for someone or something inside a building, room, or container:
  *... heard shouting **in** the manager's office.*
  *Do you keep your credit cards **in** this wallet?*

***On* is used:**

- for a point on a fixed line (e.g. a road, the coast):
  *... Napier, **on** the west coast ...*
  *They were called to the bank **on** the High Street.*

- for a point on a surface:
  *... Christchurch, **on** the south island ...*
  *There's a hook **on** the wall for coats.*

- with *floor* and *ceiling*:
  *There's a spider **on** the ceiling.*

- for public transport vehicles, such as buses, trains or planes:
  *They met **on** a plane.*
  *I can't read **on** the bus.*
  ⚠ but we use *in* for cars and taxis:
  *He came home **in** a taxi.*

***At* is used:**

- when we think about a place in terms of its function or as a meeting place:
  *... then have talks **at** the White House.*
  *I keep my tennis racket **at** the sports club.*
  *I'll see you **at** the theatre.*

- for an event:
  *He will remain **at** the conference ...*
  *There were a lot of strangers **at** the party.*

#### *Across* and *over*

There are many places where either *across* or *over* can be used:

*... a footbridge **across** / **over** the motorway ...*

but compare:

*Their eyes met **across** the table.*
*... her attempt to sail alone **across** the Pacific.*

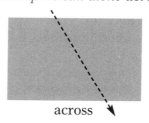

across

*The children climbed **over** the wall.*

over

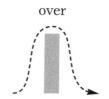

#### *Above* and *over*

*Above* or *over* is used if one thing is higher than another:
*The workshop is **above** / **over** the garage.*

*Over* is used when one thing covers another:
*Put this rug **over** that old chair.*

*Above* is used when the two things are not directly on top of each other:
*The hotel is **above** the beach.*

*Above* is used in documents:
*Please don't write **above** the line.*

## Under and below

*Under* or *below* is used if one thing is lower than another:
*The garage is **below** / **under** the workshop.*

*Under* is the opposite of *over*:
*There's a beautiful old chair **under** that rug.*

*Below* is the opposite of *above*:
*The beach is **below** the hotel.*

*Below* is used in documents:
*Please don't write **below** the line.*

## Along and through

*Along* is used for something which follows a line:
*We strolled **along** the riverbank at dusk.*
*There were cheering crowds **along** the route of the procession.*

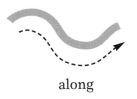

along

*Through* means from one side of something to the other side of it:
*The motorway passes **through** Birmingham.*
*I struggled **through** the crowd to reach a telephone.*
*We could see the sea **through** the trees.*

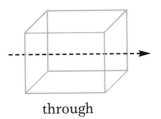

through

## By and beside

*By* can be used in the same way as *beside*, meaning 'next to':
*... a security man standing **by** / **beside** the door of the bank ...*
*I'd love to live **by** / **beside** a lake.*

## Between and among

*Between* is used when we talk about two places, things or people:
*The dictionary is **between** the grammar book and the atlas.*

*... the motorway **between** London and Oxford ...*

*Among* is used to identify something as part of a group:
*Is there a dictionary somewhere **among** these books?*

## Beyond and behind

*Beyond* is used for somewhere further away from us than something else. We may or may not be able to see it:
*... traffic jams stretching **beyond** the beginning of the motorway.*
*You can't see the lake, it's **beyond** the forest.*

*Behind* is used for somewhere which is partly or completely hidden by an object in front of it:
*The robber stood **behind** the door, hoping he wouldn't be seen.*

## 2 Prepositions of time

### *At, on* and *in*

*At* is used:

♦ for a point of time:
  ... *at* the start of her attempt to sail alone across the Pacific.

♦ for the time of day:
  *at* six o'clock, *at* dawn, *at* lunchtime

♦ for seasonal holidays:
  *at* Christmas, *at* Easter

♦ for the following expressions:
  *at* the weekend, *at* first, *at* last, *at* present (= now), *at* the moment (= now), *at* times (= sometimes), *at* once (= immediately)

**On** is used for dates and days (including special days):

*on* Monday, *on* 3rd December (note that we say: on **the** third **of** December), *on* New Year's Day, *on* Christmas Day, *on* my wedding anniversary

**In** is used for all or part of a period of time:
*in* the afternoon, *in* winter, *in* the twenty-first century, *in* the Middle Ages

### *By* and *until*

*By* means that something happens not later than, and possibly before, the time mentioned:
... *she* still intends to be in Chile **by** the end of the year. (= at the end of the year, or possibly before)

Can we finish this work **by** four o'clock? (= not later than four o'clock)

*Until* means that something continues up to, but not later than, the time mentioned:
... part of the motorway will remain closed **until** this afternoon. (= it will open this afternoon)

*Until* is often used with a negative, meaning 'not before':
We can't eat **until** all the guests arrive. (= we can eat when they are all here)

### *In, during* and *for*

*In* and *during* are often used with the same meaning:
**In / During** the summer we often go for long walks.

but *during* shows a particular event against the background of a period of time:
The manager was released **during** the night ...

especially if it is an interruption:
They walked out of the hall **during** the speech.

*For* shows how long something lasts:
He will remain at the conference **for** two days ...
We went to Spain **for** the summer.

*In* shows how soon something happens:
**In** less than an hour we had heard all about his adventures.
I'll meet you **in** ten minutes.

## C Grammar exercises

**1** Sara is on the train and she's phoning her friend Rebecca. Complete
the conversations with the prepositions in the box.

| at | at | by | by | during | for | in | in | ~~on~~ | over | until |

*In Rebecca's office, 11.30 am.*

Rebecca:   Rebecca White.

Sara:       Hi, it's Sara. I'm ..........on.......... (1) the train. Can you meet me ...................... (2) the station?

Rebecca:   What time?

Sara:       Three.

Rebecca:   I think so. The car's got a puncture. If I can arrange to get it fixed ...................... (3) my break, I'll be there.

Sara:       Thanks, that's great.

*At the garage, 1.40 pm.*

Rebecca:   Can you fix this puncture for me?

Mechanic:  Yes, probably. But my assistant won't be back from lunch ...................... (4) half an hour and I'll be working on this other job ...................... (5) then.

Rebecca:   Well, I've got to collect someone from the station ...................... (6) three.

Mechanic:  Oh, that's no problem. We'll have it done ...................... (7) half past two easily.

Rebecca:   Thanks. I'll be back ...................... (8) an hour, OK?

Mechanic:  Fine. See you then.

*On the train, 2.10 pm.*

Sara:       Hello?

Rebecca:   The car's being fixed now. I'll wait for you ...................... (9) the main door of the station, so I can help carry your stuff.

Sara:       Don't worry. I haven't got anything heavy. I'll see you ...................... (10) the car park. It's just ...................... (11) the footbridge, isn't it?

Rebecca:   Yes, all right. See you there.

Sara:       Bye.

**2** Fill in the gaps in this postcard with suitable prepositions.

Dear Rhiannon,
How are you? I'm enjoying this trip to Cornwall.
...At... (1) the moment, we're staying
.................. (2) the pretty little town of St Ives
.................. (3) the north coast. There are lots of
art galleries .................. (4) the town, so we visit
one of them each morning and then .................. (5)
the afternoon we go to the beach .................. (6)
an hour or two. .................. (7) the weekend, we
plan to drive to the south coast. From there we'll
fly to the Scilly Isles and stay there .................. (8)
two nights. There are some famous gardens
.................. (9) one of the islands that I'm looking
forward to seeing. We'll leave .................. (10)
Monday and we hope to be .................. (11) London
.................. (12) Tuesday.
See you then.
    Much love,
      Emily

**3** In eight of these sentences there is at least one wrong preposition.
Underline each mistake and write the correction.

1 She hid <u>below</u> the bed until the visitors had gone. ...under the bed...

2 We arrived to our destination in dawn. ..................

3 Shall we meet at the bus stop on the Oxford Road? ..................

4 At the night, we heard strange noises in the room over us. ..................

5 The gymnast sailed along the air and landed lightly to the mat. ..................

6 We took the mirror out of its frame and found a seventeenth-century painting beyond it.
..................

7 The detective found an earring in the path along the pool and the house. ..................

8 I put your socks in the drawer. ..................

9 The prisoners managed to get across the fence and ran away into the forest.
..................

10 I need to use the cash machine so I'll see you outside the cinema by ten minutes.
..................

**4** A hotel owner is showing some visitors round his new premises. Fill in the gaps with suitable prepositions.

We're now standing ........in........ **(1)** the lounge, a beautiful room, with paintings
.................... **(2)** the ceiling and a wonderful view .................... **(3)** the park to the hills
.................... **(4)** it. The cellar is being decorated .................... **(5)** present, but we will
open it as a restaurant .................... **(6)** a few months' time. .................... **(7)** then we are
serving meals .................... **(8)** the dining-room only.

Do you see the trees planted all .................... **(9)** the sides of the road up to the front
door? They are going to be hung with coloured lights .................... **(10)** special
occasions. If we go .................... **(11)** that gate, we'll reach the rose garden, where you
can see a number of interesting sculptures on display .................... **(12)** the bushes.

## D Exam practice

⚠ This task tests grammar from the rest of the book as well as the grammar in this unit.

### Use of English

For questions **1–15**, read the text below and look carefully at each line. Some of the lines are correct, and some have a word which should not be there. If a line is correct, put a tick (✓). If a line has a word which should **not** be there, write the word. There are two examples at the beginning (**0** and **00**).

### A DAY OUT

| | | |
|---|---|---|
| **0** | ✓ | We visited an arts centre on the road between Salisbury and |
| **00** | on | Winchester last week. It used to be on a farm and the new |
| **1** | | owners have made the clever use of some old barns, stables |
| **2** | | and other buildings. There are several small studios of which |
| **3** | | can be rented so cheaply by local painters, sculptors, potters and |
| **4** | | other artists to work in. The barn has been turned into a most |
| **5** | | attractive designed gallery. The current exhibition has some lovely |
| **6** | | modern glass from Scotland. The gallery is used to show of the |
| **7** | | work of the artists who use the studios in addition to holding |
| **8** | | exhibitions by more than famous artists from other parts of the |
| **9** | | country. Most of all the artists were in their studios when we |
| **10** | | visited that and we were able to talk to them about what |
| **11** | | occupations they were doing. One potter told us that it can |
| **12** | | be quite a lonely job at some times, so she is happy to be in a |
| **13** | | place where she feels she is among people who understand her |
| **14** | | work. They can go across the yard for have coffee and a chat |
| **15** | | and share their problems one with each other. |

After you have checked your answers to the exam task, read the text carefully once more. Then fill in the gaps with the correct prepositions without looking back at the text.

1 The arts centre is ......*on*...... the road ..................... Salisbury and Winchester.

2 The artists were ..................... their studios when we visited.

3 The potter said it can be quite a lonely job ..................... times.

4 She said she was happy to be ..................... people who understood her work.

5 The artists go ..................... the yard for coffee.

# Writing

Your family is exchanging homes with some English friends for a fortnight's holiday. Your English friends have visited your country before, but they have not been to your area. You decide to leave a letter telling them about places to visit and when they are open. Write a **letter** in **120–180** words in an appropriate style. Do not write any addresses.

**This task gives you a chance to practise:**
using prepositions for places and times.

**Useful words and expressions**
*bank, gallery, local shop, museum, sports hall, supermarket, swimming pool
in the (city) centre, just up the road, not far from, on the outskirts
at weekends, on weekdays*

# Prepositions 2

prepositions which follow verbs and adjectives; prepositions
to express *who*, *how* and *why*; expressions with prepositions

# 22

## A  Context listening

**1** You are going to hear a man called Andy telling his wife, Dawn, about a fire.
Before you listen, look at the pictures. What is happening in each one?

1 .....................................     2 .....................................     3 .....................................

**2** 🎧 **22** Listen and decide which picture best fits what Andy tells Dawn. What is wrong
with the other two pictures? .....................................

**3** 🎧 **22** Listen again and fill in the gaps.

1 ... what's happened ...*to*......... your jacket?

2 ... there's no need to shout .................. me.

3 ... an adventure .................. the way home.

4 I called the fire brigade .................. my mobile ...

5 I got in .................. breaking a window.

6 ... smashed a window .................. hitting it ...

7 I covered my face .................. a handkerchief.

8 You could have been .................. real danger.

9 ... the fire brigade were .................. control ...

10 ... they thanked you .................. saving their property.

11 ... do you forgive me .................. being late?

12 I can't be angry .................. you now.

13 I'll make a really nice supper .................. you.

14 I'm looking forward .................. eating it ...

**4** Look at your answers to questions 5 and 6 in Exercise 3. Which preposition is used to
show how something is done? .....................................

## B Grammar

### 1 Prepositions which follow verbs and adjectives

#### Verb + preposition

Some verbs are nearly always followed by a particular preposition.
These include:

◆ *approve of*: She doesn't **approve of** smoking.

◆ *enquire about*: We **enquired about** our hotel reservation.

◆ *insist on*: My boss **insists on** not having plants in the office.

◆ *look forward to*: I'm really **looking forward to** eating it.

◆ *succeed in*: Did you **succeed in** finding accommodation?

Notice that prepositions are followed by a noun or by the *-ing* form:
*We enquired **about booking** a room.*
*We enquired **about our hotel** reservation.*

#### Verb + object + preposition

Some verbs are nearly always followed by an object and a particular
preposition. These include:

◆ *accuse someone of*: They **accused the girl of** taking the parcel.

◆ *congratulate someone on*: He **congratulated me on** passing the exam.

◆ *forgive someone for*: She can't **forgive that man for** all the lies he told.

◆ *prevent someone / something (from)*: I tried to **prevent the box (from)**
   slipping off the seat.

◆ *suspect someone of*: I **suspect her of** being dishonest.

#### Verb + different prepositions

Some verbs are followed by different prepositions, which change the
meaning. These include:

◆ *agree with someone* and *agree about something*:
   *I quite **agree with** you, I think you're right.* (= a person)
   *My father and **I don't agree about** politics.* (= a subject)

◆ *ask for something* and *ask about something*:
   *He **asked** me **for** some money.* (= he requested)
   *She **asked** me **about** my plans for the summer.* (= she enquired)

◆ *laugh about* and *laugh at*:
   *I was late but he wasn't angry, he just **laughed about** it.* (= found it funny)
   *I can't wear this hat. Everyone will **laugh at** me.* (= made fun of – unkindly)

- *think of* and *think about*:
  What do you **think of** my new jacket? It's great. (= what is your opinion?)
  What are you **thinking about**? Lunch − I'm hungry! (= what is in your mind?)

- *throw at* and *throw to* (also *shout at / point at* and *shout to / point to*):
  The little boy **threw** the ball **to** his father. (= part of a game)
  Don't **throw** toys **at** your sister, Harry, you might hurt her. (= probably angry or rude)

## *To be* + adjective + preposition

Some adjectives are nearly always followed by a particular preposition. These include:

- *angry about (something):* She's **angry about** the theft of her purse.
- *angry with (someone):* He's very **angry with** his assistant.
- *good / bad at (something):* She's **good at** drawing flowers.
- *pleased about (something):* My parents **weren't pleased about** my bad report.
- *pleased with (something or someone):* Granny **was** very **pleased with** the book you sent her.
- *rude / polite to (someone):* Don't **be rude to** anyone at the party.
- *(un)kind to (someone):* The children **were** extremely **unkind to** the new boy.

## 2 Prepositions used to express *who, how* and *why*

### *By, with* and *for*

We use *by* with passive verbs, for the person or thing which does the action:
The window was smashed **by Andy**.
The fire was started **by an electrical fault**.

We use *by* + *-ing* to show how something is done:
He smashed the window **by hitting** it with a hammer.
He got in **by breaking** a window.

We use *with* + noun for a tool (or other object):
He smashed the window **with a hammer**.
He covered his face **with his handkerchief**.

We use *for* + *-ing* or a noun to explain the purpose of a tool or other object:
Hammers are normally **for knocking** in nails, not **for smashing** windows!
He keeps a bag of tools in his car **for emergencies**.

We can also use *for* + *-ing* or a noun to explain the reason for something:
The owners of the house thanked him **for saving** their property.
He received an award **for bravery**.

## 3 Expressions with prepositions

We use prepositions in the following fixed expressions:

◆ ways of travelling:
*by* air, *by* plane, *by* road, *by* car, *by* bus, *by* rail, *by* train but *on* foot

◆ ways of contacting people:
*by* post, *by* email, *by* phone but *to be* *on* the phone (= using the phone)

◆ ways things can happen:
*by* chance, *by* accident, *by* mistake but *on* purpose

◆ reasons for being somewhere:
*on* holiday, *on* / *off* duty, *on* business

◆ circumstances:
*in* love, *in* secret, *in* private, *in* public, *in* / *out of* sight, *in* / *out of* debt, *in* / *out of* danger, *in* / *out of* difficulties, *in* a hurry, *in* a temper, *in* control, *in* charge of, *at* peace, *at* war, *at* work, *at* home

⚠ Don't make mistakes with these expressions:

◆ *at least* and *at last*:
That bike must have cost **at least** five hundred pounds. (= not less than)
The work took a long time but **at last** it was finished. (= finally)

◆ *on the way* and *in the way*:
I'm going to my office so I'll call and see you **on the way**. (= between two points on a journey)
I can't move the table because that chair's **in the way**. (= blocking a path between two objects / people)

◆ *on time* and *in time*:
If the train's **on time**, I'll be home at six. (= punctual)
If we leave now, we'll be home **in time** to see the news. (= at or before the correct time)

◆ *in the end* and *at the end*:
She didn't want to come with us, but **in the end** we persuaded her.
(= the final result)
It was a great show and the audience applauded loudly **at the end**.
(= the last thing to happen)

◆ *to be the matter with* and *to be about*:
What **was the matter with** Lesley? Why was she upset?
(= something wrong)
What's that book **about**? (= subject)

◆ *to be in charge of* and *to be responsible for*:
He's **in charge of** the office and makes all the important decisions.
(= he's the boss)
I'm **responsible for** travel arrangements, but not accommodation.
(= it's my duty)

## C   Grammar exercises

**1**   Write sentences describing what happened in each of the pictures, using the words given.

1

Can you tell me what trains there are to Scotland?

*(enquired)*

He enquired about trains to Scotland.

2

Well done! You certainly deserved to win this tournament.

*(congratulated)*

3

No, you can't come in here.

*(prevented)*

4   I'm so sorry I forgot to phone you.    It's OK, I'm not angry.

*(forgave)*

5

You've been reading my diary!

*(accused)*

6   I didn't like that film at all.    No, I didn't either.

*(agreed)*

**2** In eight of these sentences there is at least one wrong preposition.
Underline each mistake and write the correction.

1   You know you shouldn't phone me <u>in</u> work! ..........._at work_..........................................................

2   Yvonne doesn't approve on wearing real fur, but Ida doesn't agree to her. ...........................................

3   Who is responsible of setting the burglar alarm? ..............................................................................

4   I asked the manager of advice for training but he just shouted angrily with me for disturbing him.

.....................................................................................................................................................................

5   Jamie and Pia were brought to the theatre by their parents. .............................................................

6   The mermaid was combing her hair by a silver comb. ......................................................................

7   No one's had any cake. What's the matter of it? ..............................................................................

8   Did you drop that dish by purpose? ....................................................................................................

9   Do you know the name of the thing you use for opening wine bottles? .........................................

10  Marco didn't understand what the play was in because there was a pillar on the way so
he couldn't see properly. .......................................................................................................................

**3** Fill in the gaps in these newspaper articles with suitable prepositions.

a

The wedding took place last Saturday of a
couple who fell ............_in_............ **(1)** love
through the internet. Penny and Peter
communicated ..................... **(2)** email for
six months until they discovered
..................... **(3)** accident that they worked
..................... **(4)** the same building.
'Actually, I had noticed her before and
liked her, but I was too shy to speak to her
..................... **(5)** public,' said blushing
Peter. 'When I realised she was my
internet friend, at first I suspected her
..................... **(6)** laughing ..................... **(7)**
me, and I was quite angry ..................... **(8)**
it. But luckily she succeeded ..................... **(9)**
persuading me that I was wrong. Now
we're looking forward ..................... **(10)**
spending our lives together.'

**b**

A FRENCH BANK ROBBER was arrested yesterday ................... (1) Edinburgh, two years after his crime. A former cashier recognised him ................... (2) chance in the hotel where she was staying ................... (3) business and reported him to the security guard ................... (4) duty. The guard accused him ................... (5) using a false name and insisted ................... (6) taking him to the hotel manager's room. The robber threw a lamp ................... (7) the guard and ran out of the hotel. Fortunately, he was not very good ................... (8) running, and the police soon caught him.

**c**

An elderly brother and sister were reunited today for the first time since they were children. Freda and Cecil Brown's parents had been ................... (1) debt and the children had been put in children's homes until their family was ................... (2) difficulties. But the country was ................... (3) war, the children were separated, and their papers were lost. Cecil's granddaughter began trying to find Freda five years ago. 'It was hard, but ................... (4) last I found the daughter of the woman who had been ................... (5) charge of the home where Freda was. She said that some of the girls were sent to Canada to be ................... (6) danger during the war and many of them never returned. When I thought I'd found Freda, I wanted to tell Dad immediately, but I decided to meet her ................... (7) secret first, in case I was wrong. But I was right.' Two days ago, Cecil travelled ................... (8) air for the first time ................... (9) his life. 'We've got a lot of catching up to do,' he said.

## D Exam practice

⚠ This task tests grammar from the rest of the book as well as the grammar in this unit.

### Use of English

For questions **1–10**, read the text below. Use the word given in capitals at the end of each line to form a word that fits in the space in the same line. There is an example at the beginning (**0**).

**THE CLOTHES WE CHOOSE TO WEAR**

The clothes we wear can be a form of (**0**) _communication_. Clothes, like a            **COMMUNICATE**

(**1**) _____ language, give out a message. This can be very simple, for example,      **SPEAK**

when we wear clothing for keeping warm, or perhaps to attend a (**2**) _____      **GRADUATE**

ceremony, announce our (**3**) _____ views or just look sexy. It isn't always       **POLITICS**

this simple, however. (**4**) _____, as with speech, our reasons for making       **FORTUNE**

any statement have a (**5**) _____ to be double or multiple. The man who       **TEND**

buys an expensive coat may simultaneously want it to offer (**6**) _____ from      **PROTECT**

bad weather, and magically surround him with the qualities of an (**7**) _____      **NATION**

film star. (**8**) _____, people rarely succeed in satisfying both these requirements   **NATURE**

at once. Even (**9**) _____ both these statements could actually be made by      **SUPPOSE**

one single coat, this (**10**) _____ item of clothing may not be available,       **IDEA**

and if it is, we may not be able to afford it.

> **Grammar focus task**
>
> **These are some extracts from the text. Without looking back at the text, fill in the gaps with the correct prepositions.**
>
> 1 The clothes we wear can be a form ........_of_........ communication.
>
> 2 ... we wear clothing _____ keeping warm ...
>
> 3 ... our reasons _____ making any statement ...
>
> 4 ... magically surround him _____ the qualities of a film star.
>
> 5 ... people rarely succeed _____ satisfying both these requirements ...
>
> 6 ... both these statements could actually be made _____ one single coat ...

# Writing

Last weekend you went to Northwold for a short winter break. When you arrived you discovered that a number of the town's attractions were not available. Your travel agent had not warned you about this. Look at the information in the brochure and the notes you made and write to the travel agent, telling him why your weekend was not as enjoyable as you had hoped and asking for compensation.

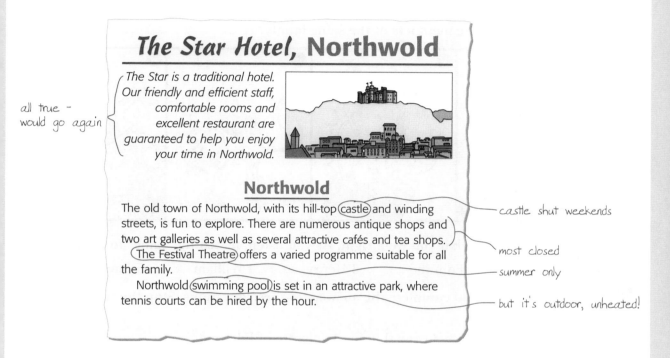

*all true – would go again*

## The Star Hotel, Northwold

The Star is a traditional hotel. Our friendly and efficient staff, comfortable rooms and excellent restaurant are guaranteed to help you enjoy your time in Northwold.

### Northwold

The old town of Northwold, with its hill-top castle and winding streets, is fun to explore. There are numerous antique shops and two art galleries as well as several attractive cafés and tea shops.

*castle shut weekends*

*most closed*

The Festival Theatre offers a varied programme suitable for all the family.

*summer only*

Northwold swimming pool is set in an attractive park, where tennis courts can be hired by the hour.

*but it's outdoor, unheated!*

Write a **letter** in **120–180** words in an appropriate style. Do not write any addresses.

| Writing hints |
| --- |

**This task gives you a chance to practise:**
describing what you did and what you could not do.
describing how you felt.
using expressions with prepositions.

**Useful words and expressions**
*to advise, to expect, to look forward to, to recommend, to be responsible for, to warn*
*annoyed, delighted, disappointed, satisfied, upset*
*the brochure said that ..., however*

# 23 Relative clauses

defining and non-defining relative clauses; relative pronouns and propositions

## A Context listening

**1** You are going to hear a man showing some visitors round the castle where he lives. Before you listen, look at each picture.

Can you guess when the people lived? .................................................................................................

Do you think they are members of the same family? ...........................................................................

**2** 🎧 23 Listen and check if you were right. As you listen, match the names to the pictures.

1 Margaret ........    2 Edmund ........    3 Henry ........    4 William ........    5 Jane ........

**3** 🎧 23 Listen again and complete the answers to these questions. Stop the recording when you need to.

1 What do we learn about the ship in the picture of Edmund?

It's the one <u>which he was captain of during a famous naval victory.</u> .................................

2 Which is the picture of Henry and William?

It's the picture ...........................................................................................................................

3 How do we know who William is?

He's the one ...............................................................................................................................

4 Which side did Henry support in the Civil War?

It was the side ...........................................................................................................................

5 Which year was the picture of Jane and her children painted?

It was the year ...........................................................................................................................

**4** Underline the first word in each of your answers to Exercise 3. They are all words which can introduce relative clauses. What does each word refer to?

1 ...................    2 ...................    3 ...................    4 ...................    5 ...................

## B Grammar

## 1 Defining relative clauses

Defining relative clauses tell us some essential information about the things or people they refer to:

*The picture **that hangs next to Margaret's portrait** is the one I like best.*

If we remove the words *that hangs next to Margaret's portrait* we don't know which picture Jasper is talking about.

**Defining relative clauses**:

- may begin with the relative pronouns *who* (for people), *which* (for things), *that* (for things and people).

- may have *who, which* or *that* as the subject or object of the relative clause:
*... the picture **which / that** hangs next to Margaret's portrait ...* (*which / that* is the **subject** of the relative clause)

*... the woman **who / that** he married ...* (*who / that* is the **object** of the relative clause, and *he* is the subject)

- very often omit the relative pronoun when it is the object of the relative clause:
*The painting we're looking at now ...* or *The painting **which / that** we're looking at now ...*

- are never separated from the rest of the sentence by commas.

- are used in writing and speaking.

## 2 Non-defining relative clauses

Non-defining relative clauses tell us some extra information about the things or people they refer to:

*The next painting shows Edmund's wife Margaret, **who he married in 1605**.*

If we remove the words *who he married in 1605*, we still know who Jasper is talking about. It is *Edmund's wife, Margaret.*

**Non-defining relative clauses**:

- always begin with the relative pronouns *who* (for people) and *which* (for things).

- may have *who* or *which* (but never *that*) as the subject or object of the relative clause:
*The building, **which** is very old, costs a lot of money to repair.* (**not** *that is very old*)

*The castle's owner, **who** we've just seen, enjoys meeting visitors.* (**not** *that we've just seen*)

- never omit the relative pronoun.

- must be separated from the rest of the sentence by commas.

- are more common in writing than in speaking.

⚠ We always omit the object pronoun (*her, him, it,* etc.) when we make a relative clause:

*We know little about **the woman that he married**.* (**not** *the woman that he married her*)

*The next painting shows Edmund's wife Margaret, **who he married in 1605**.* (**not** *who he married her in 1605*)

## 3 Relative pronouns and prepositions

Both **defining** and **non-defining relative clauses**:

◆ can begin with *whose* (instead of *his / her / their*), *when* (for times) and *where* (for places):
*William, **whose wife Jane was a famous beauty**, had nine children.*
*Here they are in this picture from the year **when the youngest was born**.*
*This has been my family home, **where we've lived for over four hundred years**, since the time of Edmund Claremont.*

◆ can begin with *whom* (for people) as the object of a clause (this is mainly in written English, and is increasingly rare):
*His girlfriend, **whom** he neglected, became very depressed.*

◆ usually have any prepositions at the end of the clause:
*It's the one **which** he was captain **of** during a famous naval victory.*
*The girl he fell in love **with** was extremely tall.*
*Peter, **who** my father used to work **with**, has become a government minister.*

◆ in formal English, sometimes have a preposition at the beginning of the clause, followed by *which* (for things) or *whom* (for people):
*It's the one **of which** he was captain during a famous naval victory.*
*The girl **with whom** he fell in love was extremely tall.*
*Peter, **with whom** my father used to work, has become a government minister.*

⚠ We cannot use *that* after a preposition in a relative clause:
*The Conference Room, **in which** the meeting was held, was not really big enough.*
(**not** ~~in that the meeting was held~~)

⚠ A defining relative clause can:

◆ begin with *why*, after the words *the reason*:
*This victory was the reason **why he became a national hero**.*

◆ omit *why* and *when*:
*That was the reason we went there. (= That was the reason **why** we went there.)*
*I remember the day I met you. (= I remember the day **when** I met you.)*

## C  Grammar exercises

**1** Fill the gaps in this letter using *who* or *which* when necessary.
If no word is necessary, write –.

Dear Mr Trotter,

I have a number of complaints about the work ........–........ (1)
your company did in my house last week.

You promised that the men .................. (2) carried out the work would
arrive by 8.00. As you know, I have to catch the bus .................. (3)
leaves at 8.15. On three days the men arrived after eight,
so I missed my bus and my boss, .................. (4) is very strict,
was extremely annoyed. The foreman lost the written instructions
.................. (5) I gave him. The paint .................. (6) he used for the
hall was the one .................. (7) should have been used in the kitchen.
The sitting-room wallpaper, .................. (8) I had chosen with great
care, was the wrong way up. My bathroom, .................. (9) you and I
agreed did not need redecorating, has been painted.

If you do not promise to put right the mistakes .................. (10)
your men have made within two weeks, I will go to my lawyer.

Yours sincerely,

Cecil J. Trubshaw

**2** Complete these sentences with your own ideas,
using the relative pronouns in the box.

| where | when | ~~which~~ | which | which | who | whose | why |

1  I don't really enjoy films which show a lot of violence.

2  I don't often go to parties .............................................

3  My teacher usually explains things .............................................

4  I can remember several occasions .............................................

5  I cannot understand the reason .............................................

6  Have you ever met anyone .............................................

7  I envy people .............................................

8  I would hate to have a job .............................................

**3** Combine each pair of sentences by making the second sentence into a non-defining relative clause.

1 My brother loves chocolate ice cream. He is rather fat.
My brother, who is rather fat, loves chocolate ice cream.

2 My uncle's cottage has been damaged by floods. We usually spend our holidays there.
..............................................................................................................................

3 My bicycle has been stolen. I only got it last week.
..............................................................................................................................

4 The chemistry exam was actually quite easy. We had been worrying about it.
..............................................................................................................................

5 The young man caused a fight in a bar. His girlfriend had left him.
..............................................................................................................................

6 During the summer there are dreadful traffic jams. Everyone goes on holiday then.
..............................................................................................................................

7 My parents enjoyed that film very much. They don't often go to the cinema.
..............................................................................................................................

**4** In eight of these sentences there is a mistake. Underline the mistakes and write the correction.

1 Have you seen the <u>folder, that</u> I keep my notes in? folder that .................................

2 My left ankle which I broke last winter is still giving me trouble. ..................................

3 Is that the man which you were talking about? ..................................

4 I'm looking for the book you lent me last week. ..................................

5 The region, where we go for our holidays, is becoming increasingly popular. ..................................

6 The friend I want to introduce you to him is away this weekend. ..................................

7 The company for whom my brother works has just opened a new factory. ..................................

8 My biggest suitcase, that had all my clothes in, was lost at the airport. ..................................

9 The principal, whose name was Somerville, gave a very amusing speech. ..................................

10 Do you remember the name of the place in that the crime was committed? ..................................

## D Exam practice

⚠ This task tests grammar from the rest of the book as well as the grammar in this unit.

### Use of English

For questions **1–10**, complete the second sentence so that it has a similar meaning to the first sentence, using the word given. **Do not change the word given.** You must use between two and five words, including the word given. There is an example at the beginning (**0**).

**0** You can only win if you enter the race.
**unless**
You _can't win unless_ you enter the race.

**1** That's the hotel where we had lunch last Sunday.
**in**
That's the hotel ............................................. last Sunday.

**2** This special offer will end on Monday!
**last**
This special offer ............................................. Monday!

**3** Being an airline employee, my girlfriend sometimes gets cheap flights.
**works**
My girlfriend, ............................................., sometimes gets cheap flights.

**4** He used a penknife to open the box.
**opened**
He ............................................. a penknife.

**5** I don't like Jim because he's so mean.
**why**
Jim's meanness ............................................. I don't like him.

**6** 'Will I be paid soon?' asked Lynda.
**if**
Lynda wondered ............................................. paid soon.

**7** Last week Gerry borrowed a book from me and now she's lost it.
**I**
Gerry's lost ............................................. last week.

**8** I intended to have a lunch break, but I had too much to do.
**going**
I ............................................. a lunch break, but I had too much to do.

**9** The concert which Ben took me to wasn't very enjoyable.
**went**
I didn't enjoy ........................................ to with Ben.

**10** The mother of that boy is a well-known actress.
**whose**
That's ........................................ a well-known actress.

## Grammar focus task

**Look at your answers to the exam task.**

1 Which of the sentences you have written contain relative clauses? ........................................

2 Are they defining or non-defining relative clauses? ........................................

3 How do you know? ........................................

## Writing

You have seen the following competition advertised in a magazine.

Write a **story** for the competition.

**Fiction Magazine**

**You are invited to enter our writing competition!**

**Write a short story in 120–180 words which ends:**

'... now at last we knew the name of the man who lived in the tower!'

## Writing hints

**This task gives you a chance to practise:**
using relative clauses to give information about people and things.
using the past simple, past continuous and past perfect to tell a story.

**Useful words and expressions**
*to be surrounded by, to discover, to notice, to recognise, to solve*
*ancient, curious, suspicious, wooden*
*building, cliff, forest, garden, gate, lane, cottage, mystery, path, secret, stranger, wall, woods*
*at once, cautiously, immediately, nervously, suddenly*

# Linking words 1

*because*, *as* and *since*; *so* and *therefore*; *in order to*, *to* +
infinitive and *so (that)*; *so* and *such*; *enough* and *too*

# 24

## A  Context listening

**1**  You are going to hear two
friends, Josie and Adam,
talking at their sports club.
Before you listen, look at
the picture. Can you guess
which sports they take part
in? ...................................................
...................................................

**2**  🎧 **24** Listen and check if you were right.

**3**  🎧 **24** Listen again and fill in the gaps. Stop the recording when you need to.

1  Josie thinks Tom Castle was chosen ..*because*.. he's the coach's nephew.

2  Adam believes that Tom is certainly ........................................ to be captain.

3  Adam suggests Josie ought to be in the team herself ................... she seems to know so
much about the subject.

4  Josie objects that she isn't ........................................ to play volleyball.

5  Adam points out that Melanie is ........................................................ that she's one of the
best players.

6  Josie says that going to judo once a week gives her ........................................ .

7  She thinks that volleyball would take ................................................................ .

8  She adds that they have ................................................................ after school.

9  Adam says that he has been training every day ............................................. be really fit.

10  The coach told Adam that he plays ........................................ .

11  Some of the older players may drop out ................... they've got
........................................................ to do.

**4**  Look at your answers to questions 2, 4, 6 and 10 in Exercise 3. Why is the word order
different in 6? ............................................................................................................................. .

## B Grammar

## 1 Expressing reason

### Because, as and since

*Because*, *as* and *since*:
- introduce the reason for something
- go at the beginning or in the middle of a sentence:
  *They had to choose him **as** / **because** / **since** he's the coach's nephew.*
  ***As*** / ***Because*** / ***Since*** *he's the coach's nephew, they had to choose him.*
  Notice that if they go at the beginning, there is usually a comma in the middle of the sentence.

*Because* is stronger than *as* and *since*, but they are often used in a similar way:
***As*** / ***Since*** / ***Because*** *I hadn't done my homework, I didn't understand the lesson.*

⚠ *Because* (but not *as* or *since*) can be used to begin the answer to a question beginning with *why*:
Question: *Why didn't you understand the lesson?*
Answer: ***Because*** *I hadn't done my homework.* (**not** ~~As / Since I hadn't done my homework.~~)

### So and therefore

*So* and *therefore*:
- introduce the result of something.

*So* usually goes in the middle of a sentence:
*They may need a new goalkeeper **so** I want to be ready.*

*Therefore* goes at the beginning of a new sentence:
*They may need a new goalkeeper. **Therefore** I want to be ready.*

We could also say:
*I want to be ready **because** they may need a new goalkeeper.*

Compare these sentences, which have the same meaning:
*I hadn't done my homework **so** I didn't understand the lesson.*
*I hadn't done my homework. **Therefore** I didn't understand the lesson.*
***As*** / ***Since*** / ***Because*** *I hadn't done my homework, I didn't understand the lesson.*

*So* is more common in speaking.
*Therefore* is more common in writing.

## 2 Expressing purpose

*(In order) to* + infinitive and *so (that)* + verb

*In order to, to, so that* and *so*:

◆ link an action and its purpose.

*So* always goes in the middle of a sentence:
*I've been training every day* **so (that)** *I'm really fit.*

*In order to* and *to* go in the middle, or occasionally at the beginning, of a sentence:
*I've been training every day* **in order to** *be really fit.*
*I've been training every day* **to** *be really fit.*
**To / In order to** *be really fit, I've been training every day.*

*In order to* and *so that* are stronger than *to* and *so*.

⚠ Sentences with *so* can sometimes have two meanings, for example:
*I've been training every day* **so** *I'm really fit.*
This could mean: *I've been training every day* **in order to be** *really fit.*
or: *I've been training every day* **therefore** *I'm really fit.*
(➤ See Grammar, part 1.)

⚠ Remember, in sentences like these, we do **not** use *for* to express purpose:
(**not** ~~I've been training every day for be really fit.~~)

## 3 Explaining cause and effect

*So* and *such*

*So* and *such* mean 'as much as this'. We can use them to talk about cause and effect:
*He walked* **so slowly that** *we arrived late.* (= we arrived late because of his slow walking speed)
*He was* **such a slow walker that** *we arrived late.*

We often omit *that*, especially in speech:
*It was* **such an untidy office** *we couldn't find our books.* = *It was* **such an untidy office that** *we couldn't find our books.*

We can use *so* and *such* after *because*:
*Her teachers sent her home* **because** *she behaved* **so badly**.
*Her teachers sent her home* **because** *she was* **such a naughty child**.

*So* is followed by:
◆ an adjective or an adverb:
*Her father is* **so rich** *that she's never travelled by bus.*
*He spoke to her* **so rudely** *that she walked out of the room.*

◆ the words *many, much* and *few*, with or without a noun:
*He's invited* **so many people** *to the party there's nowhere to sit down.*
*I've got* **so few books** *I can keep them on one shelf.*
*You complain* **so much** *that everyone gets bored.*

*Such* is followed by:

◆ *a(n)* (if necessary) + adjective + noun:
  Her father is **such a rich man** that she's never travelled by bus.
  The café always charges **such high prices** that students can't afford to eat there.

◆ *a(n)* (if necessary) + noun only:
  They were treated with **such kindness** that they were reluctant to leave.
  The concert was **such a success** they decided to give another.

◆ the expression *a lot (of)* with or without a noun:
  He's invited **such a lot of people** to the party there's nowhere to sit down.
  I **spent such a lot** last night.

➢ See Unit 8, Grammar, part 4 for other words which modify adjectives and adverbs.

## Enough and *too*

*Enough* means 'sufficient, the right quantity'. *Too* means 'more than enough'.
We can use *too* and *enough* with adjectives, adverbs and nouns, followed by:

◆ *to* + infinitive:
  This bag is **too heavy to carry**.
  I'm not **strong enough to carry** this bag.
  He wasn't running **quickly enough to catch** us.

◆ *for* something / someone:
  This bikini is **too small for** me.
  Have you got **enough money for** the car park?

*Enough*:

◆ goes before a noun:
  I've got **enough sandwiches** for lunch.
  (= as many sandwiches as I need)

◆ goes after an adjective:
  This room is **warm enough** for me.
  (= the right temperature)

◆ goes after an adverb:
  Are we speaking **loudly enough** to be heard?
  (= Can everyone hear us?)

*Too*:

◆ goes before *many / much* + a noun:
  I've got **too many books** to carry. (= I can't carry all of them)
  I've got **too much work**. (= I can't do it all)

◆ goes before an adjective:
  This room is **too warm** for us. (= the temperature is uncomfortably high)

◆ goes before an adverb:
  Are we speaking **too loudly**? (= Are we disturbing the other students?)

## C  Grammar exercises

**1**  Fill in the gaps, using the words and phrases in the box.

as    ~~because~~    enough    in order to    so    so    so that    too

1   Why are you staring at me like that?

..Because.. you've got a large black mark on the end of your nose!

2   It's only eleven o'clock. Why aren't you still at school?

We've been sent home early ..................... revise for our exam tomorrow.

3   How was the trip to the museum?

..................... several galleries were closed for repairs, it was rather disappointing.

4   What are all those students doing in the park?

The university term has ended ..................... they're having a picnic to celebrate.

5   Why are you working late today?

I want to finish this essay ..................... I'll be free to go out tomorrow.

6   Come on! If we run fast ....................., we'll catch the early train.

Sorry, I've got ..................... many bags I can't run.

Oh, never mind. If we're ..................... late for that train, we can have a drink while we wait for the next one.

**2** **In six of these sentences there is a mistake. Underline each mistake and write the correction.**

1 We're packing our cases tonight <u>so</u> we're leaving very early tomorrow. ....as..................................

2 Have you got money enough for your journey? ...................................................................

3 My father says I'm too young for have a motorbike but I don't agree. ........................

4 I've lost weight so I can wear a tight skirt at my party. ............................................

5 Since that I've never been to New York, I can't tell you much about it. ..................

6 She's been given too much advice that she doesn't know what to do. .....................

7 I've booked a table at the restaurant so we won't have to wait. ..............................

8 It was a such sad film I couldn't stop crying at the end. ...........................................

**3** **Match the beginnings and endings of these sentences.**

1 Tessa's got so much homework ...h...    **a** he should be in bed.

2 Stephen's so vain ........    **b** to make sandwiches for us all.

3 Jessie has so many hobbies ........    **c** he can buy any clothes he wants.

4 This music isn't too loud ........    **d** she neglects her schoolwork.

5 Saskia hasn't got enough money ........    **e** for us.

6 Keith earns so much money ........    **f** to come on holiday with us.

7 I think there's enough bread ........    **g** he thinks every girl fancies him.

8 Peter has such a bad cold ........    **h** she can't come out with us.

**4** **Complete these sentences using your own ideas.**

1 The bus company offers cheaper fares at weekends in order to <u>attract more passengers.</u>

2 The hotel dining-room is closed this week. Therefore guests ...................................

3 We'd better phone a qualified electrician, as we .......................................................

4 Because my brother uses a wheelchair, he often ........................................................

5 I don't have a mobile phone so my friends .................................................................

6 She has such beautiful clothes she ..............................................................................

7 We enjoyed the party so much we ..............................................................................

8 Is this box big enough to .............................................................................................

## D  Exam practice

### Use of English

For questions **1–15**, read the text below and look carefully at each line. Some of the lines are correct, and some have a word which should not be there. If a line is correct, put a tick (✓). If a line has a word which should **not** be there, write the word. There are two examples at the beginning (**0** and **00**).

**WORLD ENGLISH**

| | | |
|---|---|---|
| **0** | ✓ | If we read English language newspapers or listen to newsreaders |
| **00** | all | who use English in all different parts of the world, we will quickly |
| **1** | | develop the impression on that one form of English is so widely used |
| **2** | | that it will soon unite all the different varieties of English which |
| **3** | | exist. Is there enough evidence to support for this impression? |
| **4** | | It is in real fact misleading in several ways since a version of |
| **5** | | English which is exactly the same in everywhere and has the |
| **6** | | same high status throughout the complete world does not yet exist. |
| **7** | | For one thing, people that whose first language is English value |
| **8** | | their linguistic identity. Therefore, they try to preserve it from the |
| **9** | | influence of other forms of English. New Zealanders, for an example, |
| **10** | | do not want to speak like Australians. In addition with, there |
| **11** | | are too very many regional differences in vocabulary for the |
| **12** | | language to be the same everywhere. People need specialised |
| **13** | | words in order to discuss each local politics, business, culture |
| **14** | | and natural history. Lastly, there is the fact that learners of |
| **15** | | English may be taught by either American or British forms. |

These extracts are from the text. Without looking back at the text, fill in the gaps with the words in the box.

| enough | in order to | ~~so~~ | that | therefore | to | too |
|--------|-------------|--------|------|-----------|-----|-----|

... we will quickly develop the impression that one form of English is ...~~so~~........ (1) widely used ..................... (2) it will soon unite all the different varieties of English which exist.

Is there ..................... (3) evidence ..................... (4) support this impression?

For one thing, people whose first language is English value their linguistic identity. ..................... (5), they try to preserve it from the influence of other forms of English.

... there are ..................... (6) many regional differences in vocabulary for the language to be the same everywhere.

People need specialised words ............................................. (7) discuss local politics, business, culture and natural history.

## Writing

You see a competition advertised in a magazine and decide to enter. Read the competition and the college brochure and the notes you have made on it. Then write your application.

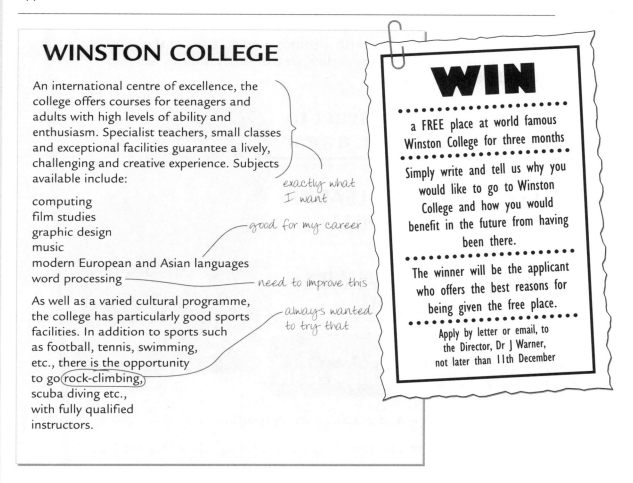

### WINSTON COLLEGE

An international centre of excellence, the college offers courses for teenagers and adults with high levels of ability and enthusiasm. Specialist teachers, small classes and exceptional facilities guarantee a lively, challenging and creative experience. Subjects available include:

*exactly what I want*

computing
film studies
graphic design
music
modern European and Asian languages
word processing

*good for my career*

*need to improve this*

As well as a varied cultural programme, the college has particularly good sports facilities. In addition to sports such as football, tennis, swimming, etc., there is the opportunity to go rock-climbing, scuba diving etc., with fully qualified instructors.

*always wanted to try that*

### WIN

a FREE place at world famous Winston College for three months

Simply write and tell us why you would like to go to Winston College and how you would benefit in the future from having been there.

The winner will be the applicant who offers the best reasons for being given the free place.

Apply by letter or email, to the Director, Dr J Warner, not later than 11th December

Write a **letter** in **120–180** words in an appropriate style. Do not write any addresses.

### Writing hints

**This task gives you a chance to practise:**
describing your plans and ambitions.
using *as, because, in order to* etc. when you explain your ideas.

**Useful expressions**
*I am writing to apply for ..., I am planning to ..., I am quite good at ...,*
*I have always wanted to ..., My mother tongue is ...*

# Linking words 2

*in spite of* and *despite*; *but*, *although* and *though*; *even though* and *even if*, participle clauses; *before* and *after* + *-ing*; *when*, *while* and *since* + *-ing*

## A    Context listening

**1**   You are going to hear an interview with a young woman. Look at the newspaper headlines from two years earlier. One of the headlines has the correct facts, the rest are wrong.

a

### New star signs contract to make three films in a year

b

### 15-YEAR-OLD GIVEN LEADING ROLE IN NEW FILM

c

### Teenage film actor wins starring part

d

### GIRL WITH NO ACTING EXPERIENCE IS NEW FILM STAR

🎧 **25** Listen to the interview and tick the correct headline.

**2**   🎧 **25** Listen again and fill in the gaps. Stop the recording when you need to.

1  ... you've been world famous _since making_ the film *Starshine* two years ago ...

2  I got the part ................................................ no film experience.

3  The director chose me to play the part ................................................ several schools.

4  I had a long talk with my parents ................................................ it.

5  I was offered two more films ................................................ *Starshine* ...

6  ... but ................................................ far from home, I sometimes felt very lonely.

7  I'd be happy to do another film later, ................................................ booked up for the next few months.

8  It's actually a comedy, ................................................ called *Dark Days*.

**3**   What form of the verb follows *since*, *in spite of*, *despite*, *after*, *before* and *while* in the sentences in Exercise 2? ................................................

## B Grammar

### 1 *In spite of* and *despite*

These words:

◆ are used to link an <u>event</u> with a situation which makes the event unlikely:
   <u>I got the part</u> **in spite of** having no experience.
   <u>We enjoyed the trip</u> **despite** the bad weather.

◆ go at the beginning or in the middle of the sentence:
   **In spite of**/ **Despite** having little money, we were very happy.
   We were very happy **in spite of**/ **despite** having little money.
   If they go at the beginning, there is usually a comma in the middle of
   the sentence.

◆ are followed by *-ing* or a noun:
   He continued to work **in spite of**/ **despite being** ill.
   He continued to work **in spite of**/ **despite his illness**.

◆ are often followed by *the fact that* + subject + verb:
   I got the part **in spite of the fact that** I had no experience.
   **Despite the fact that** I had no experience, I got the part.

*In spite of* is more common in speaking than *despite*.

### 2 *But, although* and *though*

These words contrast two events or ideas. *Though* and *although* are slightly
stronger than *but*. *Though* is weaker than *although*, and is more common
in speaking.

*But* always goes in the middle of the sentence:
*I like making films **but** I'm really a stage actor.*

*Although* and *though* can go in the middle or at the beginning of
the sentence:
*I like making films **though**/ **although** I'm really a stage actor.*
***Though**/ **Although** I'm really a stage actor, I like making films.*
(notice the comma)

⚠ We can't use *though*/ *although* and *but* in the same sentence.
(**not** ~~Though/ Although I'm really a stage actor, but I like making films.~~)

## 3 *Even though* and *even if*

These words emphasise a contrast. We use *even though* when we are certain about something:

*She was given the part **even though** she had no experience.* (= the speaker knows Gemma had no experience)

We use *even if* when we are not certain about our facts:

*I'll support my team **even if** they don't win the Cup.* (= I don't know whether they'll win the Cup, but I'll support them anyway.)

## 4 Participle clauses

The *-ing* form or the past participle:
- are used to combine two sentences when both sentences have the same subject.
- can replace the subject + verb of the first sentence:

*I **work** far from home. + **I** sometimes feel lonely.* → ***Working** far from home, **I** sometimes feel lonely.*
*Gemma **was asked** about the play. + Gemma* → ***Asked** about the play, **Gemma** said it was said it was great.*                       *great.*

These structures are more common in writing than in speaking.

**The *-ing* form**:
- can replace an active verb:
  ***We were** short of time.* → ***Being** short of time, **we** had to run for the bus.*
  *+ **We** had to run for the bus.*

- links two things happening at about the same time (present or past):
  ***The girl used** all her strength.* → ***Using** all her strength, **the girl** pushed open the
  *+ **The girl** pushed open the heavy doors.*    *heavy doors.*

**The past participle**:
- can replace a passive verb:
  ***The girls were refused** entry to the club.* → ***Refused** entry to the club, **the girls** walked
  *+ **The girls** walked slowly home.*    *slowly home.*

- links two connected events or situations:
  *'**Greensleeves**' **was written** in the* → ***Written** in the sixteenth century, '**Greensleeves**'
  *sixteenth century.*    *is still a famous song.*
  *+ '**Greensleeves**' is still a famous song.*

## 5 *Before* and *after* + *-ing*

*Before* and *after* + *-ing*:
- ◆ show the order in which things happen.
- ◆ are used to combine two sentences only when both sentences have the same subject.
- ◆ can replace the subject + verb of either sentence:

*I had* a long talk with my parents. (= first event)
+ *I accepted* the part. (= second event)

→ *I had a long talk with my parents **before** **accepting** the part.* or
*I accepted the part **after having** a long talk with my parents.*

These words can go at the beginning or in the middle of the sentence.
If they go at the beginning, there is usually a comma in the middle:
***Before accepting** the part, I had a long talk with my parents.*
***After having** a long talk with my parents, I accepted the part.*

These structures are more common in writing than in speaking.

## 6 *When, while* and *since* + *-ing*

We can use *when, while* and *since* + *-ing* in a similar way to *before* and *after* + *-ing*.

***When* + *-ing*** links two actions happening at the same time:
***When leaving** the train, passengers should ensure that they have all their possessions with them.*
*It's important to make a good impression **when starting** a new job.*

***While* + *-ing*** links a longer action to an action which happens in the middle of it:
*I was offered two more films **while making** 'Starshine'.*
***While making** 'Starshine', I was offered two more films.*

***Since* + *-ing*** links an ongoing situation or action to the event or action when it began:
***Since leaving** school, he has made a number of trips abroad.*
*She hasn't been in touch once **since moving** to New York.*

## C Grammar exercises

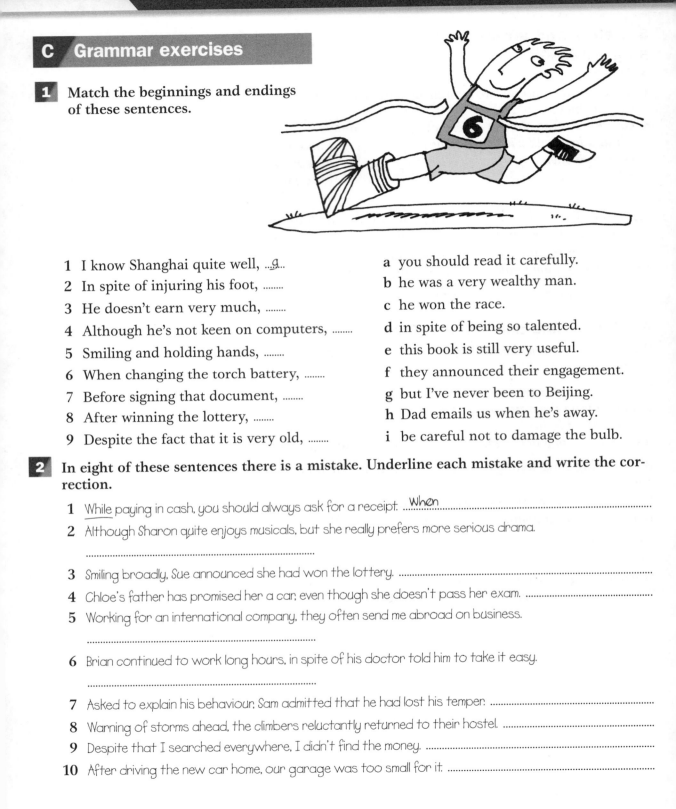

**1** Match the beginnings and endings of these sentences.

1 I know Shanghai quite well, ...g...
2 In spite of injuring his foot, ........
3 He doesn't earn very much, ........
4 Although he's not keen on computers, ........
5 Smiling and holding hands, ........
6 When changing the torch battery, ........
7 Before signing that document, ........
8 After winning the lottery, ........
9 Despite the fact that it is very old, ........

a you should read it carefully.
b he was a very wealthy man.
c he won the race.
d in spite of being so talented.
e this book is still very useful.
f they announced their engagement.
g but I've never been to Beijing.
h Dad emails us when he's away.
i be careful not to damage the bulb.

**2** In eight of these sentences there is a mistake. Underline each mistake and write the correction.

1 <u>While</u> paying in cash, you should always ask for a receipt. ....When....................................................

2 Although Sharon quite enjoys musicals, but she really prefers more serious drama.

........................................................

3 Smiling broadly, Sue announced she had won the lottery. ...............................................

4 Chloe's father has promised her a car, even though she doesn't pass her exam. ...............................

5 Working for an international company, they often send me abroad on business.

........................................................

6 Brian continued to work long hours, in spite of his doctor told him to take it easy.

........................................................

7 Asked to explain his behaviour, Sam admitted that he had lost his temper. ...........................................

8 Warning of storms ahead, the climbers reluctantly returned to their hostel. ...........................................

9 Despite that I searched everywhere, I didn't find the money. ...............................................

10 After driving the new car home, our garage was too small for it. ...............................................

**3** Combine each pair of sentences, using the *-ing* form or the past participle.

1 Arnold was faced with a difficult decision. Arnold decided to consult his boss.
Faced with a difficult decision, Arnold decided to consult his boss.

2 The singer waved to her fans. The singer got into her car.
Waving to her fans, the singer got into her car.

3 Simon grumbled about the amount of homework he had. Simon took out his grammar book.

4 The scientist felt very excited about her latest discovery. The scientist invited the journalists into the laboratory.

5 The children were puzzled by what they had heard. The children asked their teacher what it meant.

6 Wendy was a sensible girl. Wendy didn't panic when she cut her hand.

7 Paul heard cries for help. Paul dived into the water.

8 This CD was released only last week. This CD is already at the top of the charts.

**4** Complete these sentences using your own ideas.

1 I quite enjoy playing tennis, in spite of the fact that I usually lose.
2 Although Agnes is only thirteen, she ...........................................
3 While painting my room, ...........................................
4 ........................................... before attempting to run a marathon.
5 Dressed only in his underwear, ...........................................
6 I hardly ever receive any letters even though ...........................................
7 Waving ........................................... the football fans cheered their team loudly.
8 They insist they'll have a barbecue even if ...........................................
9 My grandfather swims in the lake every day despite ...........................................
10 Since arriving in this country, ...........................................

## D Exam practice

⚠ This task tests grammar from the rest of the book as well as the grammar in this unit.

### Use of English

For questions **1–15**, read the text below and think of the word which best fits each space. Use only **one** word in each space. There is an example at the beginning (**0**).

#### ANTARCTICA

It is probable that until two hundred years (**0**) ........ago........, Antarctica had never been seen by any human eyes. The first people who are known to have seen it (**1**) ..................... hunters on ships in 1819. Two years later, one of them (**2**) ..................... to land there even (**3**) ..................... conditions prevented him from exploring very far. Larger scientific expeditions later came to the Antarctic to find out more. By the end of the nineteenth century they had succeeded in mapping the coast of the continent, in (**4**) ..................... of the fact that Antarctica is almost entirely covered by a thick (**5**) ..................... of ice which in places stretches far (**6**) ..................... the edge of the land onto the sea.

There was something else which attracted people to Antarctica (**7**) ..................... scientific research. This was the South Pole. A number of attempts to reach it were (**8**) ..................... in the early years of the twentieth century, (**9**) ..................... the first person to get there was the Norwegian, Roald Amundsen, in 1911. Travelling with dogs (**10**) ..................... pull the sledges (**11**) ..................... carried his party's supplies, he arrived (**12**) ..................... the pole five weeks before his rivals, a British group (**13**) ..................... by Robert Scott.

(**14**) ..................... the terrible weather conditions, many nations now have scientific bases on Antarctica, (**15**) ..................... out research on a great range of subjects.

## Grammar focus task

**These extracts are from the text. Without looking back at the text, match the beginnings (1–5) and endings (a–e).**

1 ... one of them managed to land there even though ..b..

2 ... they had succeeded in mapping the coast of the continent, in spite of the fact that ........

3 A number of attempts to reach it were made in the early years of the twentieth century, ........

4 Travelling with dogs to pull the sledges that carried his party's supplies, ........

5 Despite the terrible weather conditions, ........

a Antarctica is almost entirely covered by a thick layer of ice

b conditions prevented him from exploring very far.

c many nations now have scientific bases on Antarctica ...

d but the first person to get there was the Norwegian, Roald Amundsen ...

e he arrived at the pole five weeks before his rivals ...

## Writing

You have been asked to write an article called 'My hero' for your class newspaper, about a man or woman whose achievements you admire. Write your **article** in **120–180** words.

## Writing hints

**This task gives you a chance to practise:**
describing how someone overcame problems.
using *because, in spite of / despite, although / but, even though.*

**Useful words and expressions**
*to accept, to bear, to carry on, to cope with, to put up with, to refuse, to succeed*

# Key

## Entry test

If you have the wrong answer, see the units indicated for more information.

1  A  (➤ Unit 1)
2  B  (➤ Unit 1)
3  C  (➤ Unit 2)
4  B  (➤ Unit 2)
5  A  (➤ Unit 3)
6  B  (➤ Unit 3)
7  B  (➤ Unit 4)
8  C  (➤ Unit 4)
9  B  (➤ Unit 5)
10  A  (➤ Unit 5)
11  A  (➤ Unit 6)
12  B  (➤ Unit 6)
13  A  (➤ Unit 7)
14  C  (➤ Unit 7)
15  A  (➤ Unit 8)
16  C  (➤ Unit 8)
17  A  (➤ Unit 9)
18  C  (➤ Unit 9)
19  A  (➤ Unit 10)
20  C  (➤ Unit 10)
21  A  (➤ Unit 11)
22  B  (➤ Unit 11)
23  C  (➤ Unit 12)
24  B  (➤ Unit 12)
25  C  (➤ Unit 13)
26  B  (➤ Unit 13)
27  A  (➤ Unit 14)
28  C  (➤ Unit 14)
29  C  (➤ Unit 15)
30  A  (➤ Unit 15)
31  B  (➤ Unit 16)
32  C  (➤ Unit 16)
33  B  (➤ Unit 17)
34  A  (➤ Unit 17)
35  A  (➤ Unit 18)
36  C  (➤ Unit 18)
37  C  (➤ Unit 19)
38  B  (➤ Unit 19)
39  C  (➤ Unit 20)
40  B  (➤ Unit 20)
41  C  (➤ Unit 21)
42  B  (➤ Unit 21)
43  A  (➤ Unit 22)
44  B  (➤ Unit 22)
45  A  (➤ Unit 23)
46  A  (➤ Unit 23)
47  A  (➤ Unit 24)
48  B  (➤ Unit 24)
49  A  (➤ Unit 25)
50  B  (➤ Unit 25)

## Unit 1

### A: Context listening

2  Millie is phoning to ask Lisa if she wants her to buy a CD.
3  2 She buys new clothes.
   3 She's looking for a new skirt / one of those new skirts.
   4 She's wearing a pair of old jeans.
   5 She's doing her homework.
   6 She looks for a special CD.
   7 She's looking at the CD (that Lisa wants).
   8 She wants Millie to buy the CD.
4  1 The present simple.
   2 The present continuous.
   3 2 and 6.
   4 1, 3, 4, 5 and 7.
   5 No. It is in the present simple but is not a regular action.

### C: Grammar exercises

1  2 *correct*  3 ~~I'm not having~~ I don't have / haven't got  4 *correct*  5 ~~I'm liking~~ I like  6 ~~I'm weighing~~ I weigh  7 ~~is going~~ goes  8 *correct* (➤ Grammar, parts 1–3)

2  2 are you wearing; looks  3 smells  4 like; don't fit  5 are you thinking  6 have; means; don't understand  7 Do / Can you see; 're (are) looking; Do you recognise; seem; 're (are) coming  8 are you doing; 'm (am) just making; don't want; are waiting; 're (are) getting  9 prefer (➤ Grammar, parts 1–3)

3  2 are enjoying  3 cost  4 are staying  5 have  6 don't like  7 serve  8 never eat  9 don't feel  10 have  11 are having  12 are visiting  13 love  14 behave  15 smile  16 says  17 is always showing (*shows* is correct but does not make clear that she is criticising)  18 come  19 realise  20 are taking (➤ Grammar, parts 1–3)

4  *Sample answers:*
   2 I listen to pop music every day.
   3 My aunt's visiting us at the moment.
   4 I have a shower before breakfast, but I don't get dressed.
   5 We're revising for our exams this term.
   6 I go on holiday once a year.
   7 I play squash or go swimming most weekends.
   (➤ Grammar, parts 1–3)

### D: Exam practice
### Listening

1 B  2 A  3 C  4 A  5 B  6 C  7 A

### Grammar focus task

2 think  3 he's actually doing  4 enjoy  5 goes  6 do you do  7 form

**Writing** *Sample answer:*

Dear Clara,

Well, here I am in England! I'm missing you a lot but I'm staying with a pleasant family who make me feel welcome.

This is a typical small town, with pretty parks. There are some nice shops too.

Some things are quite strange, though. All the shops shut at 5.30 and so do the cafés. The evenings are light, because it's summer, but the city centre is silent after six o'clock. People stay at home in the evening and work in their gardens, they don't walk about the streets.

Another difference here is meals. This family eats a big breakfast, a small lunch and a big early dinner. I'm having real problems with this! And it isn't the custom here to say anything at the beginning of the meal, like 'Enjoy your meal' for example. I always want to say something, but they tell me it's not necessary, they have no traditional way of saying this.

But don't worry, I'm enjoying my holiday and I'm beginning to make some friends. I'll write again soon.

Much love,

Blanca

## Unit 2

### A: Context listening

2  2 J  3 J  4 G  5 G  6 G  7 M  8 J
3  1 He went to London, went to the cinema, saw a famous footballer and went to a club.
   2 The past simple.
   3 She used to collect autographs, she would go up to town alone, she used to scream at pop concerts.
   4 Yes.
4  1 were travelling  2 were queuing
   3 was buying; were walking
5  The past continuous.

### C: Grammar exercises

1  2 found  3 explained  4 was  5 knew  6 wrote  7 seemed  8 ate  9 drank  10 got  11 learnt / learned  12 found  13 fed  14 gave  15 tied  16 went  17 spoke  18 met  19 read  20 had  21 spread  22 came (➢ Grammar, part 1)
2  2 travelled; always kept  3 saw; was waiting; did not / didn't see  4 filled; gave  5 was working; met; looked  6 finished; was always cancelling (*always cancelled* is also possible but it doesn't emphasise that Simon was annoyed by her behaviour)  7 was hoping; didn't get (➢ Grammar, parts 1–2)
3  2 used to feel  3 met  4 was walking  5 told  6 were breaking  7 were sitting  8 realised  9 didn't want  10 moved  11 am not used  12 thought (➢ Grammar, parts 1–3)

4  2 are used to  3 is used to  4 isn't used to / wasn't used to  5 Are you getting used to / Have you got used to / Are you used to  6 got used to (➢ Grammar, part 3)
5  *Sample answers:* 2 I didn't finish till ten.  3 ran out of the room.  4 spend a whole morning climbing trees.  5 we saw a teacher from our school.  6 travelled by train / used to travel by train / would travel by train  7 was revising for my exams.  8 borrowing his brother's car. (➢ Grammar, parts 1–3)

### D: Exam practice
### Use of English

1 A  2 B  3 C  4 C  5 A  6 D  7 A  8 C  9 A  10 B  11 D  12 C  13 B  14 A  15 C

### Grammar focus task

2 became  3 began  4 came  5 fell  6 found  7 went  8 held  9 led  10 made  11 rang  12 spent

### Writing *Sample answer:*

When I was about five, we moved from the country to the city. In those days, there was little traffic in the countryside. My friends and I used to play on the open ground between the houses. In the city we had a garden, and my mother said to me, 'You must play in the garden. Don't go outside.' I didn't understand why she said this, but I obeyed.

One day I was playing in our garden when I saw one of my friends. She was walking along the other side of the road with her father. I rushed out of the garden to meet them. A lorry was coming down the road and it nearly hit me. Luckily, I wasn't hurt. But I was very frightened.

I now realise that I forgot my mother's instructions because I didn't understand the reason for them. I clearly remember thinking about this at the time. Now I always give an explanation when I tell young children to do something.

## Unit 3

### A: Context listening

2  They live next door to each other. Mike plays a saxophone and Lucy can't concentrate on her work.
3  2 I've been at the gym.
   3 I still haven't finished it.
   4 I started it last week.
   5 I never enjoyed studying history.
   6 I've lived next door since June.
   7 I've lived here for two years.
   8 Nobody's ever complained before.
4  1 The past simple.
   2 The present perfect.
   3 3, 6 and 7.
   4 1, 4 and 5.

## C: Grammar exercises

1 2 h 3 d 4 f 5 c 6 b 7 i 8 e 9 a 10 g (➤ Grammar, part 1)

2 2 slept 3 has grown 4 sent; hasn't replied 5 Did you learn
6 bought; 've (have) used 7 have you had 8 's (has) just
arrived 9 've (have) never seen 10 dreamt 11 met
12 did you get; haven't noticed (➤ Grammar, part 1)

3 2 arrived 3 felt / was 4 have already made 5 took / drove
6 went / swam 7 enjoyed / loved / liked 8 've (have) learnt
9 haven't been 10 've (have) had 11 went 12 played
(➤ Grammar, part 1)

4 2 have you been playing 3 We've played 4 we haven't
finished 5 Have you tried 6 You've been playing
7 We've read 8 we've already started 9 we've booked
(➤ Grammar, part 2)

## D: Exam practice
### Reading

1 C 2 D 3 G 4 A 5 6 B

### Grammar focus task

2 fell 3 didn't think 4 have had to 5 've been 6 didn't believe
7 has got 8 finished 9 took 10 has read

### Writing Sample answer:

Dear Mr Kennedy

I would like to apply for a job at Treetops Activity Centre. I am
19 years old and I would prefer to work as a cook or a sports
leader.

My parents own a restaurant and I have helped in the kitchen
there since I was 14 years old. I have cooked all kinds of meals
and have also worked as a waitress.

I am keen on sports. I was in the school swimming and
basketball teams and I have continued to play basketball with my
friends at weekends. I also love playing tennis. I have studied
English since I was eight years old and I spent the summer in
England when I was 15. I also speak fluent Italian, of course.

I have had lots of experience of looking after children as I
have four younger brothers and sisters. I am now at college
studying engineering and unfortunately my term does not finish
until 15 June but I am available to start work then.

I look forward to hearing from you.

Yours sincerely

Giulia Mantovani

**Note:** *As this is a letter of application the verbs are all in
their full forms (I have, not I've). We use the full forms of
verbs when we write formal letters.*

## Unit 4

### A: Context listening

2 He's been painting his room. His mother is angry because
there is paint on the carpet.

3 2 'd painted 3 ran out of 4 was 5 'd been 6 'd done
7 'd finished 8 'd been driving 9 broke down

4 1 3 happened after 1 and 2. He uses the past perfect for 1 and
2, and the past simple for 3.
2 4 happened after 5, 6 and 7. He uses the past simple for 4,
and the past perfect for 5, 6 and 7.
3 8 happened first. She uses the past perfect continuous for 8,
and the past simple for 9.

## C: Grammar exercises

1 2 hadn't been learning / studying 3 had been planning
4 'd (had) been worrying 5 'd (had) been waiting 6 'd (had)
been sending 7 hadn't been playing 8 'd (had) been saving
9 had they been looking (➤ Grammar, part 2)

2 2 No 3 Yes: it had been snowing 4 No 5 No 6 No
7 Yes: they'd been arguing 8 No (➤ Grammar, parts 1–2)

3 2 came; fainted; hadn't (had not) seen 3 had begun; arrived
4 had you been applying; got 5 Had you ever done; built
6 didn't (did not) see; 'd (had) gone 7 sat; 'd (had) left
8 'd (had) been driving; realized 9 went; stopped; looked 10
'd (had) washed; hung 11 discovered; 'd (had) believed
(➤ Grammar, parts 1–2)

4 2 'd (had) been playing 3 'd (had) ever had 4 'd (had) been
practising 5 'd (had) been moving 6 'd (had) gone
7 'd (had) arranged 8 didn't (did not) answer
9 came 10 banged 11 'd (had) been phoning
12 hadn't (had not) heard 13 arrived 14 'd (had) forgotten
(➤ Grammar, parts 1–2)

## D: Exam practice
### Reading

1 C 2 A 3 B 4 A 5 D 6 D

### Grammar focus task

2 was 3 'd been writing 4 had just sent 5 had 6 'd heard
7 gathered

### Writing Sample answer:

I pushed open the door. The house was empty but I could see
that someone had been there and had only just left. I had been
walking in the forest and I had lost my way so I had come to the
house to ask directions. To my surprise I noticed that the table
had been laid ready for a meal with glasses and plates and
somebody had been cooking because there was a lovely smell
coming from the kitchen. I ate a few spoonfuls from a saucepan
and it was delicious so I had a few more. I looked round the
house but there was nobody there.

Suddenly there was a loud noise from the back of the house. I
held my breath and tiptoed towards the door. I was too late. A
large angry man appeared in front of me at the door. He shouted
at me. I tried to explain that I had found the door open and
wanted to ask for directions. He came towards me and I thought
he might hit me so I ran away as fast as I could. But at least I had
tasted his dinner.

# Unit 5

## A: Context listening

2  1 c  2 b  3 d  4 a  Tom is a journalist.

3  2 starts  3 arrives  4 'm playing  5 'm flying  6 'm having
7 won't be  8 'll get  9 'll have  10 will be  11 won't be
12 will live

4  1 1, 2 and 3; the present simple.
2 4, 5 and 6; the *will*-future.
3 7, 8, and 9; the present continuous.
4 10, 11 and 12; the *will*-future.

## C: Grammar exercises

1  2 doesn't leave  3 stops  4 doesn't arrive  5 are staying
6 are spending  7 doesn't go  8 are having  9 leaves  10 arrives
(➤ Grammar, parts 1–2)

2  2 is leaving  3 'm (am) giving; are you giving; 'll (will)
probably get  4 're (are) moving; 'll (will) come  5 will not
continue; will not recover  6 'll (will) have  7 is staying
8 'll (will) have  9 Are you doing; is arriving; 'm (am) driving
10 'll (will) get (➤ Grammar, parts 2–3)

3  *Sample answers:*
1 Rebecca Jones will be pleased that Anna has invited her
to visit.
One of the cousins will reply to Anna and she will realise
her mistake.
Anna will be angry with herself when she finds out what
she has done and she will have to explain what happened to
her cousins.
2 There will be an argument. The teachers will insist that
the hotel manager finds them rooms. The hotel manager
will apologise.
The hotel manager will offer to find them rooms in another
hotel. He will order taxis to take them there.
The teachers and teenagers will be angry because they are
tired. (➤ Grammar, part 3)

4  2 is going to see / is seeing the doctor  3 will be 80  4 starts
5 'll (shall / will) be a teacher  6 'll (will) be flying / sitting in
an aeroplane  7 ends / finishes  8 'll (will) be skiing  9 're (are)
going  10 will lend / give me (➤ Grammar, parts 1–4)

## D: Exam practice
### Listening

1 coffee bar  2 Order / Ask for  3 7.15 / (a) quarter past seven
4 deputy manager  5 waterfall  6 (flour) mill  7 (coal) mine
8 lamps  9 windsurfing  10 strong boots

### Grammar focus task

1  2 're going  3 're travelling  4 'll probably eat  5 're making
6 'll be  7 won't be able to  8 'll probably stop  9 'll need

2  The verbs in 2, 3 and 5 are in the present continuous because
these things have already been arranged.

## Writing *Sample answer:*

Dear Headteacher,

Our college is holding an open day next month. We would like
to invite your pupils to attend.

The day begins at 10 am. Students are giving tours of the
college every 20 minutes. We are also performing a gymnastics
display, a rock concert and some drama so that our visitors can
see the kind of activities we do here. We are preparing displays in
the art room of our paintings and drawings and the gardens will
be open for visitors to enjoy. Your pupils will also be able to try
our excellent sports facilities and at the end of the day our
principal will be available to answer questions.

The canteen is open for coffee in the morning, from 12.00 to
1.30 for lunch and for tea in the afternoon.

We hope that lots of your pupils will come to our open day
and we look forward to welcoming them here.

Yours sincerely,

The students and staff

# Unit 6

## A: Context listening

2  Simon has come to interview the people on the island. Life on
the island is very tough.

3  2 Because they're fed up with the cold, the wind, the mud and
the rain.
3 As soon as possible.
4 They'll have survived longer than anyone else in a place like
Wildrock.
5 For nearly six months.
6 As soon as they find a restaurant.
7 Simon stays because the other people take his boat and
leave him!

4  1 1, 3, 6 and 7.
2 4 and 5.
3 2.

## C: Grammar exercises

1  *Sample answers:*
2 's (is) going to crash.  3 're (are) going to arrest him.
4 's (is) going to kiss him.  5 's (is) going to score a goal.
6 's (is) going to sink. (➤ Grammar, part 1)

2  2 The world's population will have doubled.  3 Computers will
have replaced most manual workers.  4 We will have used all
the oil resources on Earth.  5 Doctors will have discovered a
cure for AIDS.  6 Scientists will have invented new sources of
energy.  7 Sea temperatures will have risen by several degrees.
(➤ Grammar, part 3)

3  2 ~~we're going to get~~ we get  3 *correct*  4 ~~will have started~~ have
started  5 ~~you'll see~~ you see  6 *correct*  7 ~~she'll have found~~
she's (has) found (➤ Grammar, part 2)

4  2 The secretary will have been typing letters for four hours.
3 The manager will have been interviewing new staff for five
and a half hours.
4 The waitress will have been standing in the dining-room for
three hours.

5 The cleaner will have been vacuuming floors for seven hours.
(➤ Grammar, part 4)

5 2 's (is) going to be 3 're (are) going to stay 4 finds out
5 was going to wash 6 'm (am) going to look round
7 're (are) going to miss 8 gets 9 will have taken
10 'm (am) about to have / 'm (am) going to have
11 'm (am) going to write 12 were going to talk
13 'll (will) have finished 14 'll (will) have been working
15 'm (am) going to start / 'm (am) about to start
(➤ Grammar, parts 1–5)

## D: Exam practice
### Reading

1 E 2 A/C 3 A/C 4 B 5 C 6 A/E 7 A/E 8 D 9 A 10 D
11 B 12 D 13 C 14 E 15 A

### Grammar focus task

2 starts 3 do 4 will have taken 5 'm (am) 6 go 7 've (have) had
8 get

### Writing *Sample answer:*

Dear Mark,

Would you like to come on a weekend trip with me and two friends in ten days' time? Robin was going to come, but now she's in hospital, I'm sorry to say!

We've booked beds at the Woodlands Hostel, near the famous waterfall. On Saturday we're going to walk to the waterfall and perhaps have a picnic there. If we're not tired we're going to climb in the afternoon and then we're going to have a barbecue at the hostel in the evening. We need to take plenty of food. We also need sleeping bags. I can lend you one if you haven't got one. The hostel only charges £15 per night. We just have to spend half an hour a day helping with cleaning.

We are going to catch the 5.45 train on Friday and come back on Sunday afternoon. I know this is rather sudden but I really hope you can join us. I'm sure we're going to have a great time.

Let me know as soon as possible what you think.

Love,

Leah

## Unit 7

### A: Context listening

2 1 fitness centre 2 wildlife park 3 cleaner 4 music shop
3 1 You can become stronger, slimmer and more self-confident.
2 They're the fiercest lions, the funniest monkeys and the cleverest dolphins you've ever seen.
3 Because they have a full-time job and feel tired trying to keep the house clean.
4 Because they've got the greatest variety of CDs ever.
4 1 sensible; friendly; excellent 2 wonderful; the best; amazing; special 3 fresh; shining; (no) sticky; reasonable
4 astonishing; the latest; traditional; the most beautiful

## C: Grammar exercises

1 2 beautiful blue Chinese silk 3 magic gold 4 elegant long leather riding 5 tight yellow silk (➤ Grammar, part 4)

2 2 depressed 3 amazing 4 annoying 5 bored 6 interesting
7 excited 8 disgusting 9 relaxed (➤ Grammar, part 5)

3 2 ~~a leather old lovely one~~ a lovely old leather one 3 ~~a more earlier train~~ an earlier train 4 *correct* 5 ~~so expensive as~~ as expensive as 6 ~~rotten looked~~ looked rotten 7 ~~wasn't so enjoyable than~~ wasn't so / as enjoyable as 8 ~~small pretty peaceful~~ small, pretty and peaceful 9 ~~most far~~ the farthest
10 ~~boring~~ bored (➤ Grammar, parts 1–5)

4 2 as / so spacious as 3 more expensive than 4 worse
5 the smartest 6 the loveliest 7 the poorest 8 the most exhausted 9 the best 10 younger 11 as cheap as
12 nearer (➤ Grammar, parts 1–2)

## D: Exam practice
### Use of English

1 A 2 B 3 C 4 D 5 A 6 B 7 B 8 D 9 C 10 B 11 C 12 C 13 A
14 D 15 D

### Grammar focus task

2 old 3 college 4 good 5 different 6 small 7 young 8 longer
9 leisure 10 local

### Writing *Sample answer:*

My room is quite small. I have a special bed which is high up. I have to go up a little ladder to reach it. Under the bed I have a desk, where I do my homework, and a small bookshelf for reference books. There are two cupboards, one quite small, and one bigger one, where I keep all my clothes and other things.

The best improvement would be to have a bigger room, but that's not possible. So, I would like to have some new shelves with plenty of space for my CD player and all my CDs. I'd also like to have a giant noticeboard above my bed. I have lots of posters of my favourite singers and sports champions and I'd like to display them properly.

Lastly, I'd like to have my room painted in a better colour. It's pale blue at the moment. I'd like a more exciting colour, like red or purple. But it may be difficult to persuade my parents about that.

## Unit 8

### Context listening

2 1 stadium 2 spectator 3 whistle 4 ball 5 ground 6 quickly
7 goal 8 scored 9 loudly
3 2 in the city today; late 3 patiently in their seats 4 happily
5 steadily 6 heavily on the ground 7 rarely 8 quickly 9 well
10 Last week 11 often
4 *When:* finally; today; late; last week
*Where:* in the city; in their seats; on the ground
*How:* patiently; happily; steadily; heavily; quickly; well
*How often:* rarely; often

## C: Grammar exercises

**1** 2 gratefully 3 anxiously 4 easily 5 sincerely
(➤ Grammar, part 1)

**2** 2 complete 3 well 4 hard; fluent 5 awful 6 efficiently
7 normal 8 badly (➤ Grammar, parts 1–2)

**3** 2 Nowadays they rarely eat steak because it is so
expensive / They rarely eat steak because it is so expensive
nowadays. / They rarely eat steak nowadays because it is so
expensive.
3 My grandfather used to take us swimming in the lake in the
summer holidays. / In the summer holidays my grandfather
used to take us swimming in the lake.
4 There is usually a good film on TV on Sunday evenings.
5 My mother insisted that good manners are always terribly
important. / My mother always insisted that good manners are
terribly important. (➤ Grammar, part 5)

**4** 2 earlier 3 always 4 very / rather 5 skilfully 6 rather / very
7 hardly 8 stiffly 9 now 10 warmly (➤ Grammar, parts 1–5)

**5** 2 correct 3 careful carefully 4 never have bought have never
bought 5 correct 6 At Tony's garage I always have my car
repaired. I always have my car repaired at Tony's garage.
7 by next Friday to the library to the library by next Friday
8 speaks very well Spanish speaks Spanish very well
9 as easily than as easily as 10 hardly hard
(➤ Grammar, parts 1–5)

## D: Exam practice
## Use of English

1 scientific 2 equipment 3 qualifications 4 extremely
5 dangerously 6 calmly 7 unusually 8 announcement 9 luckily
10 amazing

## Grammar focus task

2 extremely, extreme 3 well, good 4 dangerously, dangerous
5 calmly, calm 6 hard, hard 7 unusually, (un)usual
8 luckily, lucky

## Writing *Sample answer:*

Music and Drama Festival

Ten local schools took part in the Festival last week. The
audience was entertained with several short plays and some
concerts in the city hall.

In the afternoon, there were three plays by primary schools.
The children all acted well but the children from the last school
spoke more quietly than the others and it was quite difficult to
hear them. Then children from a nursery school sang some songs.
They sang beautifully, but I'm sorry to say that some of the older
children in the audience behaved rather badly at that time.

After the interval, we saw some more drama, including a very
good comedy. We laughed continuously for forty minutes. There
was also a rather frightening play about a ghost. Some people
were looking nervously over their shoulders as they walked home!

The evening ended with a jazz concert by some high school
students. They played extremely well, and many people said
they were very impressed and that the students were as good as a
professional group.

## Unit 9

## A: Context listening

**2** Because Molly wasn't at home when he phoned.

**3** 2 Three. 3 Molly. 4 Peter. 5 By the college gate.

**4** 2 <u>Have</u> you <u>been</u> checking up on me? No, I <u>haven't</u>.
3 You <u>said</u> you'd be in tonight, <u>didn't</u> you? Yes, I <u>did</u>.
4 You <u>know</u> I love you, <u>don't</u> you? Of course I <u>do</u>.
5 And <u>do</u> you <u>love</u> me? You <u>know</u> I <u>do</u>.
6 And you'll always love me, <u>won't</u> you? Of course I <u>will</u>.
7 <u>Let's</u> meet by the college gate, <u>shall</u> we? Yes, <u>let's</u>.

## C: Grammar exercises

**1** 2 do we? have we? 3 your sister lives your sister live 4 you
can't can't you 5 correct 6 prefer you to do you prefer to
7 haven't you? didn't you? 8 correct 9 is Julie's brother look
like is Julie's brother like / does Julie's brother look like
(➤ Grammar, parts 1–4)

**2** *Sample answers:*
3 How long do you spend on your homework?
4 Have you ever tried windsurfing?
5 What do you usually do on Sunday evenings?
6 How often do you see your grandparents?
7 Did you enjoy the party last weekend?
8 Why were you late for school this morning?
(➤ Grammar, parts 1 and 3)

**3** 2 Where was he born?
3 Who did he telephone?
4 When did he telephone her / Shirley?
5 How many children do they have / have they got?
6 Why is she really pleased?
7 Who is looking forward to welcoming them back to Farley?
(➤ Grammar, part 3)

**4** 2 did they 3 wouldn't you 4 haven't I 5 shall we
6 could it 7 didn't they 8 won't she 9 can we
10 don't you (➤ Grammar, part 4)

**5** 2 c 3 h 4 g 5 a 6 f 7 b 8 e (➤ Grammar, part 5)

## D: Exam practice
## Listening

1 B 2 C 3 A 4 A 5 C 6 B 7 A 8 C

## Grammar focus task

2 did I 3 don't you 4 doesn't it 5 wasn't it 6 can't I 7 aren't I

## Writing *Sample answer:*

Dear Michael,

I have just received your name and address as a penfriend.
My name is Beatriz Lopez. I'm seventeen and I'm Spanish. In
fact, I'm living in the United States at the moment because my
father has a job here. He's teaching a course at a university here.
My mother is working for a radio station and my brother and I
are at school.

Can you write and tell me some information about yourself?
How old are you? What do you look like? Are you a student or do

you have a job? Do you have any special hobbies? I play the piano and the guitar and I like surfing the web.

I also like playing tennis and volleyball, although I'm not very good at either of them. Do you enjoy sport? What teams do you support? I support Real Madrid of course!

Next year we'll return to Spain and perhaps I'll visit England and meet you.

I hope you'll reply to me soon.

With best wishes,

Beatriz

## Unit 10

### A: Context listening

2 *Sample answers:*
   1 She's a sales executive. 2 He works for a garage. / He's a mechanic. / He drives a recovery truck. 3 He delivers pizzas. He's a pizza delivery man. 4 She's a taxi driver.

3 2 Travel. 3 Her health. 4 Fruit. 5 When they run out of petrol. 6 The police. 7 Insurance 8 He needs cash. 9 Chemistry. 10 The traffic. 11 Food and clothing. 12 There's a lot of unemployment.

4 1 Biscuits or sweets. 2 At a garage. 3 Pizzas. 4 Traffic jams. 5 A job with a reasonable salary. 6 For three years. 7 She's got three children / kids.

5 The nouns in Exercise 3 are uncountable; the nouns in Exercise 4 are countable.

### C: Grammar exercises

1a 2 cards 3 paper / glass 4 shoppers 5 glass 6 meat 7 tools 8 clothes 9 rice 10 books / paper / luggage

 b *Sample answers:*
   1 loaf / slice 2 lump / sheet / block 3 drop / litre 4 plank / splinter / block 5 speck (➤ Grammar, part 1)

2 *Always countable:* experiment; hobby; journey
   *Always uncountable:* accommodation; advice; homework; information; leisure; luck; scenery; traffic
   *Can be countable or uncountable:* cheese; coffee; experience; glass; meat; time
   (➤ Grammar, part 1)

3 2 the 3 the 4 the 5 the 6 a 7 a 8 the 9 the 10 the 11– 12 – (➤ Grammar, part 2)

4 1 Birmingham Airport 2 the Mediterranean; Naples; Corsica 3 the Sahara; the Andes; Paris 4 a ski instructor; Switzerland 5 a terrible journey; Peterborough station (➤ Grammar, part 3)

5 We had *a* great trip to ~~the~~ France last weekend. We went to *the* little hotel that you recommended and it was very pleasant. *The food* at the hotel *wasn't* so good, as you warned us, but we strolled down to *the* city centre on Saturday evening and had *a* lovely meal there. In fact, we ate so much for ~~the~~ dinner that we didn't want ~~a~~ breakfast on Sunday! Thanks again for the advice and *information*. Now I must unpack and do the *washing*. (➤ Grammar, parts 1–3)

## D: Exam practice
### Use of English

1 ✓ 2 the 3 an 4 who 5 the 6 ✓ 7 and 8 down 9 they 10 a 11 ✓ 12 have 13 to 14 ✓ 15 ✓

### Grammar focus task

2 B 3 U 4 U 5 C 6 U 7 C 8 U

### Writing *Sample answer:*

Many people nowadays are worried about their figures, so lots of us want to lose weight. Unfortunately, this is not always easy because so much of our food is not really good for us. For example, fast food, such as burgers and crisps, contains lots of fat.

Some people think that the best way to control your weight is to eat only lettuce and be miserable! In fact this is not at all good for you. It's much better to eat a diet which consists of lots of different sorts of food.

Choose good quality bread, rice, pasta and potatoes for energy. Make sure you eat lots of delicious fruit and vegetables. Meat, fish, cheese and eggs are also good but you don't need so much of these. It's most important to eat a balanced diet. If you do this and take regular exercise, you'll find it's easy to eat well and stay healthy.

## Unit 11

### A: Context listening

2 The woman went to the beach last year (picture *a*). The man would probably prefer the quiet mountain holiday (picture *c*).

3 2 myself; of mine 3 Neither 4 by myself 5 each other 6 somewhere 7 None

### C: Grammar exercises

1 2 there is 3 It is 4 there are 5 There are 6 there are 7 It is 8 It is 9 there is 10 it is (➤ Grammar, part 5)

2 2 *correct* 3 ~~the car of my teacher~~ my teacher's car 4 ~~on myself~~ by myself / on my own 5 ~~enjoyed us when~~ enjoyed ourselves when 6 ~~mothers'~~ mother's 7 ~~the leg~~ his leg 8 *correct* 9 ~~friends of him~~ friends of his 10 *correct* (➤ Grammar, parts 1–3)

3 2 each other 3 every 4 Each 5 everyone 6 Everyone 7 all the 8 one another 9 The whole 10 nobody (➤ Grammar, parts 6–8)

4 2 Both John and Rob have an earring.
   3 Neither Pete nor John has a moustache.
   4 All of them have short hair / wear glasses.
   5 They all have short hair / wear glasses.
   6 None of them has / have a beard / is bald.
   *Sample answers:*
   7 Both my mother and my sister have dark hair.
   8 Neither my father nor my grandfather is bald.
   9 All of my friends live quite nearby.
   10 None of my family wears / wear glasses.
   (➤ Grammar, parts 7 and 9)

**230**

**D: Exam practice**
**Use of English**

1 everyone / everybody  2 own  3 soon  4 there  5 mine
6 the  7 else  8 it / mine  9 when / if / whenever  10 with  11 than
12 Every  13 what  14 Neither  15 both

**Grammar focus task**

2 a name of my own  3 a close friend of mine
4 somebody else  5 all kinds of  6 neither of them seemed to
mind  7 they both agreed

**Writing** *Sample answer:*

People travel nowadays from one side of the earth to the other. It
is possible to go anywhere you want and it only takes a few hours
because of aeroplanes. This is good for tourists because they can
visit places which are very different to their own countries and
have a good holiday.

On the one hand, most countries welcome tourists because
they bring money, and tourism gives people jobs so both the
visitors and the local people benefit. On the other hand, there are
some places which have been completely spoilt and this is not
good for the people who live there. Travelling also brings
pollution and damages the environment.

International travel helps trade between countries and makes
the world a smaller place. This is very important for business and
the economy of most countries. By trading with one another,
people from different countries get to know one another and
learn one another's languages.

## Unit 12

**A: Context listening**

2  He's a chef at the Grand Hotel.
3  2 None.  3 It's his day off.  4 He has two days off every week
    instead of one.  5 He offers to show Alice the kitchens.
4  2 c 3 a 4 g 5 i 6 j 7 b 8 f 9 h 10 d
5  *Needn't* and *must* aren't followed by *to*.

**C: Grammar exercises**

1  2 doesn't have to  3 mustn't  4 'll (will) have to  5 has to
   6 didn't have to  7 must  8 Do you have to  9 mustn't
   10 must  11 had to  12 have to  13 must  14 don't have to
   (➤ Grammar, parts 1–2)
2  2 f 3 e 4 d 5 a 6 h 7 c 8 b (➤ Grammar, parts 2–3)
3  2 worn his latest designer clothes.
   3 stand in the queue.
   4 carry his luggage.
   5 walk from the car park.
   6 got angry with his driver.
   (➤ Grammar, part 3)
4  2 You needn't / don't need to / don't have to phone me before
    you come.
   3 Students must / need to buy a good dictionary.
   4 You shouldn't have taken money from my purse without
    asking.

5 I didn't need to drive to the station to pick up my sister.
6 You should help me (to) do the washing-up.
7 Students mustn't smoke in the canteen.
8 She needn't have turned the music down.
9 She shouldn't make promises which she doesn't keep.
10 You don't have to / don't need to / needn't give the tour
    guide a tip.
   (➤ Grammar, parts 1–3)

**D: Exam practice**
**Reading**

1 G  2 B  3 C  4 D  5 H  6 A  7 F

**Grammar focus task**

2 The first thing you must address is tiredness.
3 You should do a session of exercise once or twice a week in
the evenings.
4 ... walking or tennis have to be kept up for at least an hour ...
5 ... you should choose something which you like doing.
6 ... you must do it until you get so used to doing it that you
miss it when you don't do it.
7 ... you need to keep reminding yourself of the advantages.
8 ... you don't need to behave in the same way.

**Writing** *Sample answer:*

Dear Chris,

It was good to get your letter and I'm really looking forward to
seeing you here.

About this hostel, I should tell you that it's all right, but not
very luxurious. You don't need to bring towels or sheets, but you
need to have warm clothes, because the heating isn't very good.
There's a coffee machine, so we can have hot drinks at any time,
but if you want meals, you have to order them the day before.
Personally, I usually eat out, or make a sandwich in my room.
Otherwise, the rules aren't too bad. You mustn't play music after
midnight, and you mustn't smoke. You have to pay rent in
advance of course. The hostel is locked at midnight, so if you
want to come in late, you have to get a key from the warden.
That's all really.

Don't forget to bring your swimming things because there's a
lovely pool here.

See you soon.

Love,

Nathan

## Unit 13

**A: Context listening**

2  2 Can you lend me your new jacket?
   3 Can you give me a lift to town now?
   4 Will you get me some new batteries for my Walkman?
   5 Can you collect me from the city centre at midnight
    tonight?
3  2 ✗ 3 ✗ 4 ✗ 5 ✓

4 Would you please give me a lift? Could you collect me?
She asks differently the second time because she wants to be
more polite.

## C: Grammar exercises

1  2 May / Could  3 How about / What about  4 could
5 Will / Can (*Could* is more formal)  6 can / could / 'll (will)
7 shall / why don't  8 could / would (*can* is less polite)
9 Can / May  10 Can / Will (≻ Grammar, parts 1–4)

2  *Sample answers (other versions possible):*
2 You should empty the wastepaper bin.
3 You ought to tidy the filing cabinet / put the papers in the
filing cabinet.
4 You could buy a lampshade.
5 You'd better take the coat off the chair.
6 You shouldn't leave the telephone there.
7 You should repair (the glass in) the window.
8 You'd better wash the coffee cups.
(≻ Grammar, part 5)

3  2 Can I do  3 Could I see  4 I'm afraid  5 You can't have
6 Would you exchange  7 You shouldn't have  8 You should
ask  9 Shall I ask  10 You'd better not  11 You could give
(≻ Grammar, parts 1–5)

4  *Sample answers:*
2 Shall I / I could / I'll / I can help you clean the flat.
3 You could buy her some perfume or a CD.
4 You shouldn't put so much salt on your food.
5 Could / Can you order this book for me, please?
6 Can I pay by credit card?
7 You should buy a watch.
8 Shall I / I'll / I can help you clear up.
9 Can you get me a film for my camera?
10 Could / Would you give me a lift home?
(≻ Grammar, parts 1–5)

## D: Exam practice
### Listening

1 F  2 D  3 A  4 E  5 C

## Grammar focus task

2 O  3 A  4 F  5 F  6 O  7 A  8 A

## Writing *Sample answer:*

The trip last term was successful. Twelve people came and we
travelled by minibus. The gallery had a lot of interesting
paintings in it and we enjoyed seeing the ones we had been
learning about. There were a few problems on the journey home,
but luckily no disasters.

My advice for future trip organisers:

You must make sure everyone knows the time and place to
meet the bus. On the journey, you ought to check that they all
know where they can buy lunch and you should also ask them if
they remember what time the bus will leave in the afternoon.
Some people are very forgetful!

You should allow extra time for the journey home. The traffic
may be heavy in the afternoon. If you've got a mobile phone,
you'd better take it with you. If there are delays, you could phone
to say that the bus will be late.

## Unit 14

### A: Context listening

2  The woman isn't his mother, but she could be his sister or his
girlfriend – Fiona and Clare aren't sure.

3  1 His mother.
2 The young woman can't be his mother because she's much
too young.
3 To walk across together and pretend they're looking in the
shop window.
4 Because the young woman could be Danny's new girlfriend.
5 She used to be Danny's girlfriend and she still likes him.

4  2 must be  3 can't be  4 might see  5 could be

5  1 Sentences 2 and 3.  2 Sentences 1, 4 and 5.

## C: Grammar exercises

1  2 couldn't / wasn't able to  3 can  4 was able to  5 will be able to
6 have never been able to  7 to be able to  8 could
9 couldn't / wasn't able to  10 can't  11 could / can
(≻ Grammar, parts 1 and 2)

2  *Sample answers:*
2 a tennis champion / fit
3 Greek / rich / married / Spanish
4 married / Spanish / Greek / rich
5 a film star / a schoolboy / 45 years old
6 rich / married / Spanish / Greek
7 45 years old / a schoolboy / a film star
8 fit / a tennis champion (≻ Grammar, part 2)

3  a 5, 6, 10
b 2, 3, 4, 7, 8, 9 (≻ Grammar, part 2)

4  2 should be swimming / must be swimming  3 can't / couldn't
have left  4 might not / may not have listened  5
might / may / could be  6 must be doing  7 should be  8 must
have grown
9 must be  10 might not / may not come (≻ Grammar, part 2)

5  *Sample answers:*
2 can't have stolen; she was with the other cleaners after 6.00.
3 could have stolen; he was there until 7.15 and alone after his
phone call.
4 must have stolen; he stayed after the gallery was shut and
he bought an expensive car.
5 may have stolen; she was alone there between 6.05 and
6.15 and nobody saw her leave.
6 couldn't have stolen; she was with the cleaners and they left
together.
(≻ Grammar, part 2)

## D: Exam practice
### Use of English

1 occasionally  2 confidently  3 assistants  4 delivery
5 instructions  6 attractive  7 fashionable  8 impression
9 actress / actor  10 unlikely

**Grammar focus task** *Sample answers:*

2 She can't be / couldn't be / might not be / may not be
3 She must be  4 She can't have / might not have  5 She could
be / might be / may be  6 She might have / may have / could have

**Writing** *Sample answer:*

I want to tell your readers about some letters I found in my attic.
Someone might know who wrote them. They were written by a
man who must have lived in the house. He must have worked on
the railway because he writes a lot about trains. He can't have
enjoyed his job very much because he writes about finding
another one. He might have owned the house or he might have
been a lodger.

He wrote the letters to a woman who must have been a
servant in another town. He must have been in love with her
because they are quite romantic. He can't have been rich because
he had to work very hard. He might have married her but I don't
know. He was called Walter and she was called Lily. They used to
meet on Sundays in the park on her day off.

## Unit 15

**A: Context listening**

2  1 d 2 b 3 a 4 c
3  2 were being  3 had been  4 is  5 were being  6 was  7 is
   8 was  9 had been  10 to be  11 has been  12 is
4  All of them.

**C: Grammar exercises**

1  2 ~~delaying~~ delayed  3 *correct*  4 ~~be~~ been  5 ~~prepare~~ prepared
   6 *correct*  7 ~~Was~~ Has (➤ Grammar, part 1)
2  2 had been done  3 are made / have been made / were made
   4 to be made  5 are being counted  6 to have been opened;
   was delivered  7 had been sacked  8 will be awarded
   (➤ Grammar, part 1)
3  2 has been (completely) crushed  3 has been destroyed  4 was
   captured  5 was broadcast  6 had been liberated  7 were called
   on  8 have been arrested  9 are being taken  10 will be put
   (➤ Grammar, part 1)
4  2 c; have it fixed  3 g; have it cleaned  4 a; 've (have) had it
   coloured.  5 d; have it redecorated  6 b; to have them taken in
   7 h; had it designed  8 f; 're (are) having it serviced
   (➤ Grammar, part 2)

**D: Exam practice**
**Use of English**

1 was given by the  2 in addition to going  3 flat was looked after
by  4 was not handed in  5 was accused of cheating by
6 we would often make  7 been promised his  8 the accident
could not be  9 to have / get my computer mended
10 isn't / aren't often allowed

**Grammar focus task**

Questions 1, 3, 4, 5, 7, 8, 9 and 10 test the passive.

**Writing** *Sample answer:*

Every summer there is a festival of art and music in the village
where I live. It is held at the beginning of July and people come
to the exhibitions and concerts from all over the region.

This is a good opportunity for us to bring tourists into the
village. The streets are decorated with little flags and coloured
lights are hung all round the central square. All the shops put
flowers in their windows.

Most of the concerts are held in the school hall. The art
exhibitions are usually in the old market house and sometimes
sculptures are displayed in the park. In the evenings, the village
seems to be full of people, going to concerts and sitting in the cafés.

On the Saturday night, there is a parade through the streets,
with music and dancing. It's a great change from the usual
sleepy atmosphere and everyone feels as if they are at a party.
When it is over, we are all tired, but we soon start planning for
the next year.

## Unit 16

**A: Context listening**

3  2 haven't seen  3 think I might  4 was  5 didn't sleep
   6 's; 's shining  7 can  8 'll spend  9 must get my
4  1 are you  2 think you're going  3 's the weather
   4 Can you see
5  When one speaker uses a present tense, the other reports with
   a past tense. When they use a past tense or the present
   perfect, it is reported with the past perfect.

**C: Grammar exercises**

1  2 could easily find another one.
   3 was going to travel round Africa.
   4 had lived there as a child.
   5 might get a part-time job there.
   6 was packing his bag.
   7 was really excited.
   8 would be away for a year.
   9 might stay longer.
   10 could come / go too.
   (➤ Grammar, part 1)
2  2 e 3 a 4 d 5 b 6 f (➤ Grammar, parts 3 and 5)
3  2 how old I was  3 I was studying  4 I came from
   5 whether / if I had worked  6 I played  7 whether / if I would
   work  8 whether / if I could start  9 whether / if I needed
   10 whether / if I would like (➤ Grammar, parts 1 and 5)
4  2 me (that) I could do well.
   3 if I studied every evening. / what time I went to bed. / if I
   had decided on a career yet.
   4 what time I went to bed. / if I studied every evening. / if I
   had decided on a career yet.
   5 (me) (that) I wouldn't get good marks.
   6 (that) I spent too much time with my friends.
   7 (me) if I had decided on a career yet. / what time I went to
   bed. / if I studied every evening. (➤ Grammar, parts 1, 3
   and 5)

5 *Woman:*   The same thing happened to me yesterday.
  *Suzie:*   What did you do?
  *Woman:*   Someone lent me the fare and I'm going to give it back today on the bus, so I'm happy to do the same for you. You can give the money back to me tomorrow.
  *Suzie:*   Thank you very much. I'm very glad you're here.
  (➤ Grammar, parts 1 and 3–6)

## D: Exam practice
### Use of English

1 made no attempt to  2 sun will shine  3 told me (that) he hadn't  4 don't we go  5 if she had booked  6 apart from Lucy  7 will we leave tomorrow  8 is about to  9 I can dress myself  10 whether they / we were meeting David

### Grammar focus task

Questions 0, 2, 3, 5, 7, 9 and 10 test reported speech.
1 The weatherman predicted (that) there would be sunshine all day. (question 2)
2 Paul complained (that) he hadn't heard from Helen for a long time. (question 3)
3 The little boy insisted (that) he could dress himself without any help. (question 9)

### Writing *Sample answer:*

At the beginning of the meeting we discussed when we would hold the Film Club meetings and where. Everybody said that the hall would be the best place and most people agreed that after school on Friday would be the best time.

We decided that we would make a list of films at the beginning of each term. Emma said that each class could choose one film and there would be a committee to check there was a good variety. Some people said they couldn't come every week so they didn't want to pay a membership fee for the whole term. Kerry suggested that we had a lower membership fee and then charge a small amount to see each film.

Tom suggested that it might be a good idea to have a discussion after each film and then someone could write a review for the school magazine.

## Unit 17

### A: Context listening

2 He is making a fruit cake.
3 2 adding  3 beating  4 to add  5 using  6 to use  7 to add  8 to use  9 to check  10 adding  11 to ice  12 to have
4 Some of the verbs are *to*-infinitive and some are *-ing* form.

## C: Grammar exercises

1 2 working  3 doing  4 to stay  5 working  6 to stop  7 singing  8 to tell  9 working  10 to ignore  11 going  12 to go
(➤ Grammar, parts 1 and 3)

2 2 to take  3 coming  4 to have  5 come  6 jump  7 phoning  8 to play  9 smoking  10 to become (➤ Grammar, parts 1, 2, 4, 6 and 7)

3 *Sample answers (other verbs are also possible as long as they are in the right form):*
2 to get  3 making; to read / to finish
4 to book  5 throwing  6 to inform / to tell  7 inviting
8 to leave  9 wearing  10 to talk / to speak / to chat  11 to send
12 going / travelling  13 to write  14 watching / seeing
(➤ Grammar, part 5)

4 *Sample answers:*
2 You'll enjoy seeing the paintings in the museum.
3 Don't miss going on a river boat.
4 Before you go, don't forget to buy a sunhat.
5 While you're there, try eating the sausages.
6 You must promise to visit my family.
7 Avoid travelling on the buses at night.
8 Remember to take your credit card.
(➤ Grammar, parts 1–9)

## D: Exam practice
### Use of English

1 D  2 A  3 D  4 B  5 B  6 A  7 D  8 C  9 B  10 C  11 A  12 B  13 D  14 C  15 A

### Grammar focus task

*Verbs followed by* to *infinitive:* attempt; dare; decide; demand; expect; hope; threaten; want; wish

*Verbs followed by* -ing: appreciate; consider; delay; enjoy; fancy; imagine; suggest

### Writing *Sample answer:*

Young people have more freedom today than they did one hundred years ago but it depends on the family.

Sometimes parents are too busy to make their children tell them where they are going and they allow them to stay out all night. This isn't a good idea because young people can easily get into trouble by drinking too much or mixing with the wrong people. Parents should warn their children not to drink and smoke too much and definitely not to drink and drive. On the other hand, young people must learn how to be adults. If their parents don't encourage them to do anything on their own they will never manage to be independent.

I don't think parents give their children too much freedom in most families, but it is important that parents and children discuss everything, and that there are some rules which the young people agree to keep to.

# Unit 18

## A: Context listening

2  1d  2b  3f  4a  5e  6c

3  2 get  3 count  4 back (me)  5 look  6 carry  7 call  8 get  9 go
10 throw (me)  11 give

## C: Grammar exercises

1  2 over  3 through  4 down  5 on  6 round to  7 by  8 at
9 round  10 away with (➤ Grammar, parts 1–4)

2  2 cut down  3 filled in  4 turned down  5 carried on
6 turned up  7 set off  8 rung up  9 put off  10 take in
(➤ Grammar, parts 1–4)

3  2 get  3 hands  4 make  5 work  6 are going  7 comes
8 look  9 doing (*going* is also possible)  10 fall  11 turns
12 gave / had given (➤ Grammar, parts 1–4)

4a  2 verb + adverb: broke the sculpture up  3 verb + preposition:
*no*  4 verb + adverb + preposition: *no*  5 verb + adverb: made
the excuse up  6 verb + adverb + preposition: *no*  7 verb +
preposition: *no*  8 verb + adverb: put the lights out  9 verb +
preposition: *no*  10 verb + adverb: puts its prices up
(➤ Grammar, parts 1–4)

 b  2 broke it up  3 went over it  4 run out of them  5 made it up
6 put up with it  7 looked after them  8 put them out  9 takes
after him  10 puts them up (➤ Grammar, parts 1–4)

## D: Exam practice
## Use of English

1 put the wedding off / put off the wedding  2 no point (in) asking
3 of the baby's illness / of the baby being ill  4 (that) you
(should / could) phone  5 came up against  6 looked up to
7 set out on / for / set off on / for  8 unless you hurry  9 put up
with living  10 to avoid making

## Grammar focus task

There are phrasal verbs in sentences 0 (*bring back*), 1 (*put off*),
5 (*come up against*), 6 (*look up to*), 7 (*set out / set off*) and 9 (*put up
with*).

2 By the time we *set out / set off* on our journey it was getting dark.

3 I really can't *put up with* sitting in this heat any longer.

4 This desk is for books which are being *brought back* to the
library.

5 When I'd nearly finished mending the car, I *came up against* a
problem I couldn't solve.

6 James had always *looked up to* his boss.

7 The play was *put off* for a week because the main actor was ill.

## Writing *Sample answer:*

Dear Sir / Madam

    I would like some more information about booking a room for
50 people who want to get together for an end-of-term party. Is
your room big enough? Could you please tell me how much it will
cost, what is included and if there is a reduction for students?

Do you provide snacks like nuts, crisps and sandwiches? Do
you have a list of what is available so I could look through it and
pick out what we want? If we run out during the evening, is it
possible to get more? Can we bring our own drinks or will you
provide a bar and bar staff to look after it?

    The party is on 30 June and will start at 8 pm. How long can
we carry on playing music and dancing? One of the students has
disco equipment. Is it possible for him to set it up? If not, can you
suggest what we do about music?

    Could you write back by email or ring me up? I look forward
to hearing from you.

    Yours faithfully

    Fernando Gonzalez

# Unit 19

## A: Context listening

2  Seymour wants Double X to find the man in the photo.

3  2 Because he doesn't have a better one.  3 A woman.
4 Because the woman faxed it to them.
5 If you look at it with your eyes half closed.  6 Double X.
7 *Sample answer*: Double X's former girlfriend sent it, because
she was angry with him and wanted to cause trouble!

4  1 wouldn't be giving  2 had; 'd give  3 'd told; wouldn't have
needed  4 would give; knew  5 's; look

5  1 The present simple.  2 The present simple.  3 The past
simple.  4 The past perfect.

## C: Grammar exercises

1  2 e  3 a  4 i  5 h  6 b  7 c  8 j  9 d  10 f
(➤ Grammar, parts 1–4)

2  2 want  3 cared  4 won't be  5 wouldn't have told
6 weren't  7 would have been  8 falls  9 hadn't expected
10 'll (will) discover (➤ Grammar, parts 1–4)

3  2 wouldn't have sat opposite that man.  3 If the service hadn't
been really slow  4 If she hadn't been bored  5 she wouldn't
have applied for that job. (➤ Grammar, part 4)

4  *Sample answers (notice the commas):*
    2 it wasn't spoken in so many countries.
    3 , I'll go out and celebrate with all my friends.
    4 I don't study really hard.
    5 give us so much homework every day, we'd be able to go
    out more often.
    6 forgotten my book, I would have done better in the test.
    7 wasn't so different from my own language, I wouldn't
    make so many mistakes.
    8 revise regularly if you want to pass an exam.
    9 , it really helps to improve your English.
    10 , I'll have time for a coffee.
(➤ Grammar, parts 1–4)

## D: Exam practice
### Reading

1 D   2 E   3 C   4 F   5 A   6 B

### Grammar focus task

2 f   3 e   4 c   5 b   6 a   7 d

### Writing *Sample answer:*

Dear Kai,

I've got some information about accommodation in England. There are three possibilities.

If we stayed in the Lion Hotel, it would be comfortable and also convenient for visiting the sights and enjoying ourselves. The problem is that it is very expensive and if we spend lots of money on our accommodation, we won't have much left for anything else, so I don't think we could afford it.

Alternatively, there are student flats. They're not so central but would only cost £250 a month, with electricity extra. And if we had a kitchen we would be able to cook our own food. But we'd have to do the cleaning as well!

Lastly, we could stay with a family. It's not as cheap as a flat, but the price includes two meals a day and laundry. If we stayed with a family, it would be a good way to get to know people. On the other hand, if the landlady was strict, we might not be able to enjoy ourselves so much.

What do you think? Let me know soon, and I'll make some phone calls.

All the best,

Stefan

## Unit 20

### A: Context listening

2   They're going to climb a mountain.
3   2 Provided  3 unless  4 in case  5 I'd rather  6 As long as
    7 wish  8 It's time
4   The verbs are in the present tense.

### C: Grammar exercises

1   2 They'll be here soon unless their plane is delayed.
    3 Unless you're in a hurry, you could take the bus.
    4 I won't be able to come to see you tomorrow unless my brother can give me a lift.
    5 Unless the factory increases its production, it will close down.
    6 Unless you write your address down for me, I'll forget it.
    7 I won't stay in that hotel unless it's got a good restaurant.
    8 Unless I hear from you, I'll meet you at six.
    (➢ Grammar, part 1)
2   2 if  3 if  4 in case  5 in case  6 if  7 in case  8 in case
    (➢ Grammar, part 2)
3   *Sample answers:*
    2 I wish the streets didn't all look the same.
    3 I wish I'd brought my mobile phone.

4 I wish I could speak the language.
5 I wish I'd bought a phrase book.
6 I wish I wasn't / weren't hot and thirsty. / I wish I had a drink.
7 I wish I hadn't come here alone. / I wish I'd come here with someone else.
8 I wish someone would help me.
9 I wish I hadn't come here.
10 I wish I was / were back in my hotel.
(➢ Grammar, part 4)
4   2 are  3 finishes  4 didn't bring  5 would learn  6 behaves
    7 don't know  8 can't  9 changes  10 hadn't been
    (➢ Grammar, parts 1–4)

## D: Exam practice
### Listening

1 A   2 C   3 A   4 B   5 A   6 B   7 C   8 C

### Grammar focus task

2 the manager does something about the noise.  3 it was about someone she knew.  4 he had been more careful.  5 she has a meeting.  6 the morning fog clears.  7 she has it back on Sunday.  8 he embarrasses her again.

### Writing *Sample answer:*

Last week I went to London to visit some museums. I wanted to go to the science museum to see some exhibits about space exploration. As I was leaving the house, my brother said, 'You'd better take your autograph book in case you meet someone famous in London.' Although I'm quite keen on collecting autographs, I ignored him. I wouldn't need it unless I saw someone famous in the museum, and I didn't want to have a lot of things to carry.

When I got to the museum I spent three hours looking at the rockets and other interesting exhibits. Then I had lunch. In the café I noticed that people were looking at the table next to mine. It was a family with three teenagers. Suddenly I realised it was the Prime Minister! Several people spoke to him and asked for his autograph. I was still looking for a piece of paper when they got up and left. I was really disappointed. I wish I'd had my autograph book with me.

I remembered what my brother had said when I was setting out. If only I'd listened to his advice!

## Unit 21

### A: Context listening

2   1 d; (Prime Minister in Washington)
    2 a; (lone sailor forced to stop by bad weather)
    3 c; (traffic jam)
    4 b; (bank robbery)
3   2 At the weekend.  3 To sail (alone) across the Pacific.
    4 By the end of the year.  5 Beyond the beginning of the motorway.  6 Until this afternoon.  7 By the door of the bank
    8 During the night.
4   1 at; by; until; during  2 at; across; beyond; by

## C: Grammar exercises

1   2 at  3 during  4 for  5 until  6 at  7 by  8 in  9 by  10 in
11 over (➤ Grammar, parts 1–2)

2   2 in / near  3 on  4 in  5 in  6 for  7 At  8 for  9 on  10 on
11 in  12 by / on (➤ Grammar, parts 1–2)

3   2 ~~to~~ at; ~~in~~ at  3 correct  4 ~~At the night~~ In / During the night or
At night; ~~over~~ above  5 ~~along~~ through; ~~to~~ on  6 ~~beyond~~ behind
7 ~~in~~ on; ~~along~~ between  8 correct  9 ~~across~~ over  10 ~~by~~ in
(➤ Grammar, parts 1–2)

4   2 on  3 across  4 beyond  5 at  6 in  7 Until  8 in  9 along
10 on  11 through  12 among (➤ Grammar, parts 1–2)

## D: Exam practice
### Use of English

1 the  2 of  3 so  4 ✓  5 designed  6 of  7 ✓  8 than  9 all
10 that  11 occupations  12 some  13 ✓  14 have  15 one

## Grammar focus task

1 between  2 in  3 at  4 among  5 across

## Writing Sample answer:

Dear Chris and Bill,

I hope you've had a good journey. Here's some information which I hope will be helpful.

There is an excellent local shop just up our road, or the supermarket on the outskirts of town, which isn't bad. The swimming pool is just by the supermarket. On weekdays you can use the free car park at the supermarket if you go for a swim, but not at weekends.

The bank is open from 9.30 to 4.00 on weekdays, but it shuts at 12.30 on Saturdays. It's on Market Street, between the big hotel and the museum. The museum's worth visiting, although it's only open in the afternoon.

The market is held on Tuesdays and Saturdays. You need to go early in the morning to buy fresh food, but there are also stalls with second-hand books and so on. I sometimes find good bargains among the rubbish! Those stalls are there until dusk.

Have a great time. We look forward to hearing all about it.

Love from

Nika and Peter

## Unit 22

### A: Context listening

1   1 A man is breaking a window. Fire is coming from the door.
2 A man is taking a toolbox out of a car. Fire is coming from an upstairs window.
3 A man is looking out of an upstairs window. Smoke is coming from downstairs.

2   Picture 2 fits best. Picture 1 shows the fire and the man in the wrong place, and Andy didn't put his handkerchief over his face until he was inside the house. Picture 3 also shows the fire in the wrong place, and there is someone upstairs, but Andy didn't go upstairs and there was no one else in the house.

3   2 at  3 on  4 on  5 by  6 by  7 with  8 in  9 in  10 for  11 for
12 with  13 for  14 to

4   by

## C: Grammar exercises

1   Sample answers:
2 She congratulated her on winning the tournament.
3 They prevented him from entering the disco.
4 She forgave him for not phoning her.
5 She accused him of reading her diary.
6 She agreed with him about the film.
(➤ Grammar, part 1)

2   2 ~~on~~ of; ~~to~~ with  3 ~~of~~ for  4 ~~of advice~~ for advice; ~~for training~~ about training; ~~with~~ at  5 correct  6 ~~by~~ with  7 ~~of~~ with
8 ~~by~~ on  9 correct  10 ~~in~~ about; ~~on the way~~ in the way
(➤ Grammar, parts 1–3)

3   a 2 by  3 by  4 in  5 in  6 of  7 at  8 about  9 in  10 to
b 1 in  2 by  3 on  4 on  5 of  6 on  7 at  8 at
c 1 in  2 out of  3 at  4 at  5 in  6 out of  7 in  8 by  9 in
(➤ Grammar, parts 1–3)

## D: Exam practice
### Use of English

1 spoken  2 graduation  3 political  4 Unfortunately  5 tendency
6 protection  7 international  8 Naturally  9 supposing  10 ideal

## Grammar focus task

2 for  3 for  4 with  5 in  6 by

## Writing Sample answer:

Dear Mr Wexton,

Two weeks ago you advised me about a weekend trip which my family was planning. We went by train to the Star Hotel in Northwold. There was nothing the matter with the hotel and we were very satisfied with it. In fact, we agreed that we would like to stay there again sometime.

However, we were very disappointed by Northwold. The brochure said that the town had a lot of things to do. However, you did not tell me that most of the facilities are only open in summer. The theatre, for example, was closed, and most of the antique shops, and art galleries. The only place to visit in winter is the castle, and that is shut at weekends, so we couldn't even go there. Lastly, the swimming pool is an outdoor, unheated one, as you must know. You did not tell me this. We had been looking forward to a busy and interesting weekend, but there was nothing to do.

I think you were responsible for our disappointing weekend and you should offer us some compensation.

Yours sincerely

Andrea Burnell

## Unit 23

### A: Context listening

1   They lived around 1600. They were all members of the same family.

2   1 b  2 a  3 c (boy on horse)  4 c (boy with book)  5 d

**3** 2 that hangs next to Margaret's portrait. **3** who's holding the book. **4** which lost. **5** when the youngest son was born.

**4** 1 *Which* refers to *the one* (ship). 2 *That* refers to *the picture*. 3 *Who* refers to *the one (William)*. 4 *Which* refers to *the side*. 5 *When* refers to *the year*.

## C: Grammar exercises

**1** 2 who 3 which 4 who 5 – (*which* is not necessary)
6 – (*which* is not necessary) 7 which 8 which 9 which
10 – (*which* is not necessary) (➤ Grammar, parts 1–2)

**2** *Sample answers:* 2 where people wear designer clothes.
3 which we don't understand. 4 when I felt embarrassed by my family. 5 why some people dislike cats. 6 who was very famous? 7 whose parents buy them cars. 8 which involved working at weekends. (➤ Grammar, parts 1–3)

**3** 2 My uncle's cottage, where we usually spend our holidays, has been damaged by floods.
3 My bicycle, which I only got last week, has been stolen.
4 The chemistry exam, which we had been worrying about, was actually quite easy.
5 The young man, whose girlfriend had left him, caused a fight in a bar.
6 During the summer, when everyone goes on holiday, there are dreadful traffic jams.
7 My parents, who don't often go to the cinema, enjoyed that film very much.
(➤ Grammar, parts 2–3)

**4** 2 ~~ankle which~~ ankle, which; ~~winter is~~ winter, is
3 ~~man which you~~ man that you / man who you / man you
4 *correct* 5 ~~region, where~~ region where; ~~holidays, is~~ holidays is
6 ~~to him is;~~ to is 7 ~~whom~~ which 8 ~~that~~ which
9 *correct* 10 ~~place in that~~ place in which / place where
(➤ Grammar, parts 1–3)

## D: Exam practice
### Use of English

1 in which we had lunch / which we had lunch in
2 will (only) last until / till 3 who works for an airline
4 opened the box with / by using 5 is (the reason) why
6 if she would be 7 the book I lent her 8 was going to have
9 the concert (which / that) I went 10 the boy whose mother is

### Grammar focus task

**1** Sentences 1, 3, 5, 7, 9 and 10.
**2** Sentence 3 is non-defining, all the others are defining.
**3** You can tell by the punctuation. If you remove the words between the commas in sentence 3, it still makes sense.

### Writing *Sample answer:*

Last summer, I spent the holidays with some friends in a village on the coast. The cottage where we stayed was near the top of a cliff. About five hundred metres along the lane which ran past the cottage stood a tall, ancient tower. The garden of the tower was surrounded by a high wall with a wooden gate in it, which was always shut.

We were all very curious about this building. We discovered from the woman who kept the local shop that a man lived there, but she didn't know his name.

One morning, I decided to go for a walk before breakfast. I was passing the tower when I noticed that the gate had been opened. I approached cautiously. A man was getting into a car. As he drove past me, he waved. I recognised him at once. He was a journalist whose reports we often watched on television.

Immediately, I ran back to the cottage and told my friends. The mystery was solved and now at last we knew the name of the man who lived in the tower!

## Unit 24

### A: Context listening

**2** Josie does judo and Adam plays volleyball.
**3** 2 good enough 3 since 4 tall enough 5 so quick
6 enough exercise 7 too much time 8 too many practice games 9 in order to 10 well enough 11 as; so much revision
**4** *Exercise* is a noun. *Good* and *tall* are adjectives, and *well* is an adverb.

### C: Grammar exercises

**1** 2 in order to 3 As 4 so 5 so that 6 enough 7 so 8 too
(➤ Grammar, parts 1–3)
**2** 2 ~~money enough~~ enough money 3 ~~for~~ to 4 *correct*
5 ~~Since that I've~~ Since I've 6 ~~too~~ so 7 *correct*
8 ~~a such sad~~ such a sad (➤ Grammar, parts 1–3)
**3** 2 g 3 d 4 e 5 f (*b* is also possible, though less likely)
6 c (*g* is also possible, though less likely) 7 b 8 a
(➤ Grammar, parts 4–5)
**4** *Sample answers:* 2 have to eat at a local restaurant.
3 can't fix this ourselves. 4 has problems with public transport. 5 sometimes have diffluty contacting me.
6 always looks elegant. 7 didn't notice the time.
8 hold all your books? (➤ Grammar, parts 1–5)

## D: Exam practice
### Use of English

1 on 2 ✓ 3 for 4 real 5 in 6 complete 7 that 8 ✓ 9 an
10 with 11 very 12 ✓ 13 each 14 ✓ 15 by

### Grammar focus task

2 that 3 enough 4 to 5 Therefore 6 too 7 in order to

### Writing *Sample answer:*

Dear Dr Warner,

I am writing to apply for the free place at Winston College which I have seen advertised. I feel this would be ideal for me at this stage in my career and I hope you will agree. I am seventeen years old and I am planning to study architecture at university.

My mother tongue is French, and I am quite good at English (I have had no help writing this letter) but I would really like a chance to begin Japanese as I am hoping to go there to study some of their modern buildings.

I have begun learning to use a word processor so I would like to develop this skill because it will be useful at university.

I know you offer instruction in rock-climbing. I have always wanted to try this, but until now I have been too busy with my schoolwork.

Lastly, I would like to say that if I win the place, I will make good use of such a great opportunity to make friends with people from around the world.

Yours sincerely,

Mandana Medaissi

## Unit 25

### A: Context listening

1  b (*a* is wrong because she didn't sign a contract to make more films; *c* is wrong because Gemma was not a film actor before she got the part; *d* is wrong because Gemma was already at theatre school, it was only in films that she had no experience)

2  2 in spite of having  3 after visiting  4 before accepting  5 while making  6 working  7 but I'm  8 despite being

3  The -*ing* form.

### C: Grammar exercises

1  2c 3d 4h 5f 6i 7a 8b 9e (➤ Grammar, parts 1–2 and 4–6)

2  2 ~~Although Sharon quite enjoys musicals, but she~~ Sharon quite enjoys musicals, but she *or* Although Sharon quite enjoys musicals, she 3 *correct* 4 ~~though~~ if 5 ~~they often send me~~ I am often sent 6 ~~in spite of his doctor~~ in spite of the fact that his doctor 7 *correct* 8 ~~Warning~~ Warned 9 ~~Despite that I searched~~ Despite the fact that I searched *or* Despite searching everywhere 10 ~~home, our garage~~ home, we found that our garage (➤ Grammar, parts 1–6)

3  3 Grumbling about the amount of homework he had, Simon took out his grammar book.
4 Feeling very excited about her latest discovery, the scientist invited the journalists into the laboratory.
5 Puzzled by what they had heard, the children asked their teacher what it meant.
6 Being a sensible girl, Wendy didn't panic when she cut her hand.
7 Hearing cries for help, Paul dived into the water.
8 Released only last week, this CD is already at the top of the charts.
(➤ Grammar, part 4)

4  *Sample answers:* 2 has appeared on television several times. 3 I accidentally spilt paint on the rug. 4 You must train seriously 5 Christopher ran along the hotel corridor. 6 I write lots. 7 their scarves in the air, 8 it rains. 9 being over 80. 10 I have been working for an international company. (➤ Grammar, parts 1–6)

### D: Exam practice
### Use of English

1 were  2 managed  3 though  4 spite  5 layer/sheet  6 beyond  7 besides  8 made  9 but  10 to  11 which/that  12 at  13 led  14 Despite  15 carrying

### Grammar focus task

2 a 3 d 4 e 5 c

### Writing *Sample answer:*

My hero is my cousin Benjamin despite the fact that he's only eighteen, which is quite young to be a hero. I have chosen him because about six years ago he made a difficult decision and carried on without complaining.

Unfortunately, Ben's parents divorced when he was about ten. He has a younger sister, Emily, who was about six then. Ben and Emily lived with their mother, although they saw their father regularly, and everything seemed to be going quite well for them. Then their mother became very ill.

Advised that he and Emily should go to live with their father, Ben refused. From the age of 12, he was in charge of his home. Helping his mother and looking after Emily, he had little time for himself. But he always seemed cheerful and made us all laugh at family parties, even though he was missing so much of the fun that most teenagers have.

Last year, a new treatment meant that his mother's health began to improve. Now, Ben's life is easier. But he will always be our family's hero.

# Recording scripts

## Recording 1a

Millie: Hi, Lisa – I'm in the shopping centre.

Lisa: Hi, Millie. What are you doing?

Millie: I'm looking round the shops. It is Saturday today.

Lisa: Yeah, of course. Honestly, you buy new clothes every Saturday!

Millie: Well, nearly every Saturday.

Lisa: You're always buying new clothes! So, what are you looking for today?

Millie: One of those new skirts. You know, like, everyone's wearing them this autumn.

Lisa: Well, I'm not wearing one, I'm wearing a pair of old jeans. Is there anything special you want to talk about? Because actually, I'm doing my homework.

Millie: Yes, there is, only you're being so impatient, you don't deserve to hear it.

Lisa: OK, Sorry. I'm listening.

Millie: Well, you know that special CD you want to get?

Lisa: None of the shops have it. Whenever I go into town I always look for it, but it's never there.

Millie: Well, I'm in front of the music shop window and I'm looking at that CD right now. Do you want me to buy it for you now?

Lisa: Oh, yeah. They sell really fast because they're so rare.

Millie: And that group's becoming more well known.

Lisa: I know. It'll be gone if I wait till Monday. I'll pay you when I see you.

Millie: OK.

Lisa: Oh, thank you, Millie. Sorry I was cross.

Millie: That's OK. Bye.

Lisa: Bye.

## Recording 1b

Jed: Hi everybody, this is Jed Jones, and welcome to *Study Talk*, our weekly look at news from universities around the country. And today, someone is sitting beside me to give us some info on a course he's doing. It gives people the chance to study a subject not traditionally associated with university. In fact there are some people who think it's not really a subject for serious study at all, but is only a hobby. So, I've got here with me Ellis Graham who says he's actually doing a degree in something I enjoy from time to time – now this isn't for real, is it Ellis – in surfing? Tell me you're a mathematician who goes surfing in his free time, aren't you?

Ellis: Sorry to disappoint you, Jed, it's for real.

Jed: So what do you do? You have classes on the beach?

Ellis: Well, that's possible sometimes, 'cause there is a practical element to the course, but most of it is indoors, with our books or computers. We have to study a very wide range of things.

Jed: Like where the best waves are?

Ellis: Well, yes, that's one way of describing it. We learn about weather and geographical influences on coastal regions, for example. And how waves form and grow. In fact there is quite a bit of mathematics in the course.

Jed: But, I don't want to sound rude here, but, surely surfing isn't a very academic subject, is it?

Ellis: You mean, surfers don't have very big brains?

Jed: I guess I do –

Ellis: Actually, you need really good exam results from school to be accepted on this course, because so many people want to do it, so there are many more applicants than the university has places for.

Jed: Oh, I see. So, OK, I've got to take the whole business a bit more seriously. But what I'm not clear about, is what can you do when you graduate? I mean, a degree won't make you a better surfer than if you just spend your time hanging about on the beach, will it?

Ellis: Probably not. If that's what you want, it's the practice that matters. But that's not my aim. You see, surfing is a big part of the commercial life of some parts of the world, south-west England, for example, or parts of the US and of course Australia. There are hundreds of business opportunities, some of them well known, but plenty of others are just waiting for the right person to come along and get going to make a living out of them. And a very good living.

Jed: So you're not just talking about sitting in a beach hut hiring out a few surf boards?

Ellis: By no means. But that's just my idea. Some of my fellow students will go into research and so on. There are all sorts of possibilities.

Jed: Well, I wish you all the best, Ellis. But just one last question – if I want advice on a new place to go for some really good surfing away from the crowds, would your department be able to tell me?

Ellis: That's a bit of a tricky one, actually, Jed. You see, we're looking into this for a package holiday company, so I'd be giving away confidential commercial information!

Jed: Oh, dear. I might have known! Well, thank you very much, Ellis, for filling us in ...

## Recording 2

Gran: Hello Jack! Come in.

Jack: Hello, Gran. How are you?

Gran: Fine, thanks Jack. What about you?

Jack: Oh, you know, too much college work. We had an exam on Thursday. But I went to London last Saturday with some mates. We had a great time.

Gran: Oh, yes? I suppose you spent all your money.

Jack: No, it wasn't really expensive. We caught the coach, so it was only ten pounds return.

Gran: But isn't it slow?

Jack: Well, we did some revision for our exams while we were travelling, so it didn't matter.

Gran: Well done. And where did you go?

Jack: Oh, you know, round the shops.

Gran: That's what I did too, but not in London. I was hoping to find a new jacket. But there wasn't anything I liked.

Jack: And then we went to see a film. But the brilliant thing was, when we were queuing for the cinema, we saw a really famous footballer. He was buying a burger from a stall near us like an ordinary person and all the crowds were walking past but nobody noticed him except me.

Gran: So did you get his autograph?

Jack: No, I didn't want to embarrass him.

Gran: Ooh, when I was your age, I used to collect all the autographs of film stars and singers and so on. I would go up to town on my own and wait outside the theatre till they came out.

Jack: Really?

Gran: Yes. And I used to scream at pop concerts. I really enjoyed myself when I was a teenager. But don't tell your mother. She never used to do anything like that. She was always worrying about her homework.

Jack: OK. So do you want to hear about the club we went to after the cinema?

Gran: You bet!

Jack: Well, it was really ...

## Recording 3

Lucy: Can you hold the doors a minute, Mike? I've got a big bag here.

Mike: Hi, Lucy. Nice to see you. Up to the fourth floor?

Lucy: Yes, please. Have you just finished work, Mike?

Mike: Actually, I finished at lunchtime today because they're replacing our computers. So I've been at the gym this afternoon.

Lucy: Are you going out tonight?

Mike: No I don't think so. Why? Are you inviting me somewhere?

Lucy: Oh no, I've got lots of work to do. I've actually spent all day trying to write a history essay and I still haven't finished it. I have to hand it in tomorrow. I started it last week ...

Mike: Well, sorry, I can't help you with that ... (After you.) ... I never enjoyed studying history at school and I wasn't very good at it either.

Lucy: I don't need any help with the essay. But you can help me by not playing your saxophone.

Mike: Huh?

Lucy: I'm sorry, I just can't stand it any more. I've lived next door since June and you've played the saxophone every night for at least an hour.

Mike: But I thought you liked it. I've lived here for two years. Nobody's ever complained before so I'm really surprised. This is the first time anyone has asked me not to play. Why haven't you told me this before?

| Lucy: | I've tried lots of times but I was afraid of sounding rude. |
| Mike: | So would you like me to play more quietly? |
| Lucy: | No, Mike. I don't want you to play at all. Tonight and ideally never again. |
| Mike: | I tell you what. I'll learn some new tunes. Why don't you suggest some? |
| Lucy: | Ohhhhhhh … |

## Recording 4

| Mother: | Hi, Richard. I'm home. Where are you? |
| Richard: | Upstairs, Mum. In my room. |
| Mother: | … Oh, Richard. Whatever have you been doing? |
| Richard: | I've been painting my room, Mum. |
| Mother: | Yes, I can see that. But why did you change colour halfway through? |
| Richard: | Well I'd done the ceiling, and I'd painted one wall, when I ran out of paint, so I went to the shop for some more. But then I realised the second pot was a slightly different colour. That's why it looks a bit odd. |
| Mother: | But why were you painting anyway? I thought you'd planned lots of things to do with your friends. |
| Richard: | Oh, they were all busy in the end. And yesterday afternoon I was bored. I'd been to town for a few hours – you know round the centre. I'd done the shopping – everything on your list – and I'd finished all my homework so I decided to paint my room. |
| Mother: | Mmm. Well, I suppose you can put some posters up. But look at the carpet. Why didn't you cover it up? |
| Richard: | Oh, yes, I see what you mean. |
| Mother: | I've had such a day. You know, I'd been driving for an hour when the car broke down so the journey's taken me much longer than normal. I'm just going into my room to have a lie down. |
| Richard: | Don't go in there just yet Mum. Let me tell you about … |
| Mother: | Well, come and tell me in my room so I can sit down. |

| Richard: | That's what I wanted to tell you. I've painted your room too. And it was quite difficult so you might not be too pleased … It was supposed to be a surprise … |

## Recording 5a

### Conversation 1

| Tom: | Hello? |
| Claire: | Hello, Tom. It's Claire. |
| Tom: | Hi, Claire. How are you? |
| Claire: | Fine. Are you reporting on the conference in Amsterdam? I thought maybe we could travel together. |
| Tom: | That would be good but I've already booked my flight. People are travelling from all over the world so I decided to book early. |
| Claire: | Well, maybe I can get on the same one. |
| Tom: | I'm flying with British Airways and my plane leaves Edinburgh on Tuesday at 11.05. It arrives at Amsterdam airport at 13.40. |
| Claire: | It's quick, isn't it? When does the conference actually begin? |
| Tom: | It starts on Wednesday at 9.30 so you need to get there on Tuesday. The main speaker arrives at the conference on Tuesday afternoon and I'm interviewing him at 6.30. |
| Claire: | OK, I'll let you know what I arrange. See you. |
| Tom: | Bye. |

### Conversation 2

| Steve: | Tom, hello. |
| Tom: | Hi, Steve. How are you? Oh … you're in a hurry. Where are you going? |
| Steve: | I'm playing badminton in a few minutes with Paul. But what about me and you? We haven't played for ages. What are you doing tomorrow evening? I usually play at about seven. |
| Tom: | Oh, sorry. I'll be working then. I'm flying to a conference in Amsterdam tomorrow morning. But what about the weekend? I'm not working then. I'm having my eyes tested on Saturday afternoon but I'm free the rest of the weekend. |
| Steve: | OK. Let's make it Sunday morning? About ten at the sports centre? |
| Tom: | Fine. See you there. |

Steve:   Bye, then.

Tom:   Bye.


## Conversation 3

Woman:   Good afternoon, sir. What name is it please?

Tom:   Tom Hughes.

Woman:   Ah yes. Room 341. Are you having dinner here tonight?

Tom:   I haven't decided yet. I'm interviewing someone at 6.30 so I probably won't be back in time. I think I'll get a meal in town.

Woman:   And breakfast?

Tom:   Err ... oh, I'll have breakfast in my room please.

Woman:   Here's the key then, sir. Take the lift to the third floor and turn left.

Tom:   Thank you.

Woman:   Oh, just a minute. There's a message for you, sir. It's from your newspaper office in Edinburgh.

Tom:   Oh, thanks. I'll ring them now.


## Conversation 4

Tom:   So, you got here in the end, Claire.

Claire:   Yes, but your flight was full and I couldn't get on a plane till Wednesday so I missed the first day of the conference.

Waiter:   Eherm, what would you like to drink, sir?

Tom:   I'll have some fizzy water, please. Claire?

Claire:   I'll have the same, please. Anyway, what did I miss, Tom?

Tom:   Well, the first day was mainly about the future of the planet, you know in a hundred years' time the world will be a very different place. There'll be millions more people but there won't be much oil available for energy. And people will live much longer. You know, that kind of thing. I've interviewed the main speaker and I've written my article about him. It'll be in the newspaper tomorrow.

Claire:   I'll read all about it there then. And I need to write my article about the rest of the conference tonight so I mustn't spend too long having dinner.

Tom:   Oh, right. OK then.

**Recording 5b**

Good morning. I hope you slept well and are ready to start exploring South Wales on the first day of our holiday here. Before I tell you what we are doing today, the hotel has asked me to mention a few things. Meals are served in the dining room, except breakfast which is served in the coffee bar – any time between 6.45 and 9.15. We won't actually be here to have lunch because we are going out on trips every day, so you need to order sandwiches for the next day's lunch before seven each evening from reception. Collect your lunch from the dining room in the morning. In the evening the dining room is open from 7.00p.m. until 9.30. I shall see you all in the dining room at a quarter past seven each evening because the hotel has asked if we can eat together as a group and be finished by 8.45 so please try to get there on time. There's still time to go out into town afterwards if you want to as long as you're back for breakfast the next morning!

I'm your tour guide in charge of all the trips and am looking after you while we're out. While you're in the hotel, however, if you have any problems you should talk to the deputy manager. The manager himself is off sick at the moment. The receptionist will show you where the office is.

In about ten minutes the coach is picking us up to take us on a tour of the valleys of South Wales. You may know that the area is famous for its industry but you may not realise what a lot of natural beauty there is too. Last year I visited a wonderful waterfall near here with a group and we didn't have time to explore properly so we're going back there today to have a better look. Because it rains a lot here it's quite a sight. During the 1700s, the waterfall was used to power a mill which produced flour and you can see what's left of the building and imagine what it was like.

Then we're travelling a bit further up the valley to visit a museum which has been built where there used to be a huge coal mine. They don't mine coal there any more but the museum is fascinating. There's a video you can watch and in the souvenir shop, as well as buying all the normal souvenirs, you can buy lamps which are exactly like the ones the miners carried to light their way.

We'll probably eat our lunch up there near the museum, in the coach if the weather's bad.

Then we're making our way back south to the coast to admire some more beautiful scenery. There'll be time for a walk along the cliffs or if any of you are feeling energetic you can try a bit of windsurfing. Sailing, canoeing and fishing are also popular sports in the area but we won't be able to do those today. We'll probably stop at a café on the way back to have a cup of coffee and a snack and we arrive back at the hotel by five o'clock. You'll need a coat or something to keep you dry, some strong boots because our walk might be muddy and don't forget your cameras. Now if anyone has any questions …

## Recording 5c

In about ten minutes the coach is picking us up to take us on a tour of the valleys of South Wales. You may know that the area is famous for its industry but you may not realise what a lot of natural beauty there is too. Last year I visited a wonderful waterfall near here with a group and we didn't have time to explore properly so we're going back there today to have a better look. Because it rains a lot here it's quite a sight. During the 1700s, the waterfall was used to power a mill which produced flour and you can see what's left of the building and imagine what it was like.

Then we're travelling a bit further up the valley to visit a museum which has been built where there used to be a huge coal mine. They don't mine coal there any more but the museum is fascinating. There's a video you can watch and in the souvenir shop, as well as buying all the normal souvenirs, you can buy lamps which are exactly like the ones the miners carried to light their way.

We'll probably eat our lunch up there near the museum, in the coach if the weather's bad.

Then we're making our way back south to the coast to admire some more beautiful scenery. There'll be time for a walk along the cliffs or if any of you are feeling energetic you can try a bit of windsurfing. Sailing, canoeing and fishing are also popular sports in the area but we won't be able to do those today. We'll probably stop at a café on the way back to have a cup of coffee and a snack and we arrive back at the hotel by five o'clock. You'll need a coat or something to keep you dry, some strong boots because our walk might be muddy and don't forget your cameras. Now if anyone has any questions …

## Recording 6

| | |
|---|---|
| Simon: | Good afternoon, my name is Simon Trite and I'm here from Hightime Radio Corporation to interview you! Now that you've had time to settle in, we're going to do a series about your adventures here on Wildrock. |
| | So, er, how are you finding life here in the wild? Pretty exciting, huh? |
| Woman 1: | Actually, we're about to leave. |
| Simon: | What? You can't be! You were going to stay here for at least a year. |
| Man 1: | Look, we're fed up. We're fed up with the cold. |
| Woman 2: | And the wind. |
| Woman 1: | And the mud. |
| Man 2: | And the rain. |
| Simon: | It's not raining now. |
| Man 2: | But it's going to rain soon. See those clouds over the hill? |
| Simon: | Huh? |
| Man 2: | So, we know it's going to rain. |
| Woman 1: | And it's the same almost every day. So, we're going to pack up our stuff, we're going to send a message to the mainland, and we're going to leave. |
| Woman 2: | As soon as possible. |
| Simon: | Everyone's going to be very surprised when you arrive. Aren't you embarrassed to let the weather defeat you? |
| Man 1: | By the end of this week, we'll have survived longer than anyone else in a place like this. |
| Man 2: | By the end of this week we'll have been living here for nearly six months. And that's enough. |
| Simon: | But surely it's not really that bad? |
| Woman 2: | No? |
| Man 2: | Tell you what, why don't you try it? |
| Simon: | What? |
| Man 2: | Yes, you can stay here. We're going to go to the mainland. |
| Woman 1: | We're going to eat a big hot meal as soon as we find a restaurant. |

| Man 1: | And we're not going to talk to any reporters until we've had a long sleep in warm, dry beds. |
| Simon: | Wait for me! |
| | You aren't going to leave me here all alone, are you? |
| | Hey! That's my boat! Oh no. Now what am I going to do? |

## Recording 7

1  Look in your mirror – is it time for a change? Come and work out at Transformers Fitness Centre. Together, you and Transformers can make you a stronger, slimmer and more self-confident person. Our professional advisers will help you to plan a sensible route to better health. Call in this weekend for a friendly welcome and see our excellent facilities. We're at 25 Market Street and we're open from eight in the morning till eight in the evening.

2  Looking for a really wonderful day out next summer? Come to the best wildlife park in the country. We've got the fiercest lions here at the Animal Wonder Park, in addition to the funniest monkeys and, in the water park, the cleverest dolphins you've ever seen. Phone 273156 for our amazing brochure and take advantage of our special offers for families.

3  Do you have a full-time job? Do you feel tired all the time, trying to keep the house clean as well? Don't wear yourself out – call The Sparklers. You'll come back to fresh carpets, shining sinks and surfaces and no sticky finger marks on the paintwork. Phone 273989. You'll be surprised by our reasonable prices.

4  Hurry, hurry, hurry! There's something for everyone at the Music Store in Spice Lane. We've got the greatest variety of CDs ever! And astonishing bargains! The Music Store has thousands of special deals – the latest rock and pop, traditional jazz, the most beautiful classical music. Come to the Music Store today!

## Recording 8

And here I am at the city stadium and the sun is shining. And finally the players are coming onto the pitch. As I was saying earlier there were such terrible traffic jams in the city today that the match is starting late. Most of the spectators have been waiting patiently in their seats since two o'clock but now as the players come out they're cheering happily. And the whistle goes. Rossi has the ball and is running steadily down the pitch but, oh no, the game has hardly started – only two minutes have gone – and he's fallen heavily on the ground. He's so experienced in these kinds of conditions that he rarely falls. But he's OK and he has the ball. Now Parker is running quickly towards the goal to take the ball from Rossi. Parker is playing incredibly well. But of course that's what we expect from him. Last week he scored the winning goal to take this team into the semi-final. It's often Parker who shoots that important goal. And he has, he's scored! And the crowd are roaring really loudly so it's difficult to make myself heard. That was a marvellous goal by Parker.

## Recording 9a

| Molly: | Hello? |
| Peter: | Are you home at last? |
| Molly: | Yes, I am. Why? |
| Peter: | You've been out all evening, haven't you? |
| Molly: | What are you talking about? |
| Peter: | I phoned three times and you didn't answer. |
| Molly: | Have you been checking up on me? |
| Peter: | No, I haven't. I was just worried. You said you'd be in tonight, didn't you? |
| Molly: | Yes, I did. But I had a change of plan, OK? |
| Peter: | Of course. I'm sorry. |
| Molly: | So am I. I don't want to quarrel. |
| Peter: | Neither do I. You know I love you, don't you? |
| Molly: | Of course I do. |
| Peter: | And do you love me? |
| Molly: | You know I do. |
| Peter: | And you'll always love me, won't you? |
| Molly: | Of course I will. You can meet me tomorrow, can't you? |
| Peter: | Sure. Let's meet by the college gate, shall we? |
| Molly: | Yes, let's. We'd better say goodnight, then. |
| Peter: | OK. Goodnight. Love you. |
| Molly: | Love you. Bye. |
| Peter: | Bye. |

1  *You hear a man talking to some tourists.*
   *Who is he?*

   A  *a café owner*

   B  *a tourist guide*

   C  *a street trader*

   This is a good place to sit and drink a coffee when you
   want a break and if you like you can watch the street
   market just across the way, where there's lots going on,
   plenty of local colour. Now, everybody's here I think, so
   let's order some drinks, shall we?

2  *You hear a woman and her friend in an airport.*
   *What has the woman lost?*

   A  *her handbag*

   B  *her passport*

   C  *her boarding pass*

   Man:      It leaves in five minutes and we can't get all
             the way back to the check-in – surely you put
             it inside your passport, like you usually do.

   Woman:    And that's right where I always keep it, in the
             side of my handbag, but the boarding pass
             isn't there. I didn't give it to you to hold,
             did I?

3  *You hear a man talking about his holiday.*
   *Which place did he enjoy most?*

   A  *the seaside*

   B  *Bangkok*

   C  *the north*

   We went on a sort of tour, you know the sort of thing I
   mean, don't you? We had a week by the coast to start
   with, then four days in Bangkok, and three days seeing
   something of village life in the north, which was all
   fascinating, I admit – but I get a bit tired of moving
   about, so to be honest the first week was the real holiday
   as far as I was concerned.

4  *You hear a girl talking about choosing a coat.*
   *Whose advice did she follow?*

   A  *her mother's*

   B  *her sister's*

   C  *the shop assistant's*

   Well, my mum had said I ought to get a really warm
   coat, so that's why I tried on this long one first of all,
   but my sister said the short one was more fashionable

and so did the shop assistant. But it was much more
expensive, that's why she said that. And I think my
sister was right in a way, but then she'd want to borrow
it. In the end I went for the long one, and, well, it looks
OK, doesn't it?

5  *In an office, you hear a man talking on the telephone.*
   *Where is Mr Richardson?*

   A  *in a hotel*

   B  *in America*

   C  *at home*

   I'm afraid Mr Richardson isn't available today … no, he
   took a short holiday after he got back from the States,
   and now he's home sick this week because he picked up
   a tummy bug at the hotel he stayed in. It was unlucky,
   wasn't it? Shall I get him to call you when he's back?

6  *You overhear a man telling a friend about a trip to a gym.*
   *How does the man feel?*

   A  *ashamed*

   B  *determined*

   C  *angry*

   Woman:   Have you joined that new gym?

   Man:     I've decided against it. When I went along
            there – they have these fitness trainers who
            talk to you before they let you use the
            equipment – well, he looked about fourteen
            to me – he told me I could only use their
            equipment if I went away and lost ten kilos –

   Woman:   You can do that, can't you?

   Man:     He was trying to tell me I was too old to use
            a gym really. I had to laugh because there
            was someone who looked like my son telling
            me how to organise my life. But because of
            what he said I've made up my mind that I
            really will get fit this time.

7  *You hear a woman talking to a doctor's receptionist.*
   *Why does she want an early appointment?*

   A  *because she mustn't eat before she comes in*

   B  *because she's having problems eating*

   C  *because she wants to see the doctor without taking time
      off work*

   Woman:            But I have to have an appointment first
                     thing in the morning. The doctor wants

to do some tests and I mustn't eat for twelve hours before that – I am right, aren't I?

Receptionist: Yes.

Woman: So, she said the best way is to go without breakfast and come in early.

Receptionist: Yes.

Woman: Then I can have a snack and not miss too much time at work.

8 *You hear a man talking about selling his bicycle. How did he do it?*

*A He paid for an advertisement in the newspaper.*

*B He told all his friends about it.*

*C He advertised it at work.*

Yeah – you know me, I never pay much attention to advertisements myself, you know, in the papers or in shops or whatever, so I didn't think of it. But I was talking to this colleague over the coffee break and he said, what about putting one on the notice board in the staff cloakroom? And I got three enquiries straight off! Sold it yesterday.

## Recording 10

1 I'm Angela, and I'm a sales executive for a company which makes furniture. An important part of my work is travel. I drive thousands of miles every year and that can make it quite hard to get exercise. I do care about my health though, and when I stop I usually buy fruit to eat rather than biscuits or sweets. If there's any available, that is.

2 I'm Ken and I work at a garage. I mainly drive the recovery truck – that's the vehicle that helps motorists when they break down. Some people just keep driving without thinking ahead. It's the phone calls from drivers who've run out of petrol that really annoy me. Or, the other thing is, I'm called out by the police after an accident. Some firms charge a lot of money for that, but I don't think we're too bad. Anyway, motorists have got insurance – or they should have!

3 I'm Charlie and I've got this job delivering pizzas for a fast food restaurant on a motorbike. It's OK, I can usually get round the traffic jams. I got my motorbike licence last year and I need cash. I'm a student. My subject's chemistry. I hope I won't need a job like this after I've graduated. I want to find a job with a reasonable salary.

4 I'm Hazel and I've been driving a taxi now for three years. I can't say I enjoy this sort of work. The traffic's terrible here. But I've got three kids and I've got to pay for food and clothing and so on. There's a lot of unemployment round here, so I mustn't grumble, really, I suppose.

## Recording 11

Woman: Hello. How can I help?

Man: I want to go on a week's holiday. Somewhere sunny but not too ...

Woman: Have you looked at any of our brochures? Do help yourself. Are you interested in anywhere in particular?

Man: Well, I was wondering ...

Woman: The resorts in this one, look, are all near the airport and on the coast. In fact, I went to this place myself last year with some friends of mine to see what it was really like. It's got discos, nightclubs, restaurants and it's only a few metres from the hotel to the beach. Or this place, look, has even more entertainment. Everyone's going there this year.

Man: Neither of those would suit me. I was looking for something a bit ...

Woman: I know, maybe you'd prefer some of the places on this island. My brother's friend had a holiday in this place, look, so I can really recommend it. Are you going on your own?

Man: Yes, by myself.

Woman: Well, we can book apartments which you share with three other people. That's better because you get to know each other really well. You'd have fun there. And each apartment has its own balcony with a view.

Man: I'd rather have my own apartment. I've looked at this brochure. I'm interested in either this holiday or this one on the next page.

Woman: Mmm, oh I'm sorry that's last year's brochure. It must have got on the shelf by mistake. But look at this one. The hotel itself is quite old but they are modernising it at the moment.

Man: Sounds a bit noisy. All I want is somewhere quiet – anywhere that I can relax. Maybe in the mountains. All the places near the coast seem rather busy.

| | |
|---|---|
| Woman: | Well, most of our holidays are by the sea. But here's one for you: a camping holiday in the countryside. You'd be staying in a big campsite with really good facilities. |
| Man: | I don't think you quite understand. Every brochure you've shown me contains the kind of holiday I would hate. None of the holidays look enjoyable at all. |
| Woman: | Well, you just can't please some people ... Hello madam, can I help? |

## Recording 12

| | |
|---|---|
| Chris: | Hi Alice. What are you doing walking on the beach? Shouldn't you be at school? |
| Alice: | Oh, I've left school. I'm going to college next month. I'm hoping to train to be a chef. |
| Chris: | Really? Well you know I've worked as a chef for the last five years and I work at the Grand Hotel now. In fact I'm head chef there so you need to talk to me if you want to know what the job is really like. |
| Alice: | Well, what is it really like then? I'd like to work in a hotel like the Grand. I'm sure it's really exciting and you get to meet all kinds of rich and famous people. |
| Chris: | Actually no. Chefs have to spend their time in the kitchen. Rich and famous people don't go there. |
| Alice: | But you get lots of time off, don't you? Look, you're walking on the beach now at lunchtime. |
| Chris: | Yes, but it's my day off today. I needn't think about the hotel kitchen today. |
| Alice: | Well, normally then, what's it like? You don't have to work all day, do you? |
| Chris: | I have a break in the afternoon but I need to get up early. I have to start work at 6.30 in the morning and I have to stay until all the food is cooked and served in the evening. It's late by then. |
| Alice: | Mmm, sounds like hard work. How many days off do you get? |
| Chris: | In my last job, I had to work every day except Monday. At least here I have two days off every week. In the summer I'll have to work longer hours. That's because the hotel is busier. Listen, I must go now. You must come to the hotel one day. You can have a look around. I |

| | |
|---|---|
| | can show you the kitchens and you can see what we do. |
| Alice: | Mmm, thanks. I'm not so sure any more about being a chef. |
| Chris: | Well, come and see me and we'll have another chat. |

## Recording 13a

| | |
|---|---|
| Sophie: | Mum ... |
| Mum: | Yes Sophie? |
| Sophie: | Will you lend me ten pounds? |
| Mum: | What for? |
| Sophie: | And can you lend me your new jacket? |
| Mum: | My new one? |
| Sophie: | Yes, and ... |
| Mum: | And what? |
| Sophie: | Can you give me a lift to town now? |
| Mum: | Start again. You want to borrow ten pounds, you want to borrow my new jacket and you want me to give you a lift to town now? Anything else? |
| Sophie: | Oh ... will you get me some new batteries for my Walkman? I really need to use it today. |
| Mum: | Well ... |
| Sophie: | And can you collect me from the city centre at midnight tonight? |
| Mum: | Right. Shall we go through them one by one? You can borrow ten pounds, but you already owe me ten pounds, so you'd better not spend too much. You definitely can't borrow my new jacket. |
| Sophie: | Oh Mum ... |
| Mum: | I will give you a lift to town, but not till four o'clock, because I'm busy right now. |
| Sophie: | But I need to go now. |
| Mum: | You could walk of course, or take the bus. You should get more exercise anyway. You'll go past a shop that sells batteries then. I haven't got time to do that. And you really ought to be more polite. I feel like saying no to everything when you speak to me like that. |
| Sophie: | OK, sorry, I'll wait till you're ready. So would you please give me a lift? And could you collect me from the city centre at midnight, do you think? |

| | |
|---|---|
| Mum: | Yes, I will ... but you'd better leave me to finish what I'm doing now or I'll change my mind. |
| Sophie: | OK then. |

## Recording 13b

Speaker 1: It's difficult to imagine that you'll ever be able to wear it, isn't it, when it's freezing cold here? But it's perfect for the kind of holiday you've described. And it's very reasonable too, of course. It'll be cool during the day when you're travelling around and in the evening you could put a jacket on top and wear it in the hotel for dinner. I have one very similar myself. Shall I leave you to think about it for a moment or two?

Speaker 2: You'll be surprised how cold it gets up in the mountains when it's so warm down here. I forgot to remind last week's group and it was much colder than they expected. You must bring something warm to put on when we get up there. You may not need it, of course, but you'd better all go and get a pullover or jacket or something from your rooms now before we leave. I don't want any complaints later on that someone's cold.

Speaker 3: I took all the wrong clothes of course when I went. I just didn't realise it would be so cool in the evenings. It was lovely and hot during the day but in the evenings I really needed a jacket or something. I had to go and buy one in the end. In fact I could lend it to you if you want. Why don't I pop across the road and get it? It'll only take a minute. I know exactly where it is in the wardrobe.

Speaker 4: Don't do what I did last year and sit out in the sun too long. It made me ill actually. In fact, when I got back here everyone said I looked worse than when I left, that I should have spent my holiday here at my desk. But you're more sensible than me. You'll have the right clothes, hats and things. So have a good time – don't even think about us back here looking at a computer screen all day. Oh, and don't forget what I said about the shops – you must bring one of those wonderful shirts back.

Speaker 5: At least you've been there before so you won't waste your time finding your way around. Have you got all the right clothes? You ought to take things for the daytime when it's warm and things for the evening. It can get quite cold, you know. You remember when we all went together as a family, we enjoyed walking in the evenings. I know you'll be in a group and you'll probably do different things from us. And you'd better not spend all your money in the airport shop because there are lovely things to buy when you get there.

## Recording 14

| | |
|---|---|
| Fiona: | Hey look, Clare. Isn't that Danny over there? |
| Clare: | I can't see him, Fiona. Where? |
| Fiona: | Sitting at a table in that café over there. |
| Clare: | It might be Danny. |
| Fiona: | But who's that he's with? |
| Clare: | Oh she must be his mother. He said she was coming to visit him for a few days but not till next week. They must have changed their plans. |
| Fiona: | Look Clare, she can't be his mother. She's much too young. Could you get a bit closer and see who he's with? |
| Clare: | Why don't you? |
| Fiona: | He might see me ... OK. We'll walk across together. We'll pretend we're looking in that shop window over there. |
| Clare: | OK ... No, you're right Fiona. She's much too young. Hey, we ought to get back to college now – our lecture starts in ten minutes. Shall we just go and say hi as we go past? |
| Fiona: | I don't think so. She could be his new girlfriend and I'd be embarrassed. Anyway, Clare, I'm not interested. |
| Clare: | Oh no? You must forget about him Fiona, you know. You two broke up ages ago. He's really boring anyway. Come on. We need to get back ... |

## Recording 15

Four burglars have escaped from custody only hours after being sentenced to ten years in prison. They were being transferred from the law courts in Manchester to Strangeways Prison. They had been found guilty of stealing electrical goods and money from shops in the Manchester area. It is thought that they were all members of the same gang. They escaped from the van in which they were being transported, when the driver was forced to stop because of a tree across the road. It is believed that the tree was placed there by other members of the gang, who had been informed of the route to be taken by the van. A full investigation of the events leading to the escape has been ordered and anyone with information is asked to contact the police to help with their inquiries. And now over to Simon for the weather forecast ...

## Recording 16

| | |
|---|---|
| Rachel: | Hello James. Are you there? Can you hear me? |
| James: | Hi, Rachel. Yes, I can hear you very well. |
| Rachel: | How do you feel? |
| James: | I'm fine. |
| Rachel: | Where are you now, James? |
| James: | I'm about 100 kilometres off the coast of Australia. So it's not far to the finish. |
| Rachel: | Do you think you're going to win, James? |
| James: | Well, I haven't seen another boat for a few days. It's a really amazing feeling to be alone in the middle of the ocean. I think I might win. |
| Rachel: | Could be that you're last, James, and the others have all finished! Just joking, of course! What's the weather like? |
| James: | Last week there was a terrible storm. It was really loud and quite frightening and I didn't sleep for three days but now the weather's completely different, the sea's calm, so beautiful, the sun's shining, it's almost too hot. |
| Rachel: | Can you see dolphins there? |
| James: | I can sometimes see sharks and dolphins swimming in the distance as well as so many different kinds of birds. |
| Rachel: | I'm on my way to join you, out of this noisy studio! And what's the first thing you'll do when you get to Australia? |
| James: | I'll spend two hours in a hot bath I think – oh, and I must get my hair cut. But the very first thing is to ... |

| | |
|---|---|
| Rachel: | Hello, James, are you still there? ... Oh, we've lost him, I think. Hope one of those sharks hasn't come to visit! We'll talk to James again ... |

## Recording 17

Today I'm going to explain how to make one of my own favourites – I think I enjoy making it as much as eating it. You need a large cake tin and I'll give you a complete list of ingredients at the end. First of all, beat the butter and sugar together. Continue doing this until the mixture begins to look pale and fluffy. Then pour in the eggs. Avoid adding the eggs all at the same time, you should add them slowly and keep beating all the time. Next, add the flour, and don't forget to add the baking powder, or you'll end up with a biscuit rather than a cake. Now for the fruit. I recommend using sultanas and apricots but if you prefer to use dates or raisins that's fine. Some people like to add some nuts too but you needn't include them if you prefer not to. If you decide to use nuts, chop them up small. Mix everything together and pour the mixture into the tin. Bake in the oven for about one-and-a-quarter hours. Remember to check if the fruit cake is ready after about an hour as everyone's oven is slightly different. Let the cake cool for about half an hour. If you want to ice the cake, mix up some icing sugar with water. I suggest adding a little lemon juice as well. Don't try to ice the cake until it's completely cold. If you decide not to ice it, just sprinkle some sugar on top. One word of warning, don't expect to have much fruit cake left after a couple of hours – it's delicious. My family can't resist it. And now here is the list of ingredients you need ...

## Recording 18

People are saying that I caused the group to break up and I want everyone to know the truth. It really wasn't my fault. I'd always got on with the other members. We'd been together for more than five years and I thought I could count on them as friends as well as work colleagues. I thought they would always be there to back me up when I was in trouble. I had expected them to look after me when I needed them as I would always be there for them. But last year when I came up against some problems at home I wasn't able to perform in a couple of concerts. Instead of carrying on without me – they could have managed on their own – they called the concerts off and said it was my fault. And they stopped talking to me. They would get together every Monday morning and sit round the table. They would then go over plans for the next week and not tell me anything. I put up with this for a while, then we had a big argument. They said they wanted to throw me out of the group because of what I'd done. I was so upset because I really cared about them but I don't any more. Now I'm determined that they're not going to get away with it. They're not going to treat me like that. I won't give in until they've paid me every penny they owe me. Anyway, enough of all that. Now let me tell you about my plans for ...

## Recording 19

Double X: You wanted to see me, Mr Seymour?

Seymour: Yes, come in, Double X. I have an important mission for you. I want you to follow a man and find out all about him. If you find him, I'll be extremely pleased.

Double X: Who is he, sir?

Seymour: If I knew that, I wouldn't be giving you this job! Here's a photo of him.

Double X: But this is all fuzzy. It's impossible to tell what he looks like.

Seymour: If we had a better picture, we'd give it to you. Anyway, we've had an anonymous tip-off, so we know he's a spy, and we know he works in London.

Double X: Didn't your source tell you who he works for?

Seymour: If she'd told us that, I wouldn't have needed to ask for your help.

Double X: So the source is a woman?

Seymour: Yes. She telephoned and then faxed us the photo. But we couldn't trace the number.

Double X: That's bad. It would give me somewhere to start if I knew where she'd phoned from. It's a pity we haven't got a better photo – it's just a man standing in front of a door.

Seymour: It is a bit clearer if you look at it with your eyes half closed.

Double X: Hmmm. Wait a minute. There's a number on the door. Forty-two. Oh no! It can't be. But it is.

Seymour: What? What is it?

Double X: Well, sir, this is very embarrassing. But I'm afraid that's my front door. And the man standing outside it is – me!

## Recording 20a

Is everybody here? Good. Now listen carefully. I hope you've all had a good day today. I wish the weather were better here for you. It's very unusual to have so much snow and rain here at this time of year.

Some of you were asking about tomorrow. Well, we're going unless the weather gets much worse during the night. OK? So, provided that it doesn't snow too heavily tonight, I'll see you back here at six o'clock. Set your alarms for 5.30. We'll take our breakfast with us because we won't reach the top of the mountain unless we set out early, before it's light. So be here tomorrow morning with everything you need. You've all got a list – you need a whistle in case you get separated from the rest of the group, warm waterproof clothes and gloves, and a good pair of boots. Don't forget the maps I gave you. I'd rather you didn't bring large cameras and video cameras as they'll be a nuisance.

Now, is everyone happy and looking forward to tomorrow? You all look rather worried. There's really no need. As long as we all stay together and you follow my instructions, we'll have a great time. I've never lost anyone up there yet! I wish you'd come a few weeks ago when the weather was better because we could've done so many more walks then. Never mind, there's always next year. It's time we had dinner now so if anyone has any questions, you can ask me on the way to the dining hall. Let's go in.

## Recording 20b

1   *You hear a woman telling someone about a film she has seen. What kind of film was it?*

   *A   a thriller*

   *B   a love story*

   *C   a comedy*

I wish I'd persuaded you to come with me. I must admit I really wasn't sure whether I was going to enjoy it or not so I didn't want to drag you along too but I could go again if you want to see it – although I know the ending, I'd still enjoy watching that car chase again. Someone had told me it was a romantic comedy but it's not how I would describe it. There was certainly nothing in it that made me laugh. I would have liked a bit of romance actually because it was rather exhausting sitting on the edge of your seat all the time.

**2** *You overhear a conversation in a restaurant. What is the man complaining about?*

A the food

B the service

C the noise

| | |
|---|---|
| Man: | I've been coming here for years and I've always recommended it to people. But I really haven't enjoyed my meal today. |
| Manager: | I'm sorry, sir. Can I get you something else? |
| Man: | The food is up to its usual standard, thank you. I just can't understand why you've removed the carpets and curtains from the restaurant and put down these tiles. I've brought my colleague here to discuss important business and I've only caught half of what he's said. All I can hear is other people's conversations. I complained to the waiter but of course it's not his fault. You'll have to do something about it, otherwise I shan't come here again. |
| Manager: | Well, I'm afraid there's not much I can do ... |

**3** *You hear a woman talking to a colleague. How did the woman feel?*

A upset

B ashamed

C shocked

I was standing in the queue in the canteen and there were a couple of people in front of me. They were talking about someone and I thought – Oh dear, that person's got quite a few problems. I was trying not to listen actually because I thought they might be talking about someone I knew. Then I realised they were talking about me. They turned round and they were quite embarrassed. The only person who knows all those things about me is Andrea and she must have told them. I tried not to be bothered about it but I had trusted her so it's really hurtful. I wasn't really surprised though because she never could keep a secret, could she?

**4** *You overhear a man talking to a friend on the phone. What was damaged?*

A a piece of sports equipment

B a musical instrument

C a piece of furniture

I was really cross with myself for being so careless. I was in a hurry and as I opened the car boot it just fell out. I'd got a little table in the boot too so it was probably because there wasn't enough room in there. I couldn't have my lesson – it's no good if you haven't got anything to play. I just hope it will sound all right when I've had it repaired. It'll probably cost a lot too.

**5** *You hear a couple planning to meet. When will the woman telephone the man?*

A about lunchtime

B late afternoon

C early evening

| | |
|---|---|
| Man: | You know we said we'd have a game of badminton one evening? How about today? Let's meet after work, shall we? |
| Woman: | Um, I'm not sure about today. I may have a meeting and if I do it'll run late this afternoon, but I'm not sure yet. |
| Man: | Well, I'm going out to do some deliveries now, but I'll have my mobile with me. |
| Woman: | Well, I can phone you then, can't I? I should know by around lunchtime whether I'll be able to get away early enough, then we can fix a time for the evening. |
| Man: | OK. |

**6** *You hear the weather forecast. What will the weather be like at the weekend?*

A foggy

B wet

C sunny

And here is the weather forecast for today, Friday. There's quite a lot of fog about this morning but it should clear to give a fine day with just the odd cloud in the sky. It'll be cold though. Then a change as we move into the weekend. On Saturday and Sunday we can expect heavy rain as the clouds move in. Next week there should be more sunshine – that is if the early morning fog clears. That's all from me. I'll be back at midday.

7 *Listen to a phone conversation between two women. Why is Sarah ringing Katya?*

   A *to make an apology*

   B *to offer an invitation*

   C *to make a request*

| | |
|---|---|
| Katya: | Three – four – two – seven – five – nine. |
| Sarah: | Hi, Katya. This is Sarah. |
| Katya: | Hi Sarah. |
| Sarah: | Look, I know you can't come to the party on Friday and I'm really sorry about that but I wondered if I could borrow some of your cutlery. You see, there are far more people coming than I expected. Don't worry if it's not possible. I'll ask someone else. |
| Katya: | That should be fine, Sarah, but I'll need it back on Sunday. |
| Sarah: | No problem. |
| Katya: | You'll come and get it then? And maybe we could go to the cinema next week? |
| Sarah: | Fine. |

8 *You overhear a woman talking to someone in a shop. Who is she talking to?*

   A *the shop manager*

   B *a customer*

   C *a colleague*

Well, I was serving at the time and there was a woman waiting in the queue looking very impatient. Mr Reynolds came across the shop and said to me: 'Hurry up, look, there's someone waiting. Why are you so slow?' In front of a customer too. Just like he did to you the other day. Next time he embarrasses us, we've got to stand up to him you know ... We've worked there longer than he has and we know most of the customers anyway so we have to stop and have a chat with them, don't we?

## Recording 21

Good morning. Here is the news for Wednesday the fifth of September.

The Prime Minister is in Washington to attend an international trade conference. He'll spend two days at the conference and after that he'll have talks at the White House with the President. At the weekend he'll fly to Mexico.

The lone sailor Cherry Pickles has suffered problems at the start of her attempt to sail alone across the Pacific. She started from Christchurch, on the south island of New Zealand last week, heading for Fiji, but unexpected bad weather forced her to stop at Napier, on the west coast of the north island. She says she still intends to be in Chile by the end of the year.

A footbridge over the motorway between London and Oxford has collapsed, causing serious delays, with traffic jams stretching beyond the beginning of the motorway. Emergency services are at the scene but part of the motorway will remain closed until this afternoon.

And the local news:

Police have arrested a man who was holding a bank manager hostage. They were called to the bank on the High Street late yesterday afternoon when a security man standing by the door of the bank heard shouting in the manager's office. The manager was released during the night and the gunman gave himself up early this morning.

And now back to Annie for some more music.

## Recording 22

| | |
|---|---|
| Andy: | Hi, Dawn! I'm home. |
| Dawn: | Andy! Where have you been? And what's happened to your jacket? It's filthy! |
| Andy: | OK, OK, there's no need to shout at me. Actually I had a bit of an adventure on the way home. |
| Dawn: | What happened? |
| Andy: | Well, I was driving up Wellbourne Road when I saw flames coming out of an upstairs window. I called the fire brigade on my mobile and then I thought I'd better see if I could do anything. I decided I'd better try and go in. I thought perhaps someone was in there. I got in by breaking a window. |
| Dawn: | What! How? |
| Andy: | I remembered the toolbox I keep in the car for emergencies – |
| Dawn: | Oh, yes. |
| Andy: | – and smashed a window by hitting it with a hammer. The room was full of smoke, so I covered my face with a handkerchief. There wasn't anyone on the ground floor, and I was just wondering if I could go upstairs, when a neighbour arrived and the fire brigade. They |

said the house was empty – the owners work in town.

**Dawn:** Thank God. You could have been in real danger.

**Andy:** Oh not really. Well, anyway, then the fire brigade were in control, so I went to my car. Then the owners arrived.

**Dawn:** Poor things.

**Andy:** Well, it wasn't so bad because luckily, I'd called the fire brigade before the fire had spread too far.

**Dawn:** I hope they thanked you for saving their property.

**Andy:** Oh, yes.

**Dawn:** Do they know how it was started?

**Andy:** By an electrical fault, they think. Anyway, do you forgive me for being late?

**Dawn:** Don't be silly! I can't be angry with you now. Go and have a shower and I'll make a really nice supper for you.

**Andy:** Great. I'm looking forward to eating it already.

## Recording 23

Welcome, everybody, to Claremont Castle. I'm Jasper Claremont and this has been my family's home, where we've lived for over four hundred years, since the time of Edmund Claremont, who first lived here in 1600. This room is the great hall and the paintings you can see here are our oldest portraits. The painting we're looking at now shows Edmund himself. Do you see the ship in the background? It's the one which he was captain of during a famous naval victory. This victory was the reason why he became a national hero. He was given the piece of land where Claremont Castle now stands as a reward. The next painting shows Edmund's wife Margaret, who he married in 1605. She's wearing all the family jewels. And now let's move on the picture of Henry and William, their two sons. It's the picture that hangs next to Margaret's portrait, and it's the one I like best. The one who's sitting on the horse is Henry, and William's the one who's holding the book. William, who was his mother's favourite, became a poet, while Henry, who his father preferred, was more of a man of action. He fought in the Civil War, which broke out in 1642. Unfortunately, he supported the side which lost. We don't know much about the woman he married, and he

had no heirs, but William, whose wife Jane was a famous beauty, had nine children, who all survived. Here they are in this picture from the year when their youngest son was born. Now, if I can lead you into the dining-room, where we'll see some more recent pictures …

## Recording 24

**Adam:** Hi, Josie, what's up?

**Josie:** Adam, have you heard? Tom Castle's the new captain of the volleyball team!

**Adam:** Tom Castle?

**Josie:** Yeah, and it's really bad.

**Adam:** Why?

**Josie:** They only chose him because he's the coach's nephew.

**Adam:** That's not fair. Tom's certainly good enough to be captain. I think he's an obvious choice.

**Josie:** Well, I still think it's wrong.

**Adam:** What do you mean?

**Josie:** Look, he's captain of the team. Why? Because of his uncle.

**Adam:** Perhaps you ought to be in the team yourself since you seem to know so much about the subject.

**Josie:** I'm not tall enough to play volleyball.

**Adam:** Nonsense – several people your size are in the team. Melanie, for example. She's so quick that she's one of the best players.

**Josie:** You know I'm not into team games. Going to judo once a week gives me enough exercise. Anyway, volleyball would take too much time. They have too many practice games after school.

**Adam:** Well, I've been training every day in order to be really fit. They may need some new people so I want to be ready.

**Josie:** You? You're joking.

**Adam:** No, I'm not. The coach said that I play well enough. And the exams start next term. Some of the older players may drop out as they've got so much revision to do.

**Josie:** Really? Oh. Well, good luck then. But I won't be with you.

**Recording 25**

Paul: Hello there. I'm Paul Dadley and this is Studio One with all your favourite music and entertainment news. And first off, I'm very happy to welcome actor Gemma Lewis to the studio.

Gemma: Thank you.

Paul: Actually, shouldn't I call you a film star rather than an actor? After all, you've been world famous since making the film *Starshine* two years ago, haven't you?

Gemma: Well, yes, I suppose so. I enjoyed making that film but I really want to be a stage actor.

Paul: It was quite a surprise to get the lead in *Starshine*, wasn't it?

Gemma: Yes. I got the part in spite of having no film experience.

Paul: How was that?

Gemma: I was at a theatre school. I was fifteen and I'd only acted small parts in some stage plays. The director chose me to play the part after visiting several schools. I still don't really know how he guessed I would be right for it.

Paul: And you had no hesitation in accepting?

Gemma: Oh, yes. I had a long talk with my parents before accepting it. In the end, I went for it, even though I knew I would have to spend a year away from home. It was a chance I couldn't afford to miss.

Paul: But you didn't make any more films after finishing *Starshine*. Why is that? You must have had plenty of offers.

Gemma: Yes I did. In fact I was offered two more films while making *Starshine*, but working far from home, I sometimes felt very lonely, and I wanted to develop a stage career. So I came back to England.

Paul: So, no more films?

Gemma: Oh, I don't know. I'd be happy to do another film later, but I'm booked up for the next few months.

Paul: Well, Gemma, that's good news for your fans. Now, what about the play you're appearing in at the moment?

Gemma: It's great. It's actually a comedy, despite being called *Dark Days*. It's really funny.

Paul: And it's at the Arts Theatre. So, everybody, don't miss the chance to see Gemma Lewis live! Gemma, thank you for coming to talk to us.

Gemma: Thank you.

Paul: And now some music ...

**Note:** *Although* actress *means female actor, the word* actor *is increasingly used for both men and women in modern English.*

# Appendix 1: Phrasal verbs

These are some of the most common phrasal verbs. Many phrasal verbs have more than one meaning. Check them in a good dictionary and study Unit 18 before using this list.

| | | | | | |
|---|---|---|---|---|---|
| ask after | come up against | get on with | keep back | pay off | stand up to |
| ask for | count on | get out | keep down | pay up | stay in |
| back out of | count up | get out of | keep off | pick out | stay out |
| back up | cross out | get over | keep on | pick up | stick out |
| be away | cut across | get round | keep out | point out | stop off |
| be in | cut back | get round to | keep up | pull down | stop over |
| be into | cut down | get through | keep up with | pull in | switch on |
| blow up | cut in | get together | knock down | pull off | switch off |
| break down | cut out | get up | knock out | pull out | take after |
| break in | cut up | get up to | leave in | pull up | take away |
| break off | deal with | give away | leave on | put aside | take back |
| break out | do away with | give back | leave out | put away | take in |
| break up | do out of | give in | let down | put by | take off |
| bring about | do without | give out | let in | put down | take on |
| bring back | draw in | give up | let off | put off | take over |
| bring in | draw out | go after | let out | put on | take to |
| bring out | draw up | go by | let through | put out | take up |
| bring round | drop back | go down with | live on | put through | talk over |
| bring up | drop by | go for | live through | put up | think about |
| build up | drop in on | go in for | live up to | put up with | think of |
| burst in | drop off | go off | lock up | ring back | think out |
| burst out | drop out | go on | look after | ring off | think over |
| call for | face up to | go out | look at | ring up | throw away |
| call in | fall back on | go over | look back on | rub out | throw out |
| call off | fall behind | go through | look for | run away with | try on |
| call on | fall for | go with | look forward to | run down | try out |
| care about | fall in with | go without | look in | run into | turn back |
| care for | fall out | grow out of | look into | run out of | turn down |
| carry off | fall through | grow up | look on | run over | turn into |
| carry on | feel like | hand in | look out | see about | turn off |
| carry out | feel up to | hand on | look over | see off | turn on |
| catch on | fill in | hand out | look through | see through | turn out |
| catch up with | fill out | hand over | look up | see to | turn over |
| check in | find out | hang about | look up to | send for | turn up |
| check out | fit in | hang on | make for | send out | wash up |
| check over | get across | hang up | make up | set back | watch out |
| check up | get along with | have back | make up for | set in | wear off |
| clear out | get around | have on | miss out on | set off | wear out |
| clear up | get at | have round | mix up | set out | wipe off |
| come across | get away | hold back | move in | set up | wipe out |
| come down | get away with | hold in | move out | show off | wipe up |
| come forward | get back | hold on | own up | show up | work out |
| come off | get by | hold on to | pass away | stand by | work up |
| come on | get down | hold out | pass off | stand for | write down |
| come out | get in | hold up | pass out | stand in for | write in |
| come round | get off | join in | pay back | stand out | write off |
| come up | get on | join up | pay in | stand up for | write up |

# Appendix 2: Irregular verbs

| Verb | Past simple | Past participle |
|---|---|---|
| arise | arose | arisen |
| be | was / were | been |
| beat | beat | beaten |
| become | became | become |
| begin | began | begun |
| bend | bent | bent |
| bite | bit | bitten |
| bleed | bled | bled |
| blow | blew | blown |
| break | broke | broken |
| bring | brought | brought |
| broadcast | broadcast | broadcast |
| build | built | built |
| burn | burnt | burnt |
| burst | burst | burst |
| buy | bought | bought |
| catch | caught | caught |
| choose | chose | chosen |
| come | came | come |
| cost | cost | cost |
| creep | crept | crept |
| cut | cut | cut |
| deal | dealt | dealt |
| dig | dug | dug |
| do | did | done |
| draw | drew | drawn |
| dream | dreamt | dreamt |
| drink | drank | drunk |
| drive | drove | driven |
| eat | ate | eaten |
| fall | fell | fallen |
| feed | fed | fed |
| feel | felt | felt |
| fight | fought | fought |
| find | found | found |
| fly | flew | flown |
| forbid | forbade | forbidden |
| forget | forgot | forgotten |
| forgive | forgave | forgiven |
| freeze | froze | frozen |
| get | got | got |
| give | gave | given |
| go | went | gone |
| grow | grew | grown |
| hang | hung | hung |
| have | had | had |
| hear | heard | heard |
| hide | hid | hidden |
| hit | hit | hit |
| hold | held | held |
| hurt | hurt | hurt |
| keep | kept | kept |
| kneel | knelt | knelt |
| know | knew | known |
| lay | laid | laid |
| lead | led | led |
| lean | leant | leant |
| learn | learnt | learnt |
| leave | left | left |
| lend | lent | lent |
| let | let | let |
| lie | lay | lain |

| Verb | Past simple | Past participle |
|---|---|---|
| light | lit | lit |
| lose | lost | lost |
| make | made | made |
| mean | meant | meant |
| meet | met | met |
| pay | paid | paid |
| put | put | put |
| read | read | read |
| ride | rode | ridden |
| ring | rang | rung |
| rise | rose | risen |
| run | ran | run |
| say | said | said |
| see | saw | seen |
| sell | sold | sold |
| send | sent | sent |
| set | set | set |
| sew | sewed | sewn |
| shake | shook | shaken |
| shine | shone | shone |
| shoot | shot | shot |
| show | showed | shown |
| shrink | shrank | shrunk |
| shut | shut | shut |
| sing | sang | sung |
| sink | sank | sunk |
| sit | sat | sat |
| sleep | slept | slept |
| slide | slid | slid |
| smell | smelt | smelt |
| sow | sowed | sown |
| speak | spoke | spoken |
| spell | spelt / spelled | spelt / spelled |
| spend | spent | spent |
| spill | spilt | spilt |
| spit | spat | spat |
| split | split | split |
| spoil | spoilt | spoilt |
| spread | spread | spread |
| spring | sprang | sprung |
| stand | stood | stood |
| steal | stole | stolen |
| stick | stuck | stuck |
| sting | stung | stung |
| strike | struck | struck |
| swear | swore | sworn |
| sweep | swept | swept |
| swell | swelled | swollen |
| swim | swam | swum |
| swing | swung | swung |
| take | took | taken |
| teach | taught | taught |
| tear | tore | torn |
| tell | told | told |
| think | thought | thought |
| throw | threw | thrown |
| understand | understood | understood |
| wake | woke | woken |
| wear | wore | worn |
| weep | wept | wept |
| win | won | won |
| write | wrote | written |

# Grammar glossary

**adjective**
A word which tells us about a noun:
*a **new** house; a **boring** film*

or a **pronoun**:
*She's **tired**.*
*They're **beautiful**.*

**adverb**
A word which tells us about a **verb**:
*They talked **quietly**.*
*We'll meet our friends **tomorrow**.*

or an **adjective**:
*a **very** expensive computer*

or a **sentence**:
***Luckily**, we knew all the answers.*

**auxiliary verb**
A **verb** (like *be, do, have*) which we use with a
**main verb** in some tenses:
*She **is** talking.*
*You **do** not understand.*
***Have** they arrived?*

**determiner**
A short word which goes in front of a **noun**:
***some** people; **each** person*

**imperative**
A **verb** which gives an order:
***Leave** your tray here, please.*
***Open** the door!*

**infinitive**
The basic form of a **verb** which we can use
after other verbs, often with *to*:
*I want **to see** you.*
*This is difficult **to understand**.*
*We must **leave** early.*

**main verb**
The part of a **verb** which gives its meaning
(compare **auxiliary verb**):
*She is **talking**.*
*You do not **understand**.*
*Have they **arrived**?*

**modal verb**
A special kind of **verb** which we use with an
**infinitive** to give extra meaning:
*You **can't** sit here*
*He **must** hurry.*
***May** I help you?*

**noun**
A word for a person or thing:
*a **child**; a **group** of **people**; the **place** where I
keep my **books***
*I felt great **anger** when I heard the **news**.*

**object**
The **noun** or **pronoun** (with other words like
determiners etc.) which follows a **verb**:
*He's drinking **some hot chocolate**.*
*They don't like **us**.*
*Did you solve **your problem**?*
*She gave **me a present**. (= two objects)*

## participle

The *-ing* form (e.g. *working, eating*) or the **past participle** (e.g. *worked, eaten*) of a **verb**. We use them with **auxiliary verbs** to make **tenses**:
*The boys are **working** hard.*
*We had **eaten** our meal.*

The *-ing* form and the past participle can sometimes be used as an **adjective**:
*an **exciting** story; a **frightened** animal*

The *-ing* form can sometimes be used as a **noun**:
***Swimming** is good for you.*

## phrasal verb

A **verb** made up of two or three words (**verb + adverb / preposition**):
***look after; give away; look forward to***

## preposition

A short word which usually goes in front of a **noun** or **pronoun** and links it to other words:
*Please speak **to** her.*
*He fell **off** his chair.*
*What's the meaning **of** this word?*

## pronoun

A word used in the place of a **noun**:
*The girls like volleyball so **they** play **it** every week.*
*Are **you** hungry?*

## sentence

A group of words in which there is usually a **verb** and its **subject** or **object**. In writing, sentences begin with a capital letter. A sentence can:

- make a **statement**:
  *My name is John.*

- ask a question:
  *Do you enjoy learning English?*

- give an instruction (see **imperative**):
  *Study this page.*

- be an exclamation:
  *You're very beautiful!*

## statement

A **sentence** which tells us some information:
*I like chocolate.*
*My brother doesn't live here.*

## subject

The person or thing which does the **verb**:
***My family** comes from London.*
***Smoking** is not good for your health.*
*Do **your friends** have any money?*
*Where are **they**?*

## tense

The form of a **verb** which gives extra information, for example, about the time it happens:
*She **lives** there.* (= present tense)
*She **lived** there.* (= past tense)

## verb

A word which describes what happens:
*The boy **wrote** a letter.*
*We **thought** about you.*

# CD Tracklist

| Recording | CD track | Recording | CD track |
|---|---|---|---|
| Title information | 1 | 11 | 39 |
| 1a | 2 | 12 | 40 |
| 1b | 3–4 | 13a | 41 |
| 2 | 5 | 13b | 42–43 |
| 3 | 6 | 14 | 44 |
| 4 | 7 | 15 | 45 |
| 5a, conversation 1 | 8 | 16 | 46 |
| 5a, conversation 2 | 9 | 17 | 47 |
| 5a, conversation 3 | 10 | 18 | 48 |
| 5a, conversation 4 | 11 | 19 | 49 |
| 5b | 12–13 | 20a | 50 |
| 5c | 14 | 20b, question 1 | 51–52 |
| 6 | 15 | 20b, question 2 | 53–54 |
| 7 | 16 | 20b, question 3 | 55–56 |
| 8 | 17 | 20b, question 4 | 57–58 |
| 9a | 18 | 20b, question 5 | 59–60 |
| 9b, question 1 | 19–20 | 20b, question 6 | 61–62 |
| 9b, question 2 | 21–22 | 20b, question 7 | 63–64 |
| 9b, question 3 | 23–24 | 20b, question 8 | 65–66 |
| 9b, question 4 | 25–26 | 21 | 67 |
| 9b, question 5 | 27–28 | 22 | 68 |
| 9b, question 6 | 29–30 | 23 | 69 |
| 9b, question 7 | 31–32 | 24 | 70 |
| 9b, question 8 | 33–34 | 25 | 71 |
| 10, speaker 1 | 35 | | |
| 10, speaker 2 | 36 | | |
| 10, speaker 3 | 37 | | |
| 10, speaker 4 | 38 | | |